MORNINGS

With Our

GOD

DR. LANCE BOYD

Preface

I began a journey on March 27, 2020 to read through God's Holy Word the Bible. I read a chapter each morning and then picked a verse from the chapter to write a short devotion. There are 1,189 chapter's, 31,103 verses, and 807,361 words in the Bible. I calculated it would take me around three years and 3 months to complete my work. Each day, I read from our God's Living Word at least in the morning, at lunch, and before I go to bed at night. Jesus taught us while being tempted in the wilderness that His Father's Word is what we need to use to fight spiritual battles. I firmly believe, God's Word is the greatest moral compass that we can follow. I accepted Jesus as my personal Savior in the 10th grade at Fairview United Methodist Church in Cullman, Alabama. My relationship to our Lord and Savior Jesus Christ has grown through my journey on earth from reading the Bible and consistent prayer. Mankind was created to worship God and we learn God's nature from His Word. It is my heart's desire that the ones that read these words accept the only way to our Father and that is through the acceptance of His one and only begotten Son Jesus Christ the Messiah. I pray daily for the salvation of my grandchildren and generations to come that they will find the peace and hope that comes from God's Inspired Word.

Jesus said to him, I am the way, the truth, and the life.
No one comes to the Father except through me.
John 14:6

Dr. Lance Boyd

In the beginning God created the heavens and the earth.
Genesis 1:1

Father, how wonderful a description You share with us how You created this earth and universe. We marvel at Your creation and thank You that You made us in Your image. An image to have fellowship with You.

Then the Lord God formed, a man from the dust of the ground and breathed into his nostrils the breath of life, and the man became a living being.
Genesis 2:7

Father, You breathed life into man. You created all life and all things. May we love and value life as You.

Now the serpent was more crafty than any of the wild animals the Lord God had made. He said to the woman, "Did God really say, 'You must not eat from any tree in the garden'?"
Genesis 3:1

Father, help us be alert and aware that satan is very deceptive. Just as he tempted Eve, he also seeks to bring all of mankind to hell with him. Thank You Father for Your protection.

Now Cain said to his brother Abel, "Let's go out to the field."While they were in the field, Cain attacked his brother Abel and killed him.
Genesis 4:8

After Adam and Eve displeased God by disobedience, one of their sons murdered the other. God had made mankind in His image and now life that God had breathed into Adam had been
taken from his son Abel. Father, how precious is life and may we respect it how You intend today.

When God created mankind, He made them in the likeness of God. He created them male and female and blessed them. And He named them "Mankind" when they were created.
Genesis 5:2

Father, You created us in Your likeness. We have a soul and are capable of choosing to have a relationship with You. Above all creation mankind is unique and very good. May many choose to come and accept Jesus this day.

But Noah found favor in the eyes of the Lord. Noah and the Flood. This is the account of Noah and his family.
Noah was a righteous man, blameless among the people of his time, and he walked faithfully with God.
Genesis 6:8-9

Father, man had gotten so wicked that You had regretted making mankind. But then there was Noah. Let us not do as the world this day but, like Noah, stand and walk faithfully with You.

The Lord then said to Noah, "Go into the ark, you and your whole family ,because I have found you righteous in this generation.
Genesis 7:1

Father, what a great man of God Noah was in his time on earth. Our righteousness is found in our Lord Jesus Christ. Let us shine for You this day in history.

The Lord smelled the pleasing aroma and said in His heart: "Never again will I curse the ground because of humans, even though every inclination of the human heart is evil from childhood. And never again will I destroy all living creatures, as I have done.
Genesis 8:21

Father, thank You for mercy, grace, and patience for mankind. May we make choices today pleasing to You.

Whenever I bring clouds over the earth and the rainbow appears in the clouds, I will remember my covenant between Me and you and all living creatures of every kind. Never again will the waters become a flood to destroy all life.
Genesis 9:14-15

Father, when we see the rainbow let us think of You. Your covenants always are true and stand for eternity. You are the God of truth and justices.

These are the clans of Noah's sons, according to their lines of descent, within their nations. From these the nations spread out over the earth after the flood.
Genesis 10:32

After the flood, all mankind came from Noah's family that got off the ark after 377 days. Noah's was found by God to be righteous in his generation. May our actions and choices be found pleasing to God today.

Then they said, "Come, let us build ourselves a city, with a tower that reaches to the heavens, so that we may make a name for ourselves; otherwise we will be scattered over the face of the whole earth."
Genesis 11:4

Father, as Your children it should never be about making a name for ourselves but we should be uplifting Your name. May all we say and do today bring honor and glory to Your name.

The name that is above all names: The Lord God Almighty.
I will make you into a great nation, and I will bless you; I will make your name great, and you will be a blessing.
Genesis 12:2

Father, out of Abraham You brought forth a great nation. Out of that nation, Your son Jesus would be born. Thank You Father for Your perfect plan.

There Abram called on the name of the Lord.
Genesis 13:4

Father, just as Abram called on You at Bethel where he had previously built an altar to You, we need You this day. May today be a day of service, worship, and praise to You our God

Blessed be Abram by God Most High, Creator of heaven and earth. And praise be to God Most High, who delivered your enemies into your hand."
Genesis 14:19-20

Thank You Father for Your deliverance. You can deliver in times that are impossible for man.

"Do not be afraid, Abram. I am your shield, your very great reward."
Genesis 15:1

Father, may we live this day in assurance that You are our shield.

Abram agreed to what Sarai said.
Genesis 16:2

Father, let us live our lives obeying Your words. Let us have patience and allow You to work out our journey on this earth through Your perfect timing. Lead and guide our lives to Your perfect will.

Abraham fell facedown; he laughed and said to himself, "Will a son be born to a man a hundred years old? Will Sarah bear a child at the age of ninety?"
Genesis 17:17

Father, Your plan was coming to fruition. Abraham would have a son and You told him to call his son Isaac. You would establish an everlasting covenant with him. Your timing is perfect. May we be patient and allow not our timing but Your perfect timing to be done in our lives.

Is anything too hard for the Lord?
Genesis 18:14

Father, You are sovereign and can do what You want, when You want, and how You want. You created all and can defy the laws of the universe You created.
With man this is impossible but with You all things are possible. What great peace knowing we are Your children in Your hands.

When he hesitated, the men grasped his hand and the hands of his wife and of his two daughters and led them safely out of the city, for the Lord was merciful to them.
Genesis 19:16

Father, just as with Lot, You show great mercy to Your children today. May many receive Your hand today and follow the road that leads to safety.

But God came to Abimelek in a dream one night.
Genesis 20:3

Father, You came to Abimelek in a dream. To others through: a burning bush, pillar of fire, the tabernacle, a still small voice, the temple, Your creation, and through Your beloved Son Jesus Christ. Today You allow mankind to have the Holy Spirit to dwell within us and counsel us each day on earth. What a great time on earth we live having our bodies as a temple for Your dwelling.

God heard the boy crying, and the angel of God called to Hagar from heaven and said to her, "What is the matter, Hagar? Do not be afraid; God has heard the boy crying as he lies there.
Genesis 21:17

Father, You hear a little baby as it cries. You are omnipotent and see and hear all things. You have at Your disposal countless angels to do your will. What peace comes over us when we think of Your greatness.

"Do not lay a hand on the boy," he said. "Do not do anything to him. Now I know that you fear God, because you have not withheld from me your son, your only son."
Genesis 22:12

Father, You did not withhold Your beloved Son Jesus for the sacrifice of mankind. If there had been any other way to prevent Jesus from being the sacrifice You would have provided. May many come to You through the blood of Jesus today. May we obey and tell others about the gospel of our Lord and Savior Jesus Christ.

Sarah lived to be a hundred and twenty-seven years old.
Genesis 23:1

Sarah was 90 when she and Abraham were told they would have a baby Isaac. What joy and happiness they must have felt to have a child. She got to watch the child grow and turn into a man for around the next 37 years. Father, what a blessing you give us watching our children grow and develop a relationship with You.

After she had given him a drink, she said, "I'll draw water for your camels too, until they have had enough to drink."
Genesis 24:19

Father, Rebecca, who You had chosen to be Isaacs future wife, not only gave the servant a drink from her jar but went back and forth down to the spring getting over 200 gallons of water for ten camels. May we go this day with a servant heart like Rebecca.

Isaac prayed to the Lord on behalf of his wife, because she was childless. The Lord answered his prayer, and his wife Rebekah became pregnant.
Genesis 25:21

Isaac was 40 years old when he married Rebecca and 60 until they had Esau and Jacob. Unlike his father Abraham, he waited on You Father. It is unfortunate that he loved Esau and Rebecca loved Jacob. May we look upon mankind as Jesus.

They were a source of grief to Isaac and Rebekah.
Genesis 26:35

Father, our decisions can lead to good or bad. Even when we are in Your will we still May go through very hard trials. May our decisions today regardless of difficulty be in Your will for our lives.

"Are you really my son Esau?" he asked. "I am," he replied.
Genesis 27:24

Jacob had lied to get his father Isaac's blessing. Esau's birthright and now blessing from being firstborn was now Jacob just like prophecy said. Father, may our choices today be to honor you not through lies and cunning but by honesty and integrity.

I am with you and will watch over you wherever you go.
Genesis 28:15

Father, just as You were with Jacob, You also watch over us. Thank You for the Holy Spirit that resides in us once we accept Jesus as our Lord. We can have peace and no fear knowing that You are our God.

When morning came, there was Leah! So Jacob said to Laban, "What is this you have done to me? I served you for Rachel, didn't I? Why have you deceived me?"
Genesis 29:25

Just as Jacob had deceived Esau, now we see that Jacob was deceived by his uncle and father in law Laban. Father, may our actions be pleasing to You today. Let our choices glorify Your Holy Name.

Then God remembered Rachel; he listened to her and enabled her to conceive.
Genesis 30:22

Just as Sarah did not wait on the Lord, Rachel had her servant Bilhah become a wife to Jacob because she could not have children. When it was God's timing, Rachel had her baby Joseph. Father, Your will is what matters and we are Your vessels.

When Laban had gone to shear his sheep, Rachel stole her
father's household gods.
Genesis 31:19

Jacob was leaving Laban after 20 years of working for him.
Rachel made a bad choice in stealing and taking his man-made
gods. Father, the world offers so many false gods to entice us
away from You. May we look only to You: the one true God.

I am unworthy of all the kindness and faithfulness you have
shown your servant.
Genesis 32:10

Father, Jacob has left with his two wives, two servants, eleven
sons and possessions. God has blessed Jacob and is with him.
That you for Your kindness and faithfulness in our lives and
always knowing You are with us.

But Esau ran to meet Jacob and embraced him; he threw his arms around his neck and kissed him. And they wept.
Genesis 33:4

After 20 years of being apart, Esau had ran to embrace rather than kill his brother Jacob. Father, it is wonderful to see the change of heart in mankind. You are God who changes hearts and allows forgiveness.

And Shechem said to his father Hamor, "Get me this girl as my wife."
Genesis 34:4

What a sad story of Jacob's daughter Dinah. Greed and lust are terrible sins against God. Father, thank You for showing us in Your word and through Jesus what true love is. Let us treat others today with respect and dignity.

So Jacob said to his household and to all who were with him, "Get rid of the foreign gods you have with you, and purify yourselves and change your clothes.
Genesis 35:2

Father, we wish to worship You and You alone. We put our trust in You. Praise the name of Jesus for allowing our bodies to be purified from sins by being atonement for our sins on the Cross once and for all time. Help us Holy Spirit to guide and make choices that honor God just as Jacob.

Esau took his wives from the women of Canaan.
Genesis 36:2

To displease his father, Esau took Canaanite wives. For hundreds of years, this rebellion would cause conflicts with Israel. Father, may we learn from Esau and not make choices today for selfish or retaliation reasons. Let our choices be to please You and bring honor to Your name.

Now Israel loved Joseph more than any of his other sons,
because he had been born to him in his old age; and he made an
ornate robe for him.
Genesis 37:3

Jacob showed more love to Joseph and one day the ornate robe
would be brought back to Jacob by his other sons in deception;
torn and shattered because of their hate toward Joseph. Father,
if we follow your commandments to love You with all our
heart, soul, and mind and love our neighbor as ourself there can
be no jealousy. Your love is boundless.

And he was named Perez.
Genesis 38:29

Father, through Perez Your Son Jesus was born one day. The
story of Perez dad and mom Judah and Tamar who are also
listed in the genealogy of Jesus is a wonderful example of how
we can learn of Your redemption.

The warden paid no attention to anything under Joseph's care, because the Lord was with Joseph and gave him success in whatever he did.
Genesis 39:23

Joseph was thrown in jail by false accusations from Potiphar' wife. Father, Your perfect plan is weaving through the messes of a fallen world through the life of Joseph. Even while Joseph is in jail, You are with him and giving him success. Help us this day to not get discouraged and remember You make good out of the bad.

"We both had dreams," they answered, "but there is no one to interpret them." Then Joseph said to them, "Do not interpretations belong to God? Tell me your dreams."
Genesis 40:8

Father, Joseph used the ability You gave him to interpret dreams. May we use our talents that You give us to also bring honor to Your name and fulfill the will You have for our lives.

Pharaoh asked them, "Can we find anyone like this man, one in whom is the spirit of God?"
Genesis 41:38

Father, because of You Joseph went from being a slave to second in Egypt. Pharaoh recognized the work You did through Joseph. May we work for your glory today.

Then ten of Joseph's brothers went down to buy grain from Egypt. Genesis 42:3

Joseph's brothers now stand before their brother that they had abandoned. Instead of retaliation and retribution, Joseph chooses mercy and forgiveness. A wonderful picture into the future life of Jesus on this earth. Father, may we display the same actions as Joseph today.

Deeply moved at the sight of his brother, Joseph hurried out and looked for a place to weep. He went into his private room and wept there.
Genesis 43:30

Joseph was so happy to see his brothers. Now for the first time, Joseph was seeing his youngest brother Benjamin that shared the same mother Rachel. Joseph had all life could offer but now he had back his brethren. Father, thank You for our family.

Then the steward proceeded to search, beginning with the oldest and ending with the youngest. And the cup was found in Benjamin's sack.
Genesis 44:12

Father, how Judah's heart must have sank when the cup of Joseph was found in Benjamin's sack. The brothers had mistreated Joseph and now Benjamin would not be going back to his father. May we live today and not have greed or selfishness like Joseph's brothers. May we show love and kindness this day.

And now, do not be distressed and do not be angry with yourselves for selling me here, because it was to save lives that God sent me ahead of you.
Genesis 45: 5

Father, Your plans will be carried out. Praise Your name for always watching and caring for Your children in a fallen world.

I will go down to Egypt with you, and I will surely bring you back again. And Joseph's own hand will close your eyes."
Genesis 46:4

Father, Your chosen people were having to leave the promised land to travel to Egypt due to famine. You told Jacob that they would return one day which they did. You are always in control. Please help us weave to the path you have for us today. Let Your will be done.

There was no food, however, in the whole region because the famine was severe; both Egypt and Canaan wasted away because of the famine.
Genesis 47:13

The 7 year famine that God had revealed through Joseph was at hand. Father, give us this day our daily bread just as You provided for Joseph. You are the great provider.

Joseph said to him, "No, my father, this one is the firstborn; put your right hand on his head."
Genesis 48:18

Jacob blessed Joseph's sons Manasseh and Ephraim. He told Joseph the younger would be greater than the older. Father, You are sovereign and can deviate proper order. May we be flexible as You lead our paths.

The scepter will not depart from Judah, nor the ruler's staff from between his feet, until he to whom it belongs shall come and the obedience of the nations shall be his.
Genesis 49:10

Jacob was nearing death and had gathered his sons to tell them what would happen to them. His son Judah's lineage would one day welcome to the world the Messiah. Thank you Father for allowing us to see how Your great plan of redemption unfolded. From Judah, came Your Son Jesus Christ.

But Joseph said to them, "Don't be afraid. Am I in the place of God?
Genesis 50:19

Joseph was now in a place that he could have retaliated and repaid his brothers for their treatment. Joseph knew that God was in control and through his love and obedience for God he reassured no harm would come to his brothers. Father, thank You for Your forgiveness, mercy, and grace.

Then a new king, to whom Joseph meant nothing, came to power in Egypt. "Look," he said to his people, "the Israelites have become far too numerous for us.
Exodus 1:8-9

Joseph and his brothers had died and a new king felt threatened by how numerous the Israelites had become. The king ordered that the midwives kill the baby boys. They feared God and deceived the king resulting in God allowing the midwives to have families of their own. However, the king then ordered that every Hebrew boy must be thrown into the Nile, but let every girl live.
Father, how selfishness and power corrupts. Murder of innocent babies had been ordered by the king of Egypt. Nothing is more innocent than a child. May we learn and treat each child as a priceless creation from You; born in Your image.

So God looked on the Israelites and was concerned about them.
Exodus 2:25

Father, knowing You love and are concerned for Your children gives peace. You are the God who can do as You please. Watch over us today Father with Your hand of protection and may we show compassion in Your name.

When the Lord saw that he had gone over to look, God called to him from within the bush, "Moses! Moses!"
Exodus 3:4

Father, You spoke to Moses within the burning bush, Jesus spoke to mankind as He walked along this earth, and the Holy Spirit speaks to Your children's hearts daily. May Your living word found in the Bible speak to us as we read and search through scripture. You told Moses " I will be with you." You are our Father: the God of Abraham, the God of Isaac, and the God of Jacob. "I am who I am" is Your name. May we worship You, our Father, this and every day.

At a lodging place on the way, the Lord met Moses and was about to kill him.
Exodus 4:24

Moses' wife Zipporah saved Moses' life. Father, thank you for our spouses, family, and friends that help us on this journey on earth. The encouragers and ones that keep us accountable to live and make choices that are pleasing to You. Thank You for sending the Holy Spirit that helps Your children in ways we don't even imagine. May we go this day and walk for You.

Pharaoh said, "Who is the Lord, that I should obey him and let Israel go? I do not know the Lord and I will not let Israel go."
Exodus 5:2

Moses and Aaron had gone to Pharaoh but he would not let the people go on a three day journey to wilderness to hold festivals and offer sacrifices. Pharaoh told the slaves they were lazy and demanded for men to produce the same quota of brick without the Egyptians providing the straw. The Israelite overseers were beaten by the slave drivers. Moses went to God and asked why all these events were happening.
Father, You had told Moses and Aaron that Your children would leave their slavery but it did not happen until Your timing. Let us be patient and endure as Your plans unfold in our lives and on this day we walk today.

Moreover, I have heard the groaning of the Israelites, whom the Egyptians are enslaving, and I have remembered my covenant.
Exodus 6:5

Father, thank You for the assurance You always keep Your covenants. We have peace that as Your children we will be with You forever.

You are to say everything I command you, and your brother Aaron is to tell Pharaoh to let the Israelites go out of his country.
Exodus 7:2

Father, thank You for the people in our lives that help and encourage along life's journey. Moses' brother Aaron was allowed to help Moses as they went before Pharaoh. May we be encouragers today.

Then the Lord said to Moses, "Go to Pharaoh and say to him, 'This is what the Lord says: Let my people go, so that they may worship me.
Exodus 8:1

Father, You caused Aaron's staff to become a snake and sent plagues of blood, frogs, gnats, and flies but still pharaoh's heart was hardened. Pharaoh would not allow Your people to go worship You in the wilderness. My God, since when has impossible ever stopped You. We were made to worship You. May our faith abound today and hardened hearts accept Your great love and redemption that comes through Your Son Jesus Christ.

The only place it did not hail was the land of Goshen, where the Israelites were.
Exodus 9:26

Father, You sent plaques on livestock, boils, and hail on Egyptians. The children of God were protected from the hail. Thank You Father for being our shield.

So Moses and Aaron went to Pharaoh and said to him, "This is what the Lord, the God of the Hebrews, says: 'How long will you refuse to humble yourself before me? Let my people go, so that they may worship me.
Exodus 10:3

Plagues of locusts and darkness covered Egypt but God's children were still not allowed to leave. How Egypt's people and land were ravaged because of greed and selfishness. Father, may we humble ourselves to You this day and live not for ourselves but for You. Let us bring honor and glory to Your name through Your Son Jesus Christ our Lord.

Every firstborn son in Egypt will die, from the firstborn son of Pharaoh, who sits on the throne, to the firstborn son of the female slave, who is at her hand mill, and all the firstborn of the cattle as well.
Exodus 11:5

What a terrible price the Egyptians paid for their treatment of God's people. Father, thank You for life and life abundantly that comes from following You. May many come to You today and escape separation from You through sin.
Father, may we learn from the Egyptians and never put anything before worship of You.

Then they are to take some of the blood and put it on the sides and tops of the doorframes of the houses where they eat the lambs.
Exodus 12:7

Father, You passed over the houses that had the blood of the lamb. Jesus became the Lamb at the Cross of Calvary once and for all time. Praise the name of Jesus.

By day the Lord went ahead of them in a pillar of cloud to guide them on their way and by night in a pillar of fire to give them light, so that they could travel by day or night.
Exodus 13:21

The pillar of cloud by day and the pillar of fire by night never left its place in front of the people. Father, thank You for always being with us. Thank You Holy Spirit for dwelling inside us. Father, may we keep our eyes on You this day.

Raise your staff and stretch out your hand over the sea to divide the water so that the Israelites can go through the sea on dry ground.
Exodus 14:16

Father, what a sight it was when You sent a strong east wind and drove back the waters of the sea all that night. The angel of God and the pillar of cloud moved from in front of Your children to behind to stand between the Israelites and Pharaoh's chariots, horsemen, and troops. You are the great deliverer.

"The Lord is my strength and my defense; he has become my salvation. He is my God, and I will praise him, my father's God, and I will exalt him.
Exodus 15:2

Just as we sing songs to You Father, Moses and the Israelites sang this song after being delivered from pharaoh and the Egyptians. You are the great delivery. Praise the name of Jesus for being our deliverance from sins. May we sing and give honor and glory to Your Son Jesus this day and forever more.

Then the Lord said to Moses, "I will rain down bread from heaven for you. The people are to go out each day and gather enough for that day. In this way I will test them and see whether they will follow my instructions.
Exodus 16:4

God provided manna in the morning and quail in the afternoon. For 40 years, God provided manna for His children of Israel in the wilderness. The children were to gather enough for each day at a specific time. Each morning dew around the camp formed and then turned into thin flakes like frost. The manna was white like coriander and tasted like wafers made with honey. They were to gather twice as much, about six pounds, on the sixth day so they could rest on the seventh. God wanted them to listen and follow His instructions. Father, You are the great provider. May we listen, follow Your instructions, and trust in You this day.

I will stand there before you by the rock at Horeb. Strike the rock, and water will come out of it for the people to drink." So Moses did this in the sight of the elders of Israel.
Exodus 17:6

The Israelites began to quarrel with Moses when no water was to be found. God provided their needs with water from the rock. Father, thank You for providing for our needs. Protect us today and deliver us from the evil one. May we give You honor, praise, and our best this day.

But select capable men from all the people-men who fear God, trustworthy men who hate dishonest gain-and appoint them as officials over thousands, hundreds, fifties and tens.
Exodus 18.21

Moses' father in law Jethro made this suggestion to Moses on the stipulation If God so commands. Moses received help as he helped the people with their disputes. Father, I pray for Godly leaders today and that their decisions will be trustworthy and upright. May each decision made be pleasing to You.

You yourselves have seen what I did to Egypt, and how I carried you on eagles' wings and brought you to myself.
Exodus 19:4

Father, may we be carried on eagles wings. May we fly above the temptations and snares put in front of us.

"You shall have no other gods before me."
Exodus 20:3

This was the first commandment that God spoke to his chosen people on Mount Sinai. Father, may we honor You this day and our lives show our devotion and love for You. May we offer our best.

Anyone who beats their male or female slave with a rod must be punished if the slave dies as a direct result.
Exodus 21:20

Father, thank You for allowing us to live in a country where we have human rights. Thank You for the brave men and women who have sacrificed to enable us to be free. You have truly blessed our country and may we do our part this day to continue as one nation under God.

Do not take advantage of the widow or the fatherless.
Exodus 22:22

Father, thank You for Your great love for mankind. You see the heart of man and know our innermost heart. May we look to others today and treat all we come in contact with a heart as Jesus.

But I will not drive them out in a single year, because the land would become desolate and the wild animals too numerous for you.
Exodus 23:29

Father, Your ways are the best ways. Help us this day to trust not in ourselves but in Your ways and timing.

Then Moses entered the cloud as he went on up the mountain. And he stayed on the mountain forty days and forty nights.
Exodus 24:18

Moses would receive the tablets of stone from God with the law and commandments for their instruction. Father, thank You for the Holy Spirit that helps us keep your laws and commandments. On our own, we are not able to live a life that allows a relationship with You. Your Son Jesus came to fulfill the law and not abolish them. Only by the blood of Jesus are we worthy to be called Your children. May we live for only You this day.

Then put in the ark the tablets of the covenant law, which I will give you.
Exodus 25:16

Father, the ark was to contain the tablets that Moses would receive from You on Mount Sinai. You wanted Your chosen people to live and worship only You. May we live for only You today and make choices that reflect our devotion to Your Holy wishes.

Put the atonement cover on the ark of the covenant law in the Most Holy Place.
Exodus 26:34

Father, Your Instructions for the tabernacle were so detailed and precise. You are such a perfect God. We are not. Thank You for Your patience and forgiveness. We know that our sins and failures have been covered by the blood of Jesus. Help us this day as we stumble doing Your work. We know that You only expect our best.

In the tent of meeting, outside the curtain that shields the ark of the covenant law, Aaron and his sons are to keep the lamps burning before the Lord from evening till morning. This is to be a lasting ordinance among the Israelites for generations to come.
Exodus 27:21

Father, may we keep our lamps burning for You this day. From morning to evening and evening to morning, may we shine bright for You.

Also, put the Urim and the Thummim in the breastpiece, so they may be over Aaron's heart whenever he enters the presence of the Lord. Thus Aaron will always bear the means of making decisions for the Israelites over his heart before the Lord.
Exodus 28:30

Father, we your children bear the means of the Holy Spirit that dwells within us to help and guide our decisions. May we not look to the world or ourselves but trust in only Your perfect will for our lives. Let each decision we make on this day be pleasing to You.

Then I will dwell among the Israelites and be their God.
Exodus 29:45

Father, You alone are God. No more sacrifices are to be made. Jesus became our sacrifice once and for all on the Cross of Calvary. Our sins are washed away forever by the acceptance of Your perfect son. Now You dwell among Your children who have accepted forgiveness of their sins through the blood of Jesus. Praise the name of Jesus.

Put the altar in front of the curtain that shields the ark of the covenant law before the atonement cover that is over the tablets of the covenant law where I will meet with you.
Exodus 30:6

Around 1,400 years later, the curtain of the temple would be torn in two from top to bottom as Jesus cried out in a loud voice and gave up his spirit on the Cross of Calvary. Father, praise the name of Your Son Jesus. Who died that we may live. You no longer meet Your people in the Holy of Holies but Your Holy Spirit resides in Your children who accept the gift of salvation through Your Son Jesus. Oh praise the one who paid our debts

When the Lord finished speaking to Moses on Mount Sinai, he gave him the two tablets of the covenant law, the tablets of stone inscribed by the finger of God.
Exodus 31:18

Father, You are Holy and perfect in every way. Hallowed be Your name. Your kingdom come, Your will be done. On earth as it is in heaven. May we go this day and tell others about You through our words and actions.

When the people saw that Moses was so long in coming down from the mountain, they gathered around Aaron and said, "Come, make us gods who will go before us. As for this fellow Moses who brought us up out of Egypt, we don't know what has happened to him."
Exodus 32:1

Moses had been on Mount Sinai for 40 days and the people of Israel had made them a golden calf as an idol. God was going to wipe them out but Moses interceded. The Levites took the side of Moses when he came down from the mountain and with swords in hand killed 3,000 and God sent a plague on the rest. God did blot out the sins of the people from His book. Moses broke the 2 commandment tablets written on the front and back by God himself. Father, You relented Your full wrath from Your chosen people. Thank You for allowing us to also be forgiven in Your book from our sins against You. Let us go today and not fashion any idols but only worship You.

And the Lord said, "I will cause all my goodness to pass in front of you, and I will proclaim my name, the Lord, in your presence. I will have mercy on whom I will have mercy, and I will have compassion on whom I will have compassion.
Exodus 33:19

Father, You are a good good Father. You are sovereign. May You do with our lives Your perfect will. You know what is best for us. May Your goodness, mercy, and compassion follow us all the days of our lives.

Do not worship any other god, for the Lord, whose name is Jealous, is a jealous God.
Exodus 34:14

Father, thank You for another day on Your creation. We stand in awe at Your greatness and majesty. We worship and bow only to You and give You our best today.

All the Israelite men and women who were willing brought to the Lord freewill offerings for all the work the Lord through Moses had commanded them to do.
Exodus 35:29

Thank You Father for another day to serve You. May we bring our best and do our best for You.

And said to Moses, "The people are bringing more than enough for doing the work the Lord commanded to be done."
Exodus 36:5

The skilled workers came to Moses and said the people needed to restrain from bringing more because what they had was already more than enough to build the tabernacle. Father, may we bring and do our best for You today like the people of Israel did in building Your tabernacle. May we work with a joyful heart to help build Your kingdom

Bezalel made the ark of acacia wood-two and a half cubits long, a half wide, and a cubit and a half high.
Exodus 37:1

The ark contained the 2 tablets of the 10 commandments, Aaron's rod, and a pot of the manna God provided for the Israelites to eat. The ark was about 3 3/4 ft long 21/4 ft wide and 21/4 ft high. It was made of acacia wood and covered with a sheet of gold. The Mercy Seat was the top of the ark with two cherubim on each end. The ark was placed in the Tabernacle covered by a veil in the Holy of Holies and the high priest went in once a year to offer the blood of sacrifice and incense to God. Father, how elaborate Your ark was and how beautiful. I pray that we recognize Your beauty and majesty this day and bring our best to only You. We are now able through Your Son Jesus to have a relationship with You. The final blood sacrifice was made at Calvary and now we Your children offer incense of prayers and acknowledgement of You. How wonderful is the name of Jesus.

The total amount of the gold from the wave offering used for all the work on the sanctuary was 29 talents and 730 shekels, according to the sanctuary shekel.
Exodus 38:24

There were counted 603,550 men of Israel. There was a little over a ton of gold used to build the sanctuary. There were 3 3/4 tons of silver and 2 1/2 tons of bronze. Such skill was used to build the sanctuary. Father, help us use our skills and talents to help others today and support our families. You have put us where we are and let us serve You wholeheartedly.

So all the work on the tabernacle, the tent of meeting, was completed. The Israelites did everything just as the Lord commanded Moses.
Exodus 39:32

Father, we Your children are now Your temple. You had met with Your people in the Holy of Holies but now live within us through the Holy Spirit. How beautiful the tabernacle must have been but we are created in Your image and are Your most precious creation. Thank You Father for Your unspeakable love.

So the cloud of the Lord was over the tabernacle by day, and fire was in the cloud by night, in the sight of all the Israelites during all their travels.
Exodus 40:38

Father, what peace knowing that You watch over us in our travels and wherever we go. Not a second goes by that You do not see and know our every move. Protect us this day and provide our needs as only You can.

The Lord called to Moses and spoke to him from the tent of meeting. He said,
Leviticus 1:1

Father, You spoke and Moses not only listened but took action. You spoke to Moses from the tent of meeting. The Holy Spirit within us and Your Living Word through the Bible speaks daily to us each day. Having human missteps along the way, Moses did Your will and led Your children after 40 years to Cannan. Father, may we not only see and listen to what You say in Your Word but also take action overcoming our own human missteps

"'When anyone brings a grain offering to the Lord, their offering is to be of the finest flour."
Leviticus 2:1

Father, just as the Israelites were to bring their finest flour for a grain offering, may we choose to bring our best to You this day. May our actions and choices be focused on Your will and not ours. May Your kingdom come and Your will be done on earth as it is in heaven.

"'If your offering is a fellowship offering, and you offer an animal from the herd, whether male or female, you are to present before the Lord an animal without defect."
Leviticus 3:1

Father, the offering of animals and birds is over. No more blood is to be shed for the forgiveness of sins. Praise the name of Jesus for dying once and for all for the sins of the world. We are washed from our sins by the blood of Jesus. We are free, free indeed.

He shall dip his finger into the blood and sprinkle it before the Lord seven times in front of the curtain.
Leviticus 4:17

Father, the blood of Jesus now covers our sins. Praise the name of Jesus for making the sacrifice on the Cross of Calvary. He is the High Priest.

"It is a guilt offering; they have been guilty of wrongdoing against the Lord."
Leviticus 5:19

Father, thank You for the peace in knowing our wrongdoings against You have been atoned for through the blood of Your Son Jesus. We are forgiven through believing in Jesus and come to You by faith. Praise the name of Jesus today and through eternity.

The fire must be kept burning on the altar continuously; it must not go out.
Leviticus 6:13

Father, we no longer go to the altar to offer sacrifices. When Your son Jesus came to earth and died for our sins on the cross, the last sacrifice was made. We are now able to enter Your presence white as snow through the washing of the blood of Jesus from our sins. Thank You Jesus for Your perfect sacrifice and Your love for us.

But if anyone who is unclean eats any meat of the fellowship offering belonging to the Lord, they must be cut off from their people.
Leviticus 7:20

Father, just as back in the days of Moses You want us to trust and worship You. I pray that we will honor Your name today and many will accept and turn to You today. May we show Your love toward others today.

What has been done today was commanded by the Lord to make atonement for you.
Leviticus 8:34

Moses, Aaron, and his sons did exactly what God commanded. Father, may we live by Your word today and please You. Let us not get distracted by satan and the ones that are against You. There is peace and joy knowing we serve a living God who loves us and will live us for eternity.

Fire came out from the presence of the Lord and consumed the burnt offering and the fat portions on the altar. And when all the people saw it, they shouted for joy and fell facedown.
Leviticus 9:24

Father, we offer You our best today in all we say and do. One day all mankind will fall facedown and acknowledge Your son Jesus as the King of Kings and Lord of Lord. May many make the most important decision in their life today by believing and accepting Jesus as their Lord.

Moses then said to Aaron, "This is what the Lord spoke of when he said: '"Among those who approach me I will be proved holy; in the sight of all the people I will be honored."'
Aaron remained silent.
Leviticus 10:3

Two of Aaron's sons were consumed by fire for offering unauthorized fire before the Lord, contrary to His command. Father, help us this day in the age of grace to be safe leasing to You. We want to do and be the person who is in Your will. May our prayers be sweet incense and our offerings of worship and praise be pleasing to You our Father. Thank You for Your great love for us.

I am the Lord, who brought you up out of Egypt to be your
God; therefore be holy, because I am holy.
Leviticus 11:45

Father, help us today to make choices that will honor You. As
we go through this day, may we be in continual prayer and
fellowship with You. We worship You Father and know that
You have us in the palm of Your hands. If You are for us then
who can stand against us.

"But if she cannot afford a lamb, she is to bring two doves or
two young pigeons,one for a burnt offering and the other for a
sin offering. In this way the priest will make atonement for her,
and she will be clean."
Leviticus 12:8

Jesus has made atonement for the sins of the world. He is our
High priest. We are clean by the blood of Jesus. Father, may we
live this day knowing we are clean and can do nothing to make
You love us more than You already do. You are love and
through Jesus we have been atoned once and forever for our
sins. We are Your children for eternity.

"Anyone with such a defiling disease must wear torn clothes, let their hair be unkempt, cover the lower part of their face and cry out, 'Unclean! Unclean!'
Leviticus 13:45

Father,even though our outsides may be unclean and dysfunctional, our eternal souls are washed white as snow. These mortal bodies are just shells that start to wear down from the time of birth. One day we will be in our glorified bodies with You. What a day that will be when my Jesus I shall see.

These are the regulations for anyone who has a defiling skin disease and who cannot afford the regular offerings for their cleansing.
Leviticus 14:32

Father, You made a way for the Israelites, including their poor to be cleansed. Today, by the blood of Jesus all mankind can be cleaned. You make a way when there seems to be no way.
Thank You Father

"'You must keep the Israelites separate from things that make them unclean, so they will not die in their uncleanness for defiling my dwelling place, which is among them.'"
Leviticus 15:31

Father, thank You for a beautiful morning and sunrise. Another day to enjoy Your creation and see Your mighty works and wonders. May we live today and make choices that keep us in a right relationship with You. Thank You for the promises that nothing can separate us from You and Your love for us.

The Lord said to Moses: "Tell your brother Aaron that he is not to come whenever he chooses into the Most Holy Place behind the curtain in front of the atonement cover on the ark, or else he will die. For I will appear in the cloud over the atonement cover.
Leviticus 16:2

Father, as Your children we no longer have to go to a tabernacle or temple to offer sacrifices. The temple curtain was torn from top to bottom when Jesus died for our sins on the cross of Calvary. May our prayers and petitions continually enter Your throne room today and be pleasing to You.

For the life of a creature is in the blood, and I have given it to you to make atonement for yourselves on the altar; it is the blood that makes atonement for one's life.
Leviticus 17:11

Father, we are cleansed by the blood of Jesus. We are washed in the blood.

And if you defile the land, it will vomit you out as it vomited out the nations that were before you.
Leviticus 18:28

Marriage is an institution from God and this chapter shows what God expects from His children about keeping oneself free from detestable practices and in a relationship with not only spouses but with Our Father. Father, marriage is a covenant before You. We pray that we will uphold our promises and love and respect our spouses. One day, the bridegroom Jesus will come for His bride, the Church. May we look to Jesus and the church as our guide to the meaning of true love.

The Lord said to Moses, "Speak to the entire assembly of Israel and say to them: 'Be holy because I, the Lord your God, am holy.
Leviticus 19:1

Father, You set forth how we should live but the Israelites could not keep the covenant. We today can't keep Your laws but praise the name of Jesus we are washed from our sins and one day Your children will stand before judgment and be found spotless from transgressing against You because we had asked forgiveness from our sins by believing and putting our trust and hope in You perfect Son Jesus. May we strive to tell others today about our hope that comes from Your great love and grace and mercy.

I myself will set my face against him and will cut him off from his people; for by sacrificing his children to Molek, he has defiled my sanctuary and profaned my holy name.
Leviticus 20:3

Father, may we see all mankind as your creation made in Your image. Let us show respect to all we come in contact with today and treat all as You intend.

So Moses told this to Aaron and his sons and to all the
Israelites.
Leviticus 21:24

Father, may we tell others of You today and how You have
forgiven us of our trespasses and sins against You. Your love,
forgiveness, grace, and mercy are offered to all who will
receive and believe in Your Son Jesus Christ. May many come
to know You today.

Do not profane my holy name, for I must be acknowledged as
holy by the Israelites. I am the Lord, who made you holy.
Leviticus 22:32

Father, may Your holy name be worshiped and honored this
day. You are our Lord and God. The beginning and the end. All
that we are that is good comes from You.

"'There are six days when you may work, but the seventh day is a day of sabbath rest, a day of sacred assembly. You are not to do any work; wherever you live, it is a sabbath to the Lord.
Leviticus 23:3

The Jews observed the sabbath from Friday evening until Saturday evening. Father, we come this Sunday and proclaim it as a sabbath day of rest to You. We observe the sabbath and recognize You are first in our lives and in all we do is for You. We come to sing praises and learn from Your holy word. May our work done Monday through Saturday support our families, community, and nation but most of all help build Your kingdom.

Outside the curtain that shields the ark of the covenant law in the tent of meeting, Aaron is to tend the lamps before the Lord from evening till morning, continually. This is to be a lasting ordinance for the generations to come.
Leviticus 24:3

Father, surround us with Your light and goodness this day. Let Your light shine a path as we journey through this day. We will look only to Jesus as He is the light of the world

Do not take advantage of each other, but fear your God. I am the Lord your God.
Leviticus 25:17

Father, may we go out this day not to harm but to help. Let us build up and not tear down. May all we do further Your kingdom on earth as it is in heaven.

These are the decrees, the laws and the regulations that the Lord established at Mount Sinai between himself and the Israelites through Moses.
Leviticus 26:46

Father, thank You for allowing us not to have to pay for our trespasses against You. Praise the name of Jesus for taking on our sins at the Cross of Calvary. By faith we believe and accept Your free gift of forgiveness through Your son Jesus Christ. A free gift that took Your begotten Son to come to earth from heaven and die for our sins once and for all. May we go on this day and obey Your teachings and worship only You. For You are a Holy God and none or nothing comes before You.

No person devoted to destruction may be ransomed; they are to be put to death.
Leviticus 27:29

Father, as Your children we see through Your word the Bible that in the beginning You created and it was very good. We can see through Your creation the wonder of life and to never take a day for granted. May we be focused on the building of Your kingdom rather than destruction this day.

You and Aaron are to count according to their divisions all the men in Israel who are twenty years old or more and able to serve in the army.
Numbers 1:3

Father, You could have wiped out the enemies of Your chosen people but you instead formed an army out of Israel. The total numbering is 603,550. I pray we will stand and fight for You today against injustice and for the poor. May many choose to believe and accept Jesus today.

But the Kohathites must not go in to look at the holy things,
even for a moment, or they will die.
Numbers 4:20

Only Aaron and his sons were allowed to touch or look at the
holy things of the tent of meeting. Once covered and wrapped
by Aaron and his sons, the Kohathite branch of the Levites
numbered 2,750 from the age of 30-50 and were assigned to
carry articles of the tent of meeting. Father, just a glimpse into
Your holiness is beyond understanding. That You would allow
us to have fellowship with You shows us Your love beyond
describing. May we carry Your word and live our lives for You
with as much care as the Kohathite clan carried the articles of
the tent of meeting.

Say to the Israelites: Any man or woman who wrongs another
in any way and so is unfaithful to the Lord is guilty.
Numbers 5:6

Father, may we be a light for You with the people You created
today. We know from Your word that whosoever believes in
Jesus should not perish but have eternal life. May we be faithful
and Jesus and our love for You shine through us this day.

The Lord bless you and keep you; the Lord make his face shine on you and be gracious to you; the Lord turn his face toward you and give you peace.
Numbers 6:24-26

Father, thank You for blessing us this day with Your love and care. May we be in perfect fellowship with Your will. May nothing come between our service to You. Thank You for allowing us to have joy and peace as we are Your children and committed to You.

When Moses entered the tent of meeting to speak with the Lord, he heard the voice speaking to him from between the two cherubim above the atonement cover on the ark of the covenant law. In this way the Lord spoke to him.
Numbers 7:89

Father, thank You for letting us know You through Your word and creation. You, Jesus, and the Holy Spirit are three in one. You spoke directly to Moses. We have the words of Jesus written in the Bible and now the Holy Spirit dwells in Your children that have believed and accepted Jesus as their Lord. Your words are alive and will be forevermore.

The Lord said to Moses: "Take the Levites from among all the Israelites and make them ceremonially clean.
Numbers 8:5-6

Father, as Your children we have been washed in the blood of our Savior Jesus. Only by the washing of our sins, may we enter heaven and spend the rest of eternity with You and others that have accepted Jesus as our Lord and Savior. We were once as dirty as filthy rags but now are white as snow.

Whenever the cloud lifted from above the tent, the Israelites set out; wherever the cloud settled, the Israelites encamped.
Numbers 9:17

During the day a cloud covered the tabernacle, the tent of the covenant law, from evening till morning the cloud looked like fire. Whenever the cloud moved, the Israelites that surrounded the tabernacle would move. Father, may we not settle and not move when You have us to move. May we not be complacent and not hear Your call. Let us be content with Your many blessings but be willing to do Your perfect will for our lives. Your kingdom come and Your will be done.

Whenever the ark set out, Moses said, "Rise up, Lord!
May your enemies be scattered; may your foes flee before you.
Numbers 10:35

Father, may we set out this morning as Your children and
scatter Your love to a fallen world. May we show the mercy and
grace that You have extended to us. A love that transcends any
barrier that the evil one builds. Only through acceptance of
Your Son Jesus, can true peace fill the heart of man and break
the chains of sin. May many believe and accept Jesus this day.

Now the people complained about their hardships in the hearing
of the Lord, and when he heard them his anger was aroused.
Numbers 11:1

The Israelites complained about their hardships and the rabble
complained about the manna and they wanted meat. They were
not satisfied and missed melons, garlic, cucumbers, etc from
their slavery in Egypt. Moses complained of his hardships and
the Lord provided 70 elders and put the power of the Spirit that
was on Moses and put it on them also. God provided for His
chosen people with quail to eat. The Lord's anger did result in
fire coming down and consuming some of the outskirts of the
camp and then a severe plaque that came while meat was in
their teeth that killed people that craved other meat. Father, may
we be content and not arouse Your anger. We are blessed with
life and a relationship with You. May we not be gluttonous and
be satisfied with our many blessings that You provide. You are
the great provider. You know our needs.

Now Moses was a very humble man, more humble than anyone else on the face of the earth.
Numbers 12:3

Father, may we walk this earth today and let all honor and glory be lifted to You. May we come before You this day in humble obedience and do Your will.

Then Caleb silenced the people before Moses and said, "We should go up and take possession of the land, for we can certainly do it."
Numbers 13:30

Father, I pray we see through the eyes of Caleb this day. May we take promise in You and Your word and see through human obstacles of man and physics. You are a God that does the impossible. What seems like barriers, You can make a way. May our trust be in You and may we follow Your will.

Not one of you will enter the land I swore with uplifted hand to make your home, except Caleb son of Jephunneh and Joshua son of Nun.
Numbers 14:30

Father, may we learn from Caleb and Joshua who saw Your glory and knew and believed nothing can stand against You. When You speak, we are to listen and go. For their faithfulness, they were allowed to enter the promised land forty years later. One day, we will be allowed to enter the promise of heaven.

I am the Lord your God, who brought you out of Egypt to be your God. I am the Lord your God.
Numbers 15:41

Father, You said these words to Your chosen people the Israelites that You led out of slavery from Egypt while they were in the wilderness. Through the blood of Your son Jesus Christ, we also call You Lord our God. Let today be a day we continue to do Your will for our lives while on this earth.

They went down alive into the realm of the dead, with everything they owned; the earth closed over them, and they perished and were gone from the community.
Numbers 16:33

Father, may we honor and bring glory to You this day. Thank You for the promise of heaven for Your children. May we learn from Korah and the others that became prideful and the earth opened up and swallowed them.

The next day Moses entered the tent and saw that Aaron's staff, which represented the tribe of Levi, had not only sprouted but had budded, blossomed and produced almonds.
Numbers 17:8

Father, may we grow this day in wisdom that comes from knowing and having a relationship with You. A relationship made possible through Your Son Jesus. Praise the name of Jesus, our High Priest, whose staff leads and protects His sheep.

You must present as the Lord's portion the best and holiest part
of everything given to you.
Numbers 18:29

Father, may we give our best in all we do today to further Your
kingdom on earth. May You be pleased in our efforts and
service to You.

Anything that an unclean person touches becomes unclean, and
anyone who touches it becomes unclean till evening.
Numbers 19:22

Father, we are clean by the blood of Jesus. What was once
separated from You, is now restored. Since when has
impossible ever stopped You. You make all things new. Thank
You for another day to be with family, a new sunrise, and hope
that only comes from being Your child through the forgiveness
of sin that comes from Jesus our Savior.

But the Lord said to Moses and Aaron, "Because you did not trust in me enough to honor me as holy in the sight of the Israelites, you will not bring this community into the land I give them.
Numbers 20:12

Father, may all honor and glory come to You this day. Let all we do this day be to honor You and not ourselves. We give thanks for our many blessings and know You are the source that provides.

They traveled from Mount Hor along the route to the Red Sea, to go around Edom. But the people grew impatient on the way.
Numbers 21:4

Father, may we stay the course You have set before us. Let us finish the race strong and look up to You as distractions come our way. I pray we will have the patience like You display to us.

That night God came to Balaam and said, "Since these men have come to summon you, go with them, but do only what I tell you.
Numbers 22:20

Father, may we only do what You tell us through Your word and the guidance of The Holy Spirit that dwells inside us. Let us be a light for You and help the ones around us as Jesus taught. May our actions and deeds be pleasing to You this day.

He answered, "Must I not speak what the Lord puts in my mouth?
Numbers 23:12

Father, may we speak Your truth in the world today. Let us share Your love that You have richly bestowed upon us. A love that shatters hate, prejudice, and social classes. May our actions speak louder than our words.

Now leave at once and go home! I said I would reward you handsomely, but the Lord has kept you from being rewarded.
Numbers 24:11

Father, our rewards are not found in silver and gold, power or prestige. Our rewards come from running and finishing the race strong through living and telling about Your son Jesus Christ. May we go this day and spread the gospel of Jesus.

He and his descendants will have a covenant of a lasting priesthood, because he was zealous for the honor of his God and made atonement for the Israelites.
Numbers 25:13

Father, may have zeal for the honor of You this day. May we stand on Your word and our choices be according to Your will. Thank You for the Bible and the Holy Spirit to guide our path with Truth. Thank You Jesus for being the way and the truth and the life and allowing us a path to our Father.

Not one of them was among those counted by Moses and Aaron the priest when they counted the Israelites in the Desert of Sinai.
Numbers 26:64

Now there are 601,730 men of Israel to go into the promise land. The Lord had told the other Israelites they would surely die in the wilderness. Only Caleb and Joshua were left for their trust in the Lord.
Father, may we walk in Your will this day and like Caleb and Joshua stand when others turn from You. Let our trust be in You and not the world. Like Caleb and Joshua who were allowed to enter the promise land, we also will one day enter the promised land of heaven.

Then the Lord said to Moses, "Go up this mountain in the Abarim Range and see the land I have given the Israelites.
Numbers 27:12

Moses and his brother Aaron were not allowed to go into the promised land because of disobeying God's command to honor Him as holy before the eyes of the Israelite community at the Desert of Zin. Father, may we honor You at all times this day. May all honor and glory go to You. All we are and ever will be and accomplish is a result of the talents and spirit You give and provide. May You be pleased with the service we do for You this day.

This is the regular burnt offering instituted at Mount Sinai as a pleasing aroma, a food offering presented to the Lord.
Numbers 28:6

Father, may we offer our best this day to You. May the name of Jesus be proclaimed from our mouths and the Holy Spirit guidance followed. Jesus is the Lamb that was slain and never again will a burnt offering be required. Through the blood of Jesus, sin and death are forever defeated. Oh praise the one who paid our debt.

In addition to what you vow and your freewill offerings, offer these to the Lord at your appointed festivals: your burnt offerings, grain offerings, drink offerings and fellowship offerings.
Numbers 29:39

Father, all we have or ever will obtain is not ours but Yours. May we offer our best to You this day and May You be pleased with our efforts. Our best efforts could not keep us from sin, so You sent Your Son Jesus who knew no sin to live a perfect life on this earth. Through acceptance of Jesus, we are accepted as Your child. Praise the name of Jesus forever and ever.

When a man makes a vow to the Lord or takes an oath to obligate himself by a pledge, he must not break his word but must do everything he said.
Numbers 30:2

Father, Your words and promises never have an end. Your words are living and will transcend to the end of this earth to eternity. Your love endures forever. May we keep our oaths and promises on this day.

Moses was angry with the officers of the army-the commanders of thousands and commanders of hundreds-who returned from the battle.
Numbers 31:14

Father, may we follow You and our actions and deeds be to only please and honor Your Holy name. May You lead us by Your Spirit. Let us learn from Your word and not deviate from the teachings of Jesus Your beloved son. May we go this day and proclaim peace on earth and goodwill toward men.

Because they have not followed me wholeheartedly, not one of those who were twenty years old or more when they came up out of Egypt will see the land I promised on oath to Abraham, Isaac and Jacob.
Numbers 32:11

Father, may we follow You wholeheartedly this day. May You be pleased with our choices and decisions. Let each be made with discernment and guidance from the Holy Spirit.

They left Pi Hahiroth and passed through the sea into the desert, and when they had traveled for three days in the Desert of Etham, they camped at Marah.
Numbers 33:8

Father, let us journey this day following the will You have for our life. A life of service to You. Your path causes even seas to part where man, woman, and child cross on dry land. We wish to be in Your perfect will for our family, friends, and most important to be pleasing to You.

These are the men the Lord commanded to assign the inheritance to the Israelites in the land of Canaan.
Numbers 34:29

Father, we as Your children have the promises of inheritance of the kingdom of heaven one day where we will be in Your presence for eternity. Where one day is like a thousand years. Praise the name of Jesus, whose sacrifice for our sins made it possible. May many come to know You this day and start their eternal relationship with You.

Anyone who kills a person is to be put to death as a murderer only on the testimony of witnesses. But no one is to be put to death on the testimony of only one witness.
Numbers 35:30

Father, only by the witness of Jesus will we enter heaven one day. We were dead in our sins but brought to eternal life through the acceptance of Your Son. Praise the name of Jesus and His testimony on our behalf.

These are the commands and regulations the Lord gave through Moses to the Israelites on the plains of Moab by the Jordan across from Jericho.
Numbers 36:13

Father, thank You for showing us Your laws of Your children Israel through Moses. May we go this day and use these words to help guide and make decisions that please You.

Except Caleb son of Jephunneh. He will see it, and I will give him and his descendants the land he set his feet on, because he followed the Lord wholeheartedly.
Deuteronomy 1:36

Father, may we follow you wholeheartedly today. Let each step bring us closer to Your perfect will for our lives.

This very day I will begin to put the terror and fear of you on all the nations under heaven. They will hear reports of you and will tremble and be in anguish because of you.
Deuteronomy 2:25

Father, when You are for us, who can be against us. May You guide each step we take today. Let our choices be made for You this day.

Do not be afraid of them; the Lord your God himself will fight for you. Deuteronomy 3:22

Father, this is how we fight our battles. Whether enemies, sickness, or spiritual, we call on You Father to fight our battles. May we put on the full armor You provide. May we praise and honor Your name. "For the spirit of heaviness" "Put on the garment of praise."

Acknowledge and take to heart this day that the Lord is God in heaven above and on the earth below. There is no other.
Deuteronomy 4:39

Father, may praise and worship come from our deepest soul today as we proclaim Your holiness. We acknowledge You as The Great I Am and bow before You. May we do honor to Your name today and obey Your laws and commands set before us in Your holy scripture.

Oh, that their hearts would be inclined to fear me and keep all my commands always, so that it might go well with them and their children forever!
Deuteronomy 5:29

Father, may we never have any gods before You. May Your name be revered and proclaimed as the one true God.

Love the Lord your God with all your heart and with all your soul and with all your strength.
Deuteronomy 6:5

Father, two thousand years later when Your Son Jesus was asked the greatest law He replied these words spoken by You through Moses. It is the greatest then as it is today. May we go on this day and keep this greatest law in our minds and hearts. Hearts that beat to serve You: the one true God.

Know therefore that the Lord your God is God; He is the faithful God, keeping His covenant of love to a thousand generations of those who love Him and keep His commandments.
Deuteronomy 7:9

Father, You are faithful and true. Your promises are kept and Your love is endless for Your children. Thank You for loving us and the assurance we will be in Your presence for eternity.

He humbled you, causing you to hunger and then feeding you with manna, which neither you nor your ancestors had known, to teach you that man does not live on bread alone but on every word that comes from the mouth of the Lord.
Deuteronomy 8:3

Father, life comes from You. Your word is life and may we search and live out this day accordingly. May we not have to be disciplined and humbled by You. Thank You for the many blessings that You provide and the abilities You give us to work and help others while here on earth.

Understand, then, that it is not because of your righteousness that the Lord your God is giving you this good land to possess, for you are a stiff-necked people.
Deuteronomy 9:6

Father, may we obey Your commands this day. For 40 days and nights, Moses ate or drank nothing and fell prostrate praying that You would not destroy the Israelites for their rebelliousness and wickedness. It was not because of their righteousness they inherited the promise land but because of Your will and purpose. May we follow You this day devoted to honoring and proclaiming Your name.

To the Lord your God belong the heavens, even the highest heavens, the earth and everything in it.
Deuteronomy 10:14

Father, it is beyond our comprehension the vastness of the heavens. You know each particle and star. You are the creator of all. We were created to serve and worship You. May we spend today enjoying Your creation and giving honor and glory to You.

Teach them to your children, talking about them when you sit at home and when you walk along the road, when you lie down and when you get up.
Deuteronomy 11:19

Father, may we go this day meditating on Your words found in the Bible. Joy and peace come from Your Holy Word in knowing You will never leave or forsake us. We are blessed beyond measure.

But be sure you do not eat the blood, because the blood is the life, and you must not eat the life with the meat.
Deuteronomy 12:23

Father, we celebrate the birth of Your begotten son Jesus. In Your creation, You gave life through the blood that ran through the arteries and veins of Your creation. It took the life saving blood of Your son Jesus to enable us Your children to be washed of our sins and one day enter the gates of heaven. The blood is the life. May many be washed from their sins in the blood of Jesus today and have their names written in The Lamb's Book of Life.

It is the Lord your God you must follow, and Him you must revere. Keep His commands and obey Him; serve Him and hold fast to Him.
Deuteronomy 13:4

Father, only You are worthy of our praise, honor, and devotion. We fall prostrate before You this day and claim You to be God. The maker of the heavens and earth. There are none before or after. May we hold fast to You this day.

For you are a people holy to the Lord your God. Out of all the peoples on the face of the earth, the Lord has chosen you to be his treasured possession.
Deuteronomy 14:2

Father, You chose the Israelites to be Your chosen people. Through the Israelites, the promises Messiah would be born in a humble manger in the town of Bethlehem. Through Your Son Jesus, now all mankind has the choice to accept Your plan of forgiveness. A plan that cost the blood of Your begotten Son. Praise the name of Jesus.

If an animal has a defect, is lame or blind, or has any serious flaw, you must not sacrifice it to the Lord your God.
Deuteronomy 15:21

Father, Your Son Jesus was the perfect sacrifice. No defects or sin were found in Your perfect Son. There are no more sacrifices to be made for the remission of man's sins. Only acceptance of Your perfect Son who came to this earth over 2,000 years ago as a baby. Lived a perfect sinless life proclaiming to be the Son of God and died for our sins once and for all on the Cross of Calvary. Praise the name of Jesus, the chosen Messiah.

Each of you must bring a gift in proportion to the way the Lord your God has blessed you.
Deuteronomy 16:17

Father, You have blessed beyond measure. We can't give You anything to repay for giving Your Son Jesus to come to earth and die for our sins. May we live today basking in Your love for us. A love that extends to each man, woman, and child. We offer ourselves to live a servant life for our Lord and Savior Jesus Christ: Your chosen Messiah.

It is to be with him, and he is to read it all the days of his life so that he may learn to revere the Lord his God and follow carefully all the words of this law and these decrees.
Deuteronomy 17:19

Father, may we read and hide in our hearts the words You have revealed in the Bible all the days of our lives. As long as we have breath on this earth, let us revere You the Lord our God and follow the teachings of Your Son Jesus our Savior. May the Holy Spirit direct our path for Your will this day.

You must be blameless before the Lord your God.
Deuteronomy 18:13

Father, through the blood of Your Son Jesus, we will stand before You blameless. May we go this day walking in Your laws and decrees. Jesus did not come to abolish the laws but fulfill them. Through Jesus, we live life abundantly and have assurance our sins and shortcomings will be covered by the atoning blood of our Lord Jesus Christ.

One witness is not enough to convict anyone accused of any crime or offense they may have committed. A matter must be established by the testimony of two or three witnesses.
Deuteronomy 19:15

Father, we will stand in judgment as all of mankind that reach accountability. At that time, the only witness that will determine if we receive our inheritance is Your Son Jesus Christ. Thank You for allowing another day to allow mankind to ask Jesus for forgiveness of sin and follow Him this day.

"For the Lord your God is the one who goes with you to fight for you against your enemies to give you victory."
Deuteronomy 20:4

Father, what have we to fear knowing You go before us today. We will have trials but we have Your promise that You hold us with Your righteous right hand. The victory is Yours.

The Levitical priests shall step forward, for the Lord your God has chosen them to minister and to pronounce blessings in the name of the Lord and to decide all cases of dispute and assault.
Deuteronomy 21:5

Father, thank You for Your many blessings and allowing Your son Jesus to become our High Priest and judge. Jesus is righteous and true. He knows man's innermost thoughts and no sin can hide from Him. Thank You Jesus for being our mediator to our Father. May we lay our sins before You today and live according to Your
will.

Do the same if you find their donkey or cloak or anything else they have lost. Do not ignore it.
Deuteronomy 22:3

Father, may we help our fellow man today. Let us not commit the sin of omission and not do things we know we should. May we see as You see and do as You wish us to do.

For the Lord your God moves about in your camp to protect you and to deliver your enemies to you. Your camp must be holy, so that he will not see among you anything indecent and turn away from you.
Deuteronomy 23:14

Father, we can learn Your ways by how You had laws for Your chosen people the Israelites. I pray that our homes are a place that are pleasing to You. May we be careful about what we let enter Your children's houses You have blessed us with so not to bring dishonor to Your name.

Do not deprive the foreigner or the fatherless of justice, or take the cloak of the widow as a pledge.
Deuteronomy 24:17

Father, we know by Your word You see and care for the poor and needy as well as all mankind. Jesus came for all mankind and welcomes all to His table in heaven one day. Glory and honor be lifted to Your throne for the opportunity for salvation and to live a life to honor You.

For the Lord your God detests anyone who does these things, anyone who deals dishonestly.
Deuteronomy 25:16

Father, Your scales are true and all Your actions are just. Let us go on this day and be fair and act accordingly to Your ways. May we humbly look our fellow man in the eye with honesty and show integrity in our actions.

Then you and the Levites and the foreigners residing among you shall rejoice in all the good things the Lord your God has given to you and your household.
Deuteronomy 26:11

Father, we bring our best before You today and place it at the feet of Jesus. All that we are and have is devoted to serving and honoring You. Thank You for our many blessings. We rejoice in Jesus, knowing salvation was made possible through His precious blood. All our hope is found through Your begotten Son.

And you shall write very clearly all the words of this law on these stones you have set up.
Deuteronomy 27:8

Father, Your laws and commands are good. May we live today obeying and looking unto You. May our choices be pleasing to You and not ourselves. May our thoughts and actions be to bring honor to You.

Do not turn aside from any of the commands I give you today, to the right or to the left, following other gods and serving them.
Deuteronomy 28:14

Father, You gave Your chosen people the Israelites the way You wished them to live, serve and honor You. You showed them what would be the blessings and curses from their choices. I pray we learn from their good and poor choices and live today not for ourselves but for You. Thank You Father for mercy, grace, joy, and hope that comes from having a relationship with Jesus. May we look to the straight and narrow path that leads to You.

Yet the Lord says, "During the forty years that I led you through the wilderness, your clothes did not wear out, nor did the sandals on your feet.
Deuteronomy 29:5

Father, what a miracle You performed for Your children Israel by their clothes and shoes not wearing out for 40 years. You are the great provider that can do the impossible. Thank You for all the miracles You do each day that we are not aware . We are Your children and rely on Your love and presence to get us through this day.

If you obey the Lord your God and keep his commands and decrees that are written in this Book of the Law and turn to the Lord your God with all your heart and with all your soul.
Deuteronomy 30:10

Father, with Your chosen children the Israelites You had a conditional if with a choice of life and prosperity or choosing death and destruction. Today mankind has a conditional if. That is the acceptance of Your Son Jesus who is the way and the truth and the life. May many accept Jesus today and forever remove the if from their eternal destination.

Be strong and courageous. Do not be afraid or terrified because of them, for the Lord your God goes with you; He will never leave you nor forsake you.
Deuteronomy 31:6

Father, thank You for the promise of being with Your children. May we be strong and courageous as we go this day into the world where the enemy seeks to destroy and cause terror. Let us be found worthy as we shine Your light in a fallen world. Our strength and resolve is found through Jesus and guidance of the Holy Spirit. Thank You Father for providing to accomplish Your will.

This is because both of you broke faith with me in the presence of the Israelites at the waters of Meribah Kadesh in the Desert of Zin and because you did not uphold my holiness among the Israelites.
Deuteronomy 32:51

Father, may we learn from Your servants Moses and Aaron. Our disobedience has consequences. We will never be abandoned once we are Your children by accepting Your Son Jesus as our Savior but our choices and decisions have consequences. May we be sensitive to Your calling today and refrain from deviating from Your word. May Your will and not ours be done.

Blessed are you, Israel! Who is like you, a people saved by the Lord? He is your shield and helper and your glorious sword. Your enemies will cower before you, and you will tread on their heights.
Deuteronomy 33:29

Father, how You love Your children. You are the one to be trusted. Abundant life is found in You. Our constant companion in all we do. May our focus be on You this day as we go into the world. A world that desperately needs a relationship with You. How great is our God.

He buried him in Moab, in the valley opposite Beth Pear, but to this day no one knows where his grave is.
Deuteronomy 34:6

Father, when Moses died he was 120 years old but his eyesight was not weak nor was his strength gone. It was in Your timing to bring Moses up to Mt Nebo and show him the wonderful land the Israelites would enter as You promised before You buried him in Moab. It would now be Joshua, who would be taking Moses' place and lead Your children Israel to the promised land. May we strive to have a relationship as Moses did with You.

Have I not commanded you? Be strong and courageous. Do not be afraid; do not be discouraged, for the Lord your God will be with you wherever you go.
Joshua 1:9

Father, just as You commanded Joshua to be strong and courageous as he took the leadership place of Moses to lead Your children of Israel in three days to the promised land, may we go today with the promise You are with us. May we be strong and courageous as we go into the world and obey Your commands and do Your will.

When we heard of it, our hearts melted in fear and everyone's courage failed because of you, for the Lord your God is God in heaven above and on the earth below.
Joshua 2:11

Father, the people of Jericho were in fear of how You totally destroyed the Amorites. Rahab knew for her family to survive that she should help the two spies that Joshua sent to look over the land they would soon take possession. I pray today that we will do nothing to hinder Your perfect will for our lives. May thy will be done.

And as soon as the priests who carry the ark of the Lord-the Lord of all the earth-set foot in the Jordan, its waters flowing downstream will be cut off and stand up in a heap.
Joshua 3:13

Father, to show that You were with Joshua just as You were with Moses You exalted Joshua before the Israelites. It was flood stage at the Jordan and You caused the river to stop flowing. It piled up in a heap a great distance away at the town called Adam. The ark went before the people and as the people crossed dry land the ark was in the middle of the dry Jordan so people could understand that You were with them. Moses led the Israelites across the dry land of the Red Sea and now You had Joshua leading the Israelites across the Jordan to the promised land 40 years later. Father, thank you for still parting obstacles today that we can't.

That day the Lord exalted Joshua in the sight of all Israel; and they stood in awe of him all the days of his life, just as they had stood in awe of Moses.
Joshua 4:14

Father, You lifted Joshua up among the people of Israel. You used a miracle in nature to show the Israelites that You would be with them and Joshua would be the next leader You would use to replace Moses. Just as You parted the Red Sea, now the Jordan in flood stage would be held back and Your chosen people would pass through the Jordan on dry ground. The priests stood in the middle of Jordan with the ark. Your presence was there for all Israelites to see as they passed through the Jordan. Twelve stones were carried from the middle of the dry Jordan to the other side and placed at Gilgal as a reminder to generations after of Your promises. You Father are our solid rock on which we stand.

The manna stopped the day after they ate this food from the land; there was no longer any manna for the Israelites, but that year they ate the produce of Canaan.
Joshua 5:12

Father, for 40 years in the wilderness, you provided manna for your children to eat. Now they are eating the produce of the land: unleavened bread and roasted grain. You are our great provider.

When you hear them sound a long blast on the trumpets, have the whole army give a loud shout; then the wall of the city will collapse and the army will go up, everyone straight in.
Joshua 6:5

Father, You gave Joshua strict instructions of how to have the people walk around the walls of Jericho with the ark. They followed Your instructions and the walls of Jericho indeed collapsed. All were killed inside but Rahab and her family. How great is our God.

Who killed about thirty-six of them. They chased the Israelites from the city gate as far as the stone quarries and struck them down on the slopes. At this the hearts of the people melted in fear and became like water.
Joshua 7:5

Father, the few men of Ai chased 3,000 fighting men of Israel and killed 36 of them. This happened because Achan, from the tribe of Judah, had taken a robe, silver, and gold from the plunder of Jericho. May we go this day not covering the things of this world but focus our devotion and service to You.

Afterward, Joshua read all the words of the law-the blessings and the curses just as it is written in the Book of the Law.
Joshua 8:34

Father, Joshua read all the words of the law- the blessings and curses- to the whole assembly of Israel. Just as it is written in the Book of the Law, he read it to the assembly of Israel including the women, children, and foreigners who lived among them. May we read Your Holy Word and keep it close to our heart. For Your Word is living water. The human body can go but just days before dying. Like the human body we need Your Word daily.

The Israelites sampled their provisions but did not inquire of the Lord.
Joshua 9:1

Father, the Israelites did not inquire to You about the people of Gibeon and were fooled by their ruse. Just as in the days of Joshua, there is much deception and sin in the world. May we learn from Your word and by guidance from the Holy Spirit not make the same mistake as the Israelites.

So the sun stood still, and the moon stopped, till the nation avenged itself on its enemies, as it is written in the Book of Jashar. The sun stopped in the middle of the sky and delayed going down for about a full day.
Joshua 10:13

Father, You were with Joshua and Your chosen people the Israelites when you caused confusion upon the 5 armies of the Amorites. You brought down hailstones that killed more fleeing than were killed by the Israelites swords.
Even the sun stopped in the sky for a full day, as the battle was completed. Father, You are the one true God and do what You want, when You want, and how You want. We have peace knowing we are Your children.

As the Lord commanded his servant Moses, so Moses commanded Joshua, and Joshua did it; he left nothing undone of all that the Lord commanded Moses.
Joshua 11:15

Father, Joshua followed You totally and did as You commanded. May we also follow You totally today. Help us Father leave nothing undone as we go to do Your will this day.

Here is a list of the kings of the land that Joshua and the Israelites conquered on the west side of the Jordan.
Joshua 12:7

Father, in Your word You describe Moses and Joshua as Your servants. Moses and the Israelites took territory from kings on the east of the Jordan. Joshua and the Israelites took territory from kings on the west of the Jordan. You worked through the Israelites to acquire the promised land You promised to Abraham. Kings of this earth come and go. Jesus is the eternal King of Kings and Lord of Lords. May we bow only to Jesus, our King, this day.

When Joshua had grown old, the LORD said to him, "You are now very old, and there are still very large areas of land to be taken over."
Joshua 13:1

Father, what a great man Joshua was while on this earth. He lived and carried out Your will. May we go this day and live a life as committed to You as Joshua.

I am still as strong today as the day Moses sent me out; I'm just as vigorous to go out to battle now as I was then.
Joshua 14:11

Father, Caleb was now 85 years old and just as vigorous as he was when he was 40 years of age when Moses Your servant sent him from Kadesh Barnea to explore the land. When the other men were afraid, Caleb stood on Your promises. May we stand as Caleb on Your promises this day.

She replied, "Do me a special favor. Since you have given me land in the Negev, give me also springs of water." So Caleb gave her the upper and lower springs.
Joshua 15:19

Father, Caleb's daughter Aksah asked for springs of water. May many ask today of the gift of living water that only comes through Jesus Your Son. Thank You Jesus for allowing mankind to drink freely through Your atonement of our sins on the Cross of Calvary.

They did not dislodge the Canaanites living in Gezer; to this day the Canaanites live among the people of Ephraim but are required to do forced labor.
Joshua 16:10

Father, one day there will be no slaves. Your kingdom that is to come will have no whips and chains. All who dwell in heaven will be free. Free to worship and praise You for eternity.

But the forested hill country as well. Clear it, and its farthest limits will be yours; though the Canaanites have chariots fitted with iron and though they are strong, you can drive them out.
Joshua 17:18

Father, You gave Joshua wisdom to deal with the many questions brought before him. Please help us today as we go and make decisions. Let them be guided by the Holy Spirit. Please clear paths that are best for us. May Your will be done.

So Joshua said to the Israelites: "How long will you wait before you begin to take possession of the land that the Lord, the God of your ancestors, has given you?
Joshua 18:3

Father, there were 7 tribes of Israel that had still not taken possession of the land you had given them. Joshua, being the leader You had put in place, took the initiative and had each tribe appoint 3 men to go survey the land. They returned to Joshua at Shiloh to cast lots before You and distribute the land that was surveyed according to tribal divisions. Father, may we like Joshua look for Your guidance and direction in our decisions and actions today. May we go and do the things in the Bible that You command.

These are the territories that Eleazar the priest, Joshua son of Nun and the heads of the tribal clans of Israel assigned by lot at Shiloh in the presence of the Lord at the entrance to the tent of meeting. And so they finished dividing the land.
Joshua 19:51

Father, just as these men sought guidance and direction from You in dividing the land, may we look to You today. May we focus only on You.

Any of the Israelites or any foreigner residing among them who killed someone accidentally could flee to these designated cities and not be killed by the avenger of blood prior to standing trial before the assembly.
Joshua 20:9

Father, one day we will all stand before judgment. By the blood of Jesus, Your children will be allowed to spend eternity with You in heaven through the washing of our sins and transgressions. Others who have not accepted Jesus, will be separated from You forever in hell. May many come to You today through the blood of Your Son Jesus.

Not one of all the Lord's good promises to Israel failed; everyone was fulfilled.
Joshua 21:45

Father, we have peace and assurance that You are in control of all things at all times. Joy comes from knowing we have received the promise of eternal fellowship with You through the acceptance of Your Son Jesus Christ our Savior. May our worship today be a sweet incense to You.

But be very careful to keep the commandment and the law that Moses the servant of the Lord gave you: to love the Lord your God, to walk in obedience to him, to keep his commands, to hold fast to him and to serve him with all your heart and with all your soul.
Joshua 22:5

Father, the Reubenites, the Gadites and the half-tribe of Manasseh had fulfilled their oath and were now going to their land on the west side of the Jordan. May we do Your will today and keep Your commands to love and share the gospel of Jesus

You yourselves have seen everything the Lord your God has done to all these nations for your sake; it was the Lord your God who fought for you.
Joshua 23:3

Father, You go before Your children clearing paths and fighting battles. You fought for the Israelites where one man defeated a thousand. May we put on Your spiritual armor this day as we go and live for You. Joshua told Your chosen people the Israelites to hold fast to the Lord your God. Father, may we hold fast to You this day.

But if serving the Lord seems undesirable to you, then choose for yourselves this day whom you will serve, whether the gods your ancestors served beyond the Euphrates, or the gods of the Amorites, in whose land you are living. But as for me and my household, we will serve the Lord.
Joshua 24:15

Father, You give us a choice to accept Your love through Your son Jesus Christ or to reject that free gift that came at Calvary. As for our houses. We will serve the Lord. May we go on this day and be servants for You. May Your will be done.

The Lord answered, Judah shall go up; I have given the land into their hands.
Judges 1:2

Father, after the death of Joshua Your chosen people asked who shall go up first and fight against the Canaanites, You said the tribe of Judah. Out of that tribe would one day be born Jesus our Lord and Savior. May the name of Jesus be lifted with honor and praise today, tomorrow, and throughout eternity.

The people served the Lord throughout the lifetime of Joshua and of the elders who outlived him and who had seen all the great things the Lord had done for Israel.
Judges 2:7

Father, what a time of peace for Your chosen people, the Israelites, when they chose to follow You and not turn to other gods and wickedness. I pray in our lives today that we will have clean hearts and minds. This is accomplished by our relationship to Your son Jesus. In whose name, is our hope, peace, joy, and salvation.

After Ehud came Shamgar son of Anath, who struck down six hundred Philistines with an oxgoad. He too saved Israel.
Judges 3:31

Father, You had left several nations to test the Israelites. During the coming years the Israelites would turn from God and war would come. Your people would look again to You and You would answer their cries when they would turn to You. May we live by Your word and learn from the past that each day should be to worship only You and not fall into the snares of satan.

Now Deborah, a prophet, the wife of Lappidoth, was leading Israel at that time.
Judges 4:4

Father, You chose two women. Deborah as a prophet and Jael to do Your will. Deborah told Barek to go into battle. Our Father uses men, women, youth, and children to carry out His will. Father, may we be obedient and answer yes when You call us into action.

"So may all your enemies perish, LORD! But may all who love you be like the sun when it rises in its strength."
Then the land had peace forty years.
Judges 5:31

Father, one day all of the angels and mankind that rejected Your love will be thrown into the lake of fire. All who love You and accept Your Son Jesus as their Savior will have peace for eternity. As the sun rises today, may many come to You before it sets.

When the angel of the Lord appeared to Gideon, he said, "The Lord is with you, mighty warrior.
Judges 6:12

Father, the Israelites did evil in Your sight and You allowed the Midianites, Amalekites and other eastern peoples to invade the country. You chose Gideon. Gideon, the weakest in his family and one who was threshing wheat in a winepress to keep it away from the Midianites. Where Gidian felt weak, You saw a mighty warrior. Only with You Father are we strong. Down on my knees I learn to stand, I can't even walk without You holding my hand.

The Lord said to Gideon, "With the three hundred men that lapped I will save you and give the Midianites into your hands.Let all the others go home.
Judges 7:7

Father, with three hundred men You used to defeat the Midianites, the Amalekites and all the other eastern peoples. Since when has impossible ever stopped You. May we go this day and by Your strength defeat evil and temptations as they come our way. May Your will be done.

But Gideon told them, "I will not rule over you, nor will my son rule over you. The Lord will rule over you.
Judges 8:23

Father, thank You for allowing us to serve and worship only You. You are our God. We bow to You Father and may all we do be pleasing and in Your perfect will this day. May Your will be done on earth as it is in heaven.

Thus God repaid the wickedness that Abimelek had done to his father by murdering his seventy brothers.
Judges 9:56

Father, Your love is beyond understanding. We were not created to sin and do wickedness but to worship You our God. Wickedness and sin will not enter our eternal home in heaven. By the precious blood of Jesus we have the remission of our wickedness and sins. May we go this day and show the love that You gave to us through the offering of Your son Jesus Christ our hope and redeemer.

Then they got rid of the foreign gods among them and served the Lord. And he could bear Israel's misery no longer.
Judges 10:16

Father, again and again Your chosen people the Israelites turned to other gods. Your love for mankind is beyond what man can fathom. Thank you Father for loving us so much that You never want us to live in misery but to live a full life of joy and peace. May we choose You and Your ways this day.

And Jephthah made a vow to the Lord: "If you give the Ammonites into my hands, whatever comes out of the door of my house to meet me when I return in triumph from the Ammonites will be the Lord's, and I will sacrifice it as a burnt offering.
Judges 11:30-31

Father, the mighty warrior Jephthah had made a vow and when he got home from war and victory, his vow was met with having to sacrifice his only child, a daughter, as a sacrifice. May we learn from Jephthah's torment for the rash words that came out of his mouth as a vow to the Lord that he could not break.

When I saw that you wouldn't help, I took my life in my hands and crossed over to fight the Ammonites, and the Lord gave me the victory over them. Now why have you come up today to fight me?
Judges 12:3

Father, just as Japhthah, we know our victories are through You. We may have struggles and setbacks on this journey on earth but we know in the end that we as Your children are on the winning team. O Victory in Jesus my Savior forever.

The woman gave birth to a boy and named him Samson. He grew and the Lord blessed him.
Judges 13:24

Father, as we go this day may we grow in our relationship to You. Thank You for Your many blessings. We know that our marriage, being a parent, or being a friend can only be as good as our relationship with You. It all starts with You.

The Spirit of the Lord came powerfully upon him so that he tore the lion apart with his bare hands as he might have torn a young goat. But he told neither his father nor his mother what he had done.
Judges 14:6

Father, it was not Samson but You that gave Samson the strength to tear the lion apart and went down to Ashkelon striking down thirty of their men. We are weak but through You we are strong. May we journey this day holding tight to Your hand. We can't even walk without You holding our hand.

Then God opened up the hollow place in Lehi, and water came out of it. When Samson drank, his strength returned and he revived. So the spring was called En Hakkore, and it is still there in Lehi.
Judges 15:19

Father, You refresh when we are tired and thirsty. Your Word gives us strength to go on this day. May we drink freely from Your endless spring.

Then Samson prayed to the Lord, "Sovereign Lord, remember me. Please, God, strengthen me just once more, and let me with one blow get revenge on the Philistines for my two eyes."
Judges 16:28

Father, just as Samson called upon You over 3,000 years ago, we call on You, our Father, to strengthen us this day. May we go this day and do Your will for our lives. Your kingdom come, Your will be done on earth as it is in heaven.

In those days Israel had no king; everyone did as they saw fit.
Judges 17:6

Father, may we look to You today. May we not do as we see fit but live and obey Your Word.

Then they said to him, "Please inquire of God to learn whether our journey will be successful.
Judges 18:5

Father, today we have a relationship with You through Your Son Jesus. All our prayers are heard and You at all times hear when we tell You our struggles and joys. You tell us in Your Word that You want us to talk with You continually. Thank You for loving us so much. Thank You Holy Spirit for helping guide and council us so we are in God's will.

But she was unfaithful to him. She left him and went back to her parents' home in Bethlehem, Judah. After she had been there for four months.
Judges 19:2

Father, what an awful story happened to this woman who had been unfaithful to her husband. May we obey Your word today and keep our hearts pure. This can only be done through a personal relationship with Jesus. Thank You Father for grace and mercy when we make choices that we say, do, or think that are displeasing to You.

So all the Israelites got together and united as one against the city.
Judges 20:11

Father, may we Your children unite this day and help our fellow man. May we go into this world and be a light for You. Guide us Holy Spirit so we may see and not be blinded by the snares of satan. Father, may Your will be done on earth as it is in heaven.

"Lord, God of Israel," they cried, "why has this happened to Israel? Why should one tribe be missing from Israel today?
Judges 21:3

Father, just as You allowed all twelve tribes of Israel to live, we Your children will live with You for eternity. Thank You Father for the assurance of our salvation. We can go this day with peace and joy knowing You are with us and will never leave us or forsake us.

But Ruth replied, "Don't urge me to leave you or to turn back from you. Where you go I will go, and where you stay I will stay. Your people will be my people and your God my God.
Ruth 1:16

Father, Ruth made a choice that day over 3,000 years ago that she would commit her life to you. That decision was the greatest she would ever make on this earth. In the generations to follow, Your son Jesus would be born in Bethlehem from the linage of Ruth. May many choose to accept Your son Jesus today. Wherever You lead, may we go.

Just then Boaz arrived from Bethlehem and greeted the harvesters, The Lord be with you!" The Lord bless you!" they answered.
Ruth 2:4

Father, Your timing is always on time. Boaz showed up just at the right time to see Ruth in the fields gleaning the leftover grain. We have assurance in Your word that all things work for good. May we show patience in the storms of life knowing that You are in control of all things at all times.

One day Ruth's mother-in-law Naomi said to her, "My daughter, I must find a home for you, where you will be well provided for.
Ruth 3:1

Father, just as Naomi wanted the best for her daughter in law Ruth, so You want the best for Your children. May we listen to You today as Ruth listened to Naomi. Thank You Father for being our great provider.

The women living there said, "Naomi has a son!" And they named him Obed. He was the father of Jesse, the father of David.
Ruth 4:17

Father, what a wonderful story of love and redemption. Through the line of Boaz and Ruth, would come the true redeemer , our savior Jesus. May many call on Your precious sons name this day. The name that is above all names: Jesus.

I prayed for this child, and the Lord has granted me what I
asked of him.
1 Samuel 1:27

Father, Hannah prayed from her heart and You remembered her.
She gave birth to a son and named him Samuel because she
asked the Lord for him. May we pray from our hearts on this
day. Not thine will, but Yours be done Father.

There is no one holy like the Lord; there is no one besides you;
there is no Rock like our God.
1 Samuel 2:2

Father, what a beautiful prayer Hannah prayed to You. You are
our solid rock. When the winds blow and the earth shakes You
are immovable. May we hold fast to You this day.

So Samuel told him everything, hiding nothing from him. Then Eli said, "He is the Lord; let him do what is good in his eyes."
1 Samuel 3:18

Father, may You do this day what is good in Your eyes with our lives. May we be a vessel that is used by You. We were all born into sin and fell short of Your glory but you allowed a way for us to be Your children by the acceptance of Your son Jesus. May all we do this day be for the honor and glory of Your name.

She said, "The Glory has departed from Israel, for the ark of God has been captured."
1 Samuel 4:22

Father, because of their disobedience Your Glory had departed from Israel. Just as You said, Eli, who had led Israel for 40 years, had two sons Hophni and Phinehas who were killed as a result of their disobedience. Disobedience has its consequences. May we live this day in obedience to You Father. Praise the name of Jesus who bore our sins and shortcomings on the cross. Our hope is found at the Cross and resurrection of Jesus our Savior.

When the people of Ashdod rose early the next day, there was Dagon, fallen on his face on the ground before the ark of the Lord! They took Dagon and put him back in his place.
1 Samuel 5:3

Father, You are the one true God. There is no one or nothing that is before You. You are the beginning and the end. We bow before You with all honor and glory. May we bring our best to You on this day.

And the people of Beth Shemesh asked, "Who can stand in the presence of the Lord, this holy God? To whom will the ark go up from here?"
1 Samuel 6:20

Father, You struck down the 70 at Beth Shemesh because they had looked inside the ark. You are holy and we humbly come before You on this day. It is beyond our understanding of holiness. Moses and others could not look upon You but mankind was able to look into the face and eyes of Jesus. They were able to touch and walk with Jesus who has always been and forever will be. One day all the questions we have will be revealed in heaven. Thank You Father for Your great love for Your children.

So the Israelites put away their Baals and Ashtoreths, and
served the Lord only.
1 Samuel 7:4

Father, Samuel continued as Israel's leader all the days of his
life. He put You first in all His ways while here on earth. May
we put away any thing we say, do, or think that is displeasing to
You this day. Praise the name of Jesus for allowing us to have
peace and assurance that our sins are forgiven. Praise the Lord
O my soul, worship His holy name.

But the people refused to listen to Samuel. "No!" they said. "We
want a king over
us.
1 Samuel 8:19

Father, Samuel's sons had become corrupt and Gods chosen
people had come to Him demanding a man become their king
like the other nations around them. It is hard to understand how
they would want a king. You had always been their provider but
over and over again they turned from You to false gods and
selfishness. Let us learn from their foolishness. May we go this
day looking only to You and bow at Your feet. You are our
alpha and omega. There is none before You.

Kish had a son named Saul, as handsome a young man as could be found anywhere in Israel, and he was a head taller than anyone else.
1 Samuel 9:2

Father, You had sent Saul from the tribe of Benjamin to Samuel. You had heard the cries of Israel and would now anoint Saul as king of Israel and deliver them from the hands of the Philistines. Even in their disobedience, you love and care for Your children. When we fail today, thank You for allowing us to seek forgiveness and allowing us to receive forgiveness through Your son Jesus. Praise the holy name of Jesus. Jesus paid it all, all to Him we owe, death had left a crimson stain, He washed it white as snow.

As Saul turned to leave Samuel, God changed Saul's heart, and all these signs were fulfilled that day.
1 Samuel 10:9

Father, just as You changed Saul's heart, our heart's were changed when we accepted Jesus as our Savior. Although we fight temptations each day, we have the assurance that the Holy Spirit will help us this day. What peace and joy started that day deep within our souls when our sins were forgiven and washed away by the blood of Jesus. Praise the name of Jesus. Our sins.were washed away and our night was turned to day.

But Saul said, "No one will be put to death today, for this day
the Lord has rescued Israel."
1 Samuel 11:13

Father, You rescued Your children the Israelites from the
Ammonites. Thank You Father for also rescuing us from the
bondage of sin. May the name of Jesus be praised. You are our
great Deliverer.

But be sure to fear the Lord and serve him faithfully with all
your heart; consider what great things he has done for you.
1 Samuel 12:24

Father, how blessed we are to be called Your children. Nothing
compares to our relationship to You. Through the acceptance of
Jesus, You call us Your own. We can go this day with the
confidence that You watch over and protect us with Your
righteous right hand.

But now your kingdom will not endure; the Lord has sought out
a man after his own heart and appointed him ruler of his people,
because you have not kept the Lord's command."
1 Samuel 13:14

Father, Saul ruled as king over Israel for 42 years. Instead of
waiting for Samuel, he felt compelled to offer the burnt
offering. If not for doing the foolish thing by not keeping the
command You gave him, his kingdom would have been
established over Israel for all time. As a result, You sought out a
man after Your own heart. May we have clean hearts that can be
used to do Your will and not ours today.

Then panic struck the whole army-those in the camp and field,
and those in the outposts and raiding parties-and the ground
shook. It was a panic sent by God.
1 Samuel 14:15

Father, Johnathan and his armor-bearer struck down some
twenty men that day. Johnathan had inquired to You and knew
that You can accomplish Your will with many or by a few. That
day it was only two men that started a conflict and You sent
panic among the Philistines that ended in victory at Beth Aven.
It took one, Your only Son, to defeat sin. Jesus was the only one
that could defeat sin and death. Praise the name of Jesus. May
we go this day and tell the gospel of Jesus.

Then Saul said to Samuel, "I have sinned. I violated the Lord's command and your instructions. I was afraid of the men and so I gave in to them.
1 Samuel 15:24

Father, may we obey your word and will this day. We are Your children and serve and worship only You. Please help us to learn from King Saul and not make the same mistakes that caused You to regret You had made him King over Israel.

But the Lord said to Samuel, "Do not consider his appearance or his height, for I have rejected him. The Lord does not look at the things people look at. People look at the outward appearance, but the Lord looks at the heart."
1 Samuel 16:7

Father, Jesse had his son Eliab and his other sons pass before Samuel but David the youngest was the one with the heart for You. May we have the same heart as David.

The Lord who rescued me from the paw of the lion and the paw of the bear will rescue me from the hand of this Philistine.
1 Samuel 17:37

Father, David knew that You were with him when he was able to seize the lion and the bear and kill them. David knew You were the source of his strength and Your will would be done. When the Goliaths come in our path today, may we remember that You are our strength and are with us.

After David had finished talking with Saul, Jonathan became one in spirit with David, and he loved him as himself.
1 Samuel 18:1

What a special bond Johnathan and David had together. To have a friend you must be a friend. Thank You Jesus for allowing us to have You as our Savior and closest friend. Father, may we work today to build friendships that please You.

Jonathan spoke well of David to Saul, his father and said to him, "Let not the king do wrong to his servant David; he has not wronged you, and what he has done has benefited you greatly.
1 Samuel 19:4

What a wonderful friend Johnathan was to David. Johnathan knew his daddy, even though being the king, was in the wrong and Johnathan spoke the truth. Father, may we also have the courage to speak truth and help those that are innocent even in the face of persecution.

But Saul hurled his spear at him to kill him. Then Jonathan knew that his father intended to kill David.
1 Samuel 20:23

Father, disobedience against You causes so much chaos and confusion. King Saul in his disobedience toward You threw a spear and tried to kill David. Now, in his anger Saul has thrown a spear at his own son Johnathan. May we live this day in total obedience to You Father.

So he pretended to be insane in their presence; and while he was in their hands he acted like a madman, making marks on the doors of the gate and letting saliva run down his beard.
1 Samuel 21:13

David had done no wrong for King Saul to be wanting to kill him. Now David is running for his life and resorting to acting like a mad man. Only if the Israelites would have obeyed and not coveted to have a leader like the ones around them. Father, may we look only to You. Only You are enough.

Ahimelek answered the king, "Who of all your servants is as loyal as David, the king's son-in-law, captain of your bodyguard and highly respected in your household?
1 Samuel 22:14

What courage Ahimelek showed when King Saul questioned him about David. That day 85 men were killed that wore the linen ephod. Father, may we have the courage and strength that comes from You this day.

And Saul's son Jonathan went to David at Horesh and helped him find strength in God.
1 Samuel 23:16

Father, may we go this day and be like Johnathan, Let us help one another in times of trouble and sorrow. May we rejoice with one another in times of joy and happiness. Most importantly, may we always help each other to always look to Your Son Jesus. Our strength comes from You.

May the Lord judge between you and me. And may the Lord avenge the wrongs you have done to me, but my hand will not touch you.
1 Samuel 24:12

Father, David could have taken the life or had one of his men kill King Saul as they were alone with him in the cave. However, David did not have King Saul killed because he was the Lord's anointed. Father, may we learn from the old saying "from evil doers come evil deeds." May we overcome evil with good this day.

His name was Nabal and his wife's name was Abigail. She was an intelligent and beautiful woman, but her husband was surly and mean in his dealings-he was a Calebite.
1 Samuel 25:3

Father, may we be peacemakers today as Abigail. Because of Abigail, all the other males belonging to Nabal were not killed by David and his men. Let us go to do good today and not evil

Then Saul said to David, "May you be blessed, David my son; you will do great things and surely triumph."
1 Samuel 26:25

Father, again Saul, had pursued David to take his life. You had caused Saul and his men to fall into a deep sleep and David took the spear and water jug beside King Saul's head as he slept. David valued Saul's life. May we go this day and value life overcoming evil with good.

But David thought to himself, "One of these days I will be destroyed by the hand of Saul. The best thing I can do is to escape to the land of the Philistines. Then Saul will give up searching for me anywhere in Israel, and I will slip out of his hand."
1 Samuel 27:1

David had thought to himself. To get away from King Saul, he went to live 1 year and 4 months in the land of the Philistines. Father, You know the best thing for us today. Go before us today Father and may we walk behind.

When Saul saw the Philistine army, he was afraid; terror filled his heart.
1 Samuel 28:5

There was a day when King Saul had no fear because You were with him Father. Because Saul did not obey You or carry out Your fierce wrath against the Amalekites, now he, his sons, and Israel will be delivered into the hands of the Philistines. Thank You Jesus for allowing us to have forgiveness of our sins and not live in fear. We seek Your mercy and grace on this day.

So David and his men got up early in the morning to go back to the land of the Philistines, and the Philistines went up to Jezreel.
1 Samuel 29:11

Father, You worked it out so David would not be fighting against the Israelites. You do so much for us that we will never know until we get to heaven. Go before us today Father and may Your will be done.

And David inquired of the Lord, "Shall I pursue this raiding party? Will I overtake them?"
"Pursue them," he answered. "You will certainly overtake them and succeed in the rescue.
1 Samuel 30:8

Father, the Amalekites had come and raided David's camp while he and his men were gone. The Amalekites had burned Ziklag and taken their wives, sons, and daughters captive. Now his men were talking of stoning him. But, David found strength in the Lord his God. When David took the ephod and inquired of You, You told him to pursue and they would certainly overtake them and succeed in the rescue. And they did. Father, go before us today and may we follow; may we not lead but follow.

So Saul and his three sons and his armor-bearer and all his men
died together that same day.
1 Samuel 31:6

Father, the king that the Israelites had wanted was now dead.
You had tried to tell them what was best for them to look to You
and not a human king. Now they are deserting their towns to be
plundered by the Philistines. May we look only to You this day
and never ever have anything before You Father.

Saul and Jonathan- in life they were loved and admired, and in
death they were not parted. They were swifter than eagles, they
were stronger than lions.
2 Samuel 1:23

Father, may we be the friend today that David was to
Johnathan. As much as we love our friends on earth, nothing
can compare to the love You have for Your children Father.
Thank You Jesus for always lifting our prayers to our Father.
Thank You Holy Spirit for dwelling inside of us and giving us
the peace that You will never leave us.

Now then, be strong and brave, for Saul your master is dead, and the people of Judah have anointed me king over them.
2 Samuel 2:7

Father, David would be king of Judah for 7 years and 6 months in Hebron. You were with David. Thank You Father for never leaving our side as Your children. May we go this day with that assurance.

The war between the house of Saul and the house of David lasted a long time. David grew stronger and stronger, while the house of Saul grew weaker and weaker.
2 Samuel 3:1

Father, our strength comes from You. Thank You for wanting to have a relationship with Your children. We are humbled that the creator of all would seek us with the offering of His Son Jesus on the Cross of Calvary. What love You have for mankind. May we grow stronger and stronger today in our love and devotion to You.

Jonathan son of Saul had a son who was lame in both feet. He was five years old when the news about Saul and Jonathan came from Jezreel. His nurse picked him up and fled, but as she hurried to leave, he fell and became disabled. His name was Mephibosheth.
2 Samuel 4:4

David loved Johnathan and would one day take Johnathans son Mephibosheth into his care and household. Mephibosheth would sit and eat with David and his family. Father, may we never forget our friends. May we learn from David and Johnathan the meaning of true friendship.

In the past, while Saul was king over us, you were the one who led Israel on their military campaigns. And the Lord said to you, 'You will shepherd my people Israel, and you will become their ruler.
2 Samuel 5:2

David would now reign over both Israel and Judah for 33 years. He had already reigned over Judah for 7 years and 3 months. Father, may we have a heart for You as David. May we go on this day and serve only You.

David said to Michal, "It was before the Lord, who chose me rather than your father or anyone from his house when he appointed me ruler over the Lord's people Israel–I will celebrate before the Lord.
2 Samuel 6:21

Father, may we honor You with thanksgiving and praise. Let our voices sing and our feet dance as David. He worshiped with his heart. May we give our best to You on this day.

What more can David say to you? For you know your servant, Sovereign Lord.
2 Samuel 7:20

Father, You know our hearts. May our hearts be clean by the blood of Jesus. Let no sin have hold over our worship and service to You. Just as David, let us sing songs of praise to You Father.

He put garrisons in the Aramean kingdom of Damascus, and the Arameans became subject to him and brought tribute. The Lord gave David victory wherever he went.
2 Samuel 8:6

Father, You gave David the victory in battle. We ask that You go before us in our battles on this earth. Battles against cancer, battles against mental illness, battles against substance abuse, battles against...This is how we fight our battles. The victory comes through Your son Jesus Christ.

Don't be afraid," David said to him, "for I will surely show you kindness for the sake of your father Jonathan. I will restore to you all the land that belonged to your grandfather Saul, and you will always eat at my table.
2 Samuel 9:7

David allowed Mephibosheth, his family, and his servant Ziba's family to restore the land that belonged to Saul. Ziba and his family were to farm the land.
Father, David never forgot his friend Johnathan. Now his son Mephibosheth will forevermore have his grandfather's Saul's land to tend and eat at King David's table. Father, may we always remember our friends and encourage and build them up as David did Mephibosheth. The same Mephibosheth who earlier addressed himself to David as a filthy dog is now restored to his place of honor.

Be strong, and let us fight bravely for our people and the cities of our God. The Lord will do what is good in his sight."
2 Samuel 10:12

Father, may we be strong today. Although David sought peace, the new king of the Ammorites was given council to go to war. May we use discernment and listen to Godly counsel. May we not be deceived by satan and evil. Let us look to Your word and guidance from the Holy Spirit all the days of our lives. Thank You Father for Your great love for Your children. May You do what is good in Your sight.

After the time of mourning was over, David had her brought to his house, and she became his wife and bore him a son. But the thing David had done displeased the Lord.
2 Samuel 11:27

Father, when David should have been off to war, he committed sins against You. The things David did displeased You just as all the sins we commit displease You. May we go this day and stay focused on You and not become idle. Let us serve as Jesus served. May we work till Jesus comes.

Then David said to Nathan, "I have sinned against the Lord." Nathan replied, "The Lord has taken away your sin. You are not going to die.
2 Samuel 12:13

Father, thank You for the forgiveness of our sins that comes from the acceptance of Your Son Jesus Christ. Thank You Jesus for defeating death at the old rugged cross. May many carry their sins and burdens and lay them at the foot of the cross this day.

'Go to bed and pretend to be ill," Jonadab said. "When your father comes to see you, say to him, 'I would like my sister Tamar to come and give me something to eat. Let her prepare the food in my sight so I may watch her and then eat it from her hand.'
2 Samuel 13:5

Father, may we be watchful and careful of the evil one. He prowls around seeking to destroy. May we surround ourselves with Godly counsel and accountability. Let us be on our guard this day.

Joab son of Zeruiah knew that the king's heart longed for Absalom.
2 Samuel 14:1

Father, thank You that in Your complete Holiness that You seek mankind to spend an eternity with You in heaven. Even though we are not worthy, You provided a way to have forgiveness of our sins and trespasses against You. Thank You Jesus for coming to earth and living a sinless life and taking our sins to the Cross of Calvary. Just as David longed for Absolom, You long for one sinner to repent and come to You. May many leave their sins at the foot of the Cross this day.

But Ittai replied to the king, "As surely as the Lord lives, and as my lord the king lives, wherever my lord the king may be, whether it means life or death, there will your servant be."
2 Samuel 15:21

Father, just as Ruth stayed with Naomi, Ittai has chosen to stay with David. When hard times come, may we choose to stand for what is right in your Word. Thank You Father for always staying with Your children through the hills and valleys of life on this earth. You walk with us and talk with us and tell us we are Your own. What a friend we have in Jesus.

The king then asked, "Where is your master's grandson?"
Ziba said to him, "He is staying in Jerusalem, because he thinks, 'Today the Israelites will restore to me my grandfather's kingdom.'"
2 Samuel 16:3

Mephibosheth did not go with David but stayed behind in Israel. Father, may we make choices today that honor You. Let us not look to the world but to You. May all we do and say today bring honor to Your Holy name.

Absalom and all the men of Israel said, "The advice of Hushai the Arkite is better than that of Ahithophel." For the Lord had determined to frustrate the good advice of Ahithophel in order to bring disaster on Absalom.
2 Samuel 17:14

Father, go before us on this day. Just as spies helped David and his people to survive from his son Absolom, go before us with Your angels and Your children to help shape the will You have for us today. Not our will but Yours be done.

The king was shaken. He went up to the room over the gateway and wept. As he went, he said: "O my son Absalom! My son, my son Absalom! If only I had died instead of you-O Absalom, my son, my son!"
2 Samuel 18:33

Father, just as David cried for the death of his son Absalom, how Mary must have cried as her Son Jesus hung on the Cross of Calvary. Three days later, her tears turned to joy as her Son, just as He had said, arose from the grave and appeared to over 500 people over a span of 40 days. We come this Easter Sunday rejoicing as Mary and praise You Jesus for defeating death and providing peace and joy for the ones that accept You as their Lord and Savior. Praise the name of Jesus. He is risen.

So the king got up and took his seat in the gateway. When the men were told, "The king is sitting in the gateway," they all came before him. Meanwhile, the Israelites had fled to their homes.
2 Samuel 19:8

Father, just as David returned to sit in the gateway after fleeing from Absalom, Your Son Jesus now sits by Your right side at your throne. What a day that will be when our Jesus we shall see. May we go this day spreading the Gospel of Jesus and living our lives so that the ones we come in contact can see the light of Jesus.

So all the men of Israel deserted David to follow Sheba son of Bikri. But the men of Judah stayed by their king all the way from the Jordan to Jerusalem.
2 Samuel 20:2

Father, may we keep our eyes on You this day. When temptations come, let us be sensitive to Your word and rebuke what is not pleasing to You in the name of Jesus. May we stand strong with strength and courage that only comes through You. Standing standing standing on the promises of God.

But Abishai son of Zeruiah came to David's rescue; he struck the Philistine down and killed him. Then David's men swore to him, saying, "Never again will you go out with us to battle, so that the lamp of Israel will not be extinguished."
2 Samuel 21:17

Father, thank You for coming to mankind's rescue and providing a way back to You. Through the Cross of Calvary, Jesus made a way. May we go this day and shine the light to others and reveal to them what Jesus has done for us. What a friend we have in Jesus.

He said: "The Lord is my rock, my fortress and my deliverer; my God is my rock, in whom I take refuge, my shield and the horn of my salvation. He is my stronghold, my refuge and my savior–from violent people you save me.
2 Samuel 22:2-3

Father, You are the foundation we stand on, all other ground is sinking sand. Protect us this day with Your mighty shield of protection. May we serve with a servant heart this day.

But Shammah took his stand in the middle of the field. He defended it and struck the Philistines down, and the Lord brought about a great victory.
2 Samuel 23:12

Father, when Israel's troop fled from the Philistines, Shammah stood his ground and You brought about a great victory. May we go this day and not live for ourselves but for You. Let us stand and Your will be done. May all be for the honor and glory of Your name.

David said to Gad, "I am in deep distress. Let us fall into the hands of the Lord, for his mercy is great; but do not let me fall into human hands."
2 Samuel 24:14

Father, Your mercy and grace is great. Thank you for allowing us to pray and worship You. For allowing us to have a relationship with Your son Jesus. For allowing us to choose this day to honor You by our choices and decisions. All to thee, we surrender.

His father had never rebuked him by asking, "Why do you behave as you do?" He was also very handsome and was born next after Absalom.
1 Kings 1:6

Adonijah, one of David's sons, said to himself that he would be king after David. Father, You love us so much and when we get out of Your will You discipline us as David should have Adonijah. I pray that we honor You today and live in Your will.

"I am about to go the way of all the earth," he said. "So be strong, act like a man, and observe what the Lord your God requires: Walk in obedience to him, and keep his decrees and commands, his laws and regulations, as written in the Law of Moses. Do this so that you may prosper in all you do and wherever you go.
1 Kings 2:2-3

Father, what wonderful words David left Solomon to live by as he became king. May we be strong on this day and walk in obedience to You.

Solomon showed his love for the Lord by walking according to the instructions given him by his father David, except that he offered sacrifices and burned incense on the high places.
1 Kings 3:3

Father, Solomon asked that you give him a discerning heart to govern Your people and to distinguish right from wrong. May we have that same discerning heart and have no exceptions as we show our love for You this day.

God gave Solomon wisdom and very great insight, and a
breadth of understanding as measureless as the sand on the
seashore.
1 Kings 4:29

Father, You gave Solomon wisdom. He also had knowledge that
caused people from other nations to come and learn about
Botany and reptiles but wisdom comes from following You.
You gave Solomon wisdom. May we seek wisdom this day.

"You know that because of the wars waged against my father
David from all sides, he could not build a temple for the Name
of the Lord his God until the Lord put his enemies under his
feet.
1 Kings 5:3

Father, thank You for salvation that comes only from Your Son
Jesus. The Holy Spirit resides in Your children that have
received the gift of forgiveness of sins that comes from the
acceptance of Jesus. One day when we enter heaven, we are
assured in Your Word that there will never again be enemies or
war or disease. Through Jesus, came victory over all sin. O
victory in Jesus, our Savior forever.

In the eleventh year in the month of Bui, the eighth month, the temple was finished in all its details according to its specifications. He had spent seven years building it.
1 Kings 6:38

Father, the temple was completed 487 years after your chosen people left the bondage of Egypt. The temple was so specific in its building that it took 7 years to complete. What a wonderful time it must have been in Solomon's life to have been able to oversee the building of the temple. May we serve You today with the same attention to detail.

When all the work King Solomon had done for the temple of the Lord was finished, he brought in the things his father David had dedicated-the silver and gold and the furnishings-and he placed them in the treasuries of the Lord's temple.
1 Kings 7:51

Father, just like Solomon, when we start something may we finish. As we journey through this life on earth, what we start let us finish according to Your will. May we finish our race strong.

Hear the supplication of your servant and of your people Israel when they pray toward this place. Hear from heaven, your dwelling place, and when you hear, forgive.
1 Kings 8:30

Father, as Solomon dedicated the temple he was knelt down with outstretched arms toward heaven. 900 years later, Jesus would come with outstretched arms on the Cross of Calvary. When He cried out in a loud voice, He gave up His spirit. The temple curtain was torn in two from top to bottom as the earth shook and rocks split. Now Your children have access to You through Jesus. We never have to travel to a temple, we always have access to You at all times at any place. Blessed be the name of Jesus.

Three times a year Solomon sacrificed burnt offerings and fellowship offerings on the altar he had built for the Lord, burning incense before the Lord along with them, and so fulfilled the temple obligations.
1 Kings 9:25

Father, thank you for allowing mankind to have a way through Jesus back to You. Jesus made the ultimate sacrifice on the Cross of Calvary and now mankind has the free gift of salvation that only comes through Your begotten Son. Praise the name of Jesus.

The whole world sought an audience with Solomon to hear the wisdom God had put in his heart.
1 Kings 10 24

Father, true wisdom comes from You. May we seek wisdom from You on this day. You tell us if we seek, we will find. You are a good good Father.

As Solomon grew old, his wives turned his heart after other gods, and his heart was not fully devoted to the Lord his God, as the heart of David his father had been.
1 Kings 11:4

Father, You had told Your children not to marry foreign women but Solomon had 700 brides of royal birth and 300 concubines that led him astray. Solomon did evil in Your sight. As a result, Israel would be torn apart when Solomon son becomes King. You would allow His son to reign over one tribe for the sake of David and Jerusalem. May we hold fast this day to Your teachings and Your will for our lives. May we not turn to the left or right but be focused solely on You Father.

But Rehoboam rejected the advice the elders gave him and consulted the young men who had grown up with him and were serving him.
1 Kings 12:8

Father, Solomon's son Rehoboam did not choose the advice of the elders resulting in Israel being in rebellion against the house of David. May we act and serve only You today Father. Go before us today our Lord and God.

The old prophet answered, "I too am a prophet, as you are. And an angel said to me by the word of the Lord: 'Bring him back with you to your house so that he may eat bread and drink water.'" But he was lying to him.
1 Kings 13:18

Father, may we look to You and obey You. By the word of You a man of God delivered a message but listed to a man who lied to him. As a result, the man was on the road home and killed by a lion and his body was not buried in the tomb of his ancestors because he did not keep the command You gave him. He was to go and tell and not eat or drink while there. When others try to lead us astray, let us hold to Your Word.

"The Lord will raise up for himself a king over Israel who will cut off the family of Jeroboam. Even now this is beginning to happen."
1 Kings 14:14

Father, You are in control at all times. Because of Jeroboam's disobedience his son would die. A son that was the only one in the house of Jeroboam that was found anything good. He was the only one allowed to be buried. May we live this day pleasing to You Father.

Asa did what was right in the eyes of the Lord, as his father David had done. He expelled the male shrine prostitutes from the land and got rid of all the idols his ancestors had made.
1 Kings 15:11

Father, may we expel all the things in our lives that are displeasing to You. May our hearts have peace this day knowing we are in a right relationship with You. This was made possible by Jesus. Only through the blood of Jesus.

Then the people of Israel were split into two factions; half supported Tibni son of Ginath for king, and the other half supported Omri.
1 Kings 16;21

Father, now there is but one true team: the team of Jesus Christ. Through Jesus, we are allowed to one day stand before Your throne. Thank You Jesus for providing a way. Jesus paid it all, all to Him we owe.

Elijah said to her, "Don't be afraid. Go home and do as you have said. But first make a small loaf of bread for me from what you have and bring it to me, and then make something for yourself and your son."
1 Kings 17:13

Father, may we not be afraid today. Jesus has overcome the world. What have we to fear. Our hope is in You Father.

The power of the Lord came on Elijah and, tucking his cloak into his belt, he ran ahead of Ahab all the way to Jezreel.
1 Kings 18:46

Father, Your prophet Elijah on Mount Carmel bent down to the ground with his face between his knees and heard the sound of a heavy rain. He sent his servant to look and after seven times a small cloud the size of a man's hand was rising from the sea after a three year famine. You are the great provider. May we run to You this day Father. When we don't know what to do, may we run to the shelter of our Father.

After the earthquake came a fire, but the Lord was not in the fire. And after the fire came a gentle whisper.
1 Kings 19:12

Father, Elijah had traveled to Mount Horeb, the mountain of God. Angels had tended to him on his journey. On the mountain, a great and powerful wind tore through and shattered rocks, then an earthquake, then fire but You were not in them. After the fire, You came to Elijah in a gentle whisper. Jesus would come to earth 2900 years later and speak as our Messiah. Now the Holy Spirit dwells in Your children that have accepted Jesus. May we do as Elijah and obey Your Word. We have been told, now may we act and obey. Trust and obey for there's no other way.

Afterward, the prophet came to the king of Israel and said, "Strengthen your position and see what must be done, because next spring the king of Aram will attack you again."
1 Kings 20:22

Father, may we be on guard for the enemy. May we strengthen our position through Your Word, prayer, and making choices pleasing to You. Let us dwell in the shelter of Your hands. Go before us Your children, on this day. May Your will be done. We need You oh how we need You. Every hour we need You. Our one defense, our righteousness. Oh Father how we need You.

There was never anyone like Ahab, who sold himself to do evil in the eyes of the Lord, urged on by Jezebel his wife.
1 Kings 21:25

Father, may we surround ourselves with accountability for You. Thank you Father for our spouses that help us keep You number one in our lives and them second. May we walk hand in hand with them this day enjoying another day on earth praising and worshiping You and enjoying Your wonderful creation.

But Micaiah said, "As surely as the Lord lives, I can tell him only what the Lord tells me."
1 Kings 22:14

Father, may we speak the truth this day. Truth that comes from Your living Word the Bible. Let the truth come from our mouth as it did Jesus: with love. Thank You Father for so many of our family members who are now with You in heaven that showed us day after day their love and devotion to You. May we do the same.

But the angel of the Lord said to Elijah the Tishbite, "Go up and meet the messengers of the king of Samaria and ask them, 'Is it because there is no God in Israel that you are going off to consult Baal-Zebub, the god of Ekron?'
2 Kings 1:3

Father, because Ahaziah sent messengers to consult false gods, he never recovered from his injury and died in bed. May we always call on You Father, the one true God. The maker of heaven and earth. Our God is an awesome God, He reigns over heaven and earth. With wisdom, power, and love our God is an awesome God.

As they were walking along and talking together, suddenly a chariot of fire and horses of fire appeared and separated the two of them, and Elijah went up to heaven in a whirlwind.
2 Kings 2:11

Father, what a sight that must have been for Elisha to see Elijah taken up into heaven to be with You for eternity. May we live this day in anticipation of the rapture of Your church. Come Lord Jesus. But until that day let us go and tell of the Gospel of Jesus, one individual at a time. The ones whom You put in our path: students, fellow workers, the ones at the grocery store... May we work till Jesus comes and our labor be pleasing to You. Your kingdom come, Your will be done on earth as it is in heaven.

The next morning, about the time for offering the sacrifice, there it was-water flowing from the direction of Edom! And the land was filled with water.
2 Kings 3:20

Father, go before us today and bring forth waters that refresh and strengthen us as we go and proclaim the name of Jesus. The land is dry and parched but Your living water brings dry bones to life. Only through the blood of Jesus, is the fountain of Living Water.

Then he set it before them, and they ate and had some left over,
according to the word of the Lord.
2 Kings 4:44

Father, with just 20 loaves of bread You fed over 100 men and
there was some left over. You are our great provider. Thank You
Father for providing a way out from the bondage of sin through
Your Son Jesus. May we go this day in service to Your will.

Elisha sent a messenger to say to him, "Go, wash yourself seven
times in the Jordan, and your flesh will be restored and you will
be cleansed."
2 Kings 5:10

Naaman, who had leprosy, was told by Elisha to go to the
Jordan and wash himself 7 times. After washing himself as
Elisha instructed, his skin turned to that of a young boy. Father,
about 2,900 years after Elisha lived on this earth, Your Son
Jesus would also go down to the Jordan to be baptized by John.
What a wonderful time when You, Jesus, and the Holy Spirit
are all mentioned in the event in the Bible. Thank You Father
for the peace and assurance that through the blood of Jesus that
our sins are washed away.

And Elisha prayed, "Open his eyes, Lord, so that he may see."
Then the Lord opened the servant's eyes, and he looked and saw
the hills full of horses and chariots of fire all around Elisha.
2 Kings 6:17

Father, when the king of Aram army had surrounded Elisha and
the city of Samaria, Elisha's servant said what shall we do.
Elisha told the servant, "Those who are with us are more than
those who are with them." What a sight that must have been for
the servants eyes to behold. Go before us today Father. Open
our eyes Father. Thank you for the peace of knowing that you
protect and love us Your children.

⊢━━━━━━━━━━━━━⊣

For the Lord had caused the Arameans to hear the sound of
chariots and horses and a great army, so that they said to one
another, "Look, the king of Israel has hired the Hittite and
Egyptian kings to attack us!
2 Kings 7:6

Father, the siege by the Arameans was horrific. For their
disobedience so many suffered and died. You did come like You
told Elisha to tell Your people, the Israelites. What a mighty
sound it must have been to cause the Aramean army to leave
their camps with all the food, silver, and gold still in their tents.
All is under Your control. Thank You for loving Your children
so much.

Nevertheless, for the sake of his servant David, the Lord was not willing to destroy Judah. He had promised to maintain a lamp for David and his descendants forever.
2 Kings 8:19

Father, for mankind's sake, You looked down from heaven and sent Your Son to die for mankind's sins. May we, Your children, worship You in a way that brings honor and glory to Your name. Let our choices and decisions be pleasing to You. All to Jesus we surrender.

When Joram saw Jehu he asked, "Have you come in peace, Jehu?" "How can there be peace," Jehu replied, "as long as all the idolatry and witchcraft of your mother Jezebel abound?
2 Kings 9:2

Father, peace comes from accepting Jesus and serving You. What joy in knowing that You are our Father. We are only a short time on this earth but will spend eternity with You in heaven. What joy that will be when our Jesus we shall see.

Yet Jehu was not careful to keep the law of the Lord, the God of Israel, with all his heart. He did not turn away from the sins of Jeroboam, which he had caused Israel to commit.
2 Kings 10:31

Father, may we go this day making choices that follow Your wishes for our lives. May we serve only You. Let us not look back and see a "yet" tonight as we reflect on our service to You this day. This is the day that You have made, we will rejoice and be glad in it.

All the people of the land went to the temple of Baal and tore it down. They smashed the altars and idols to pieces and killed Mattan the priest of Baal in front of the altars.
2 Kings 11:18

Father, may we smash things in our lives that are displeasing to You this day. Let us go and keep our eyes focused on You. As distractions and temptations come, through the guidance of the Holy Spirit let us choose Your will Father. We surrender all. All to thee our blessed Savior, we surrender all.

They did not require an accounting from those to whom they gave the money to pay the workers, because they acted with complete honesty.
2 Kings 12:15

Father, may we act this day with complete honesty. We know from Your word that honesty pleases You. May we speak truth this day. Truth is found in Your Son Jesus Christ.

Once while some Israelites were burying a man, suddenly they saw a band of raiders; so they threw the man's body into Elisha's tomb. When the body touched Elisha's bones, the man came to life and stood up on his feet.
2 Kings 13:21

Father, since when has impossible ever stopped You. This is the sound of dry bone rattling. This is the sound that makes a dead man walk again. Dry bones rattle.

You have indeed defeated Edom and now you are arrogant. Glory in your victory, but stay at home! Why ask for trouble and cause your own downfall and that of Judah also?"
2 Kings 14:10

Father, may we live in peace with our neighbor. May we choose humbleness and not arrogance. We have the choice to be content and not covet. It is not about what we accumulate on this earth but about who we surrender our life and all we have to: our Savior Jesus Christ. Count your blessings name them one by one. Count your blessings see what God has done. Let us look to You Father and Your ways and not our own this day

He did evil in the eyes of the Lord. He did not turn away from the sins of Jeroboam son of Nebat, which he had caused Israel to commit.
2 Kings 15:28

Father, so much war and so much evil happened with Your chosen people. So many kings as You predicted were corrupt and self seeking for glory and power. How patient You have been through the centuries and how Your love is evident for mankind to the ones who would seek Your will for their lives and accept Jesus as their personal Savior. May we go this day and show the patience and love you have shown us to the ones that cross our path today.

He followed the ways of the kings of Israel and even sacrificed his son in the fire, engaging in the detestable practices of the nations the Lord had driven out before the Israelites.
2 Kings 16:3

Father, Ahaz chose to do detestable practices. May we follow Your ways and not the ways of the world and satan. You created man and life. Jesus came to earth to die for man that we may have life. Jesus is the bread of life. May many choose life this day Father.

Rather, worship the Lord your God; it is he who will deliver you from the hand of all your enemies.
2 Kings 17:39

Father, You require worship from Your children. You are a jealous God and will not tolerate worship of other Gods or idols. Your chosen people again and again worshiped false Gods as You instructed them not to do. Your patience continued anticipating one day Your Son Jesus would be born into the world to be the ultimate sacrifice for man's sins. Thank You Father for allowing me and so many to call on the name of Jesus and to have our sins removed so we can have fellowship with You for eternity. Thank You Holy Spirit for second by second guidance and direction while on earth. Only through the blood of Jesus, was redemption possible. May we choose to follow Your statutes and laws this day Father. Let our choices be pleasing to You.

Hezekiah trusted in the Lord, the God of Israel. There was no one like him among all the kings of Judah, either before him or after him.
2 Kings 18:5

Father, how refreshing after king after king that had done evil and not followed Your ways to come to Hezekiah. Hezekiah trusted in You. Trust and obey for there's no other way to be happy in Jesus is to trust and obey.

That night the angel of the Lord went out and put to death a hundred and eighty-five thousand in the Assyrian camp. When the people got up the next morning-there were all the dead bodies!
2 Kings 19:35

Father, for Your sake and the sake of Your servant David You sent Your angel to the Assyrian camp and killed 185,000 of King Sennacherib, king of Assyria men. The next day they broke camp and returned to Nineveh. Father, go before us this day. May we be pleasing to You in our choices and decisions. May we serve and honor only You. May Your will be done and not our own. For You alone are the one true God.

Then the prophet Isaiah called on the Lord, and the Lord made the shadow go back the ten steps it had gone down on the stairway of Ahaz.
2 Kings 20:11

Father, You made the shadow go in the opposite direction. It would be a sign that Hezekiah would have 15 years added to his life. You are sovereign and can cause Your creation to do what You ask when You want and how You want. Thank You for sending Your son Jesus to make a way to You Father from the separation due to sin. We Your children will never again be separated and will forever be with You. Father, go before us today and may we live in Your will this day.

But the people did not listen. Manasseh led them astray, so that they did more evil than the nations the Lord had destroyed before the Israelites.
2 Kings 21:9

Father, may we be grounded in Your word and not be led astray by false teachings. Holy Spirit guide us today and lead us in the way of the Father.

He did what was right in the eyes of the Lord and followed completely the ways of his father David, not turning aside to the right or to the left.
2 Kings 22:2

Father, may we strive this day to also do what is completely right in Your eyes just as King Josiah. Let us place You first in our priorities. Thank You Father for loving Your children and the promise of always holding us with Your righteous right hand. Go before us this day Father.

Neither before nor after Josiah was there a king like him who turned to the Lord as he did-with all his heart and with all his soul and with all his strength, in accordance with all the Law of Moses.
2 Kings 23:25

Father, may we serve You with all our heart and all our soul and all our strength this day just as Josiah the King of Judah.

Including the shedding of innocent blood. For he had filled Jerusalem with innocent blood, and the Lord was not willing to forgive.
2 Kings 24:4

Father, You are the creator of life. It is one of Your Ten Commandments that we should not murder. May we value life as You.

Gedaliah took an oath to reassure them and their men. "Do not be afraid of the Babylonian officials," he said. "Settle down in the land and serve the king of Babylon, and it will go well with you.
2 Kings 25:24

Father, thank You for allowing Your children to live in a country where we are free to worship You and not bow down to a king. You are our King and Lord. May we make choices today that reflect our love and devotion to You.

Abraham was the father of Isaac. The sons of Isaac: Esau and Israel.
1 Chronicles 1:34

Father, just as You said in Your word, Jesus will descend from Abraham 400 years from this writing. You create and nothing happens without Your knowledge and permission. You are beyond human understanding and all we have is Yours. Go before us on this day and may we live according to Your will for our lives.

Jesse was the father of Eliab his firstborn; the second son was Abinadab, the third Shimea, the fourth Nethanel, the fifth Raddai, the sixth Ozem and the seventh David.
1 Chronicles 2:13-15

Father, David would be the seventh son of Jesse. You would know His heart and choose him to be in the lineage of Your begotten son Jesus. May we go this day with the same heart as David. To serve and honor You in all we say and do.

And these were the children born to him there:
Shammua, Shobab, Nathan and Solomon. These four were by
Bathsheba daughter of Ammiel.
1 Chronicles 3:5

Father, Your son Jesus would come from the lineage of David
and through his son Nathan some 1000 years later. One could
speculate that David's son Nathan was named after Your
prophet Nathan that went to David and confronted his sin. May
we also listen to the Holy Spirit on this day when He confronts
us with our sins. May we do like David and confess and repent
of the things that we say, think, and do that displease You.

The descendants of Judah: Perez, Hezron, Karmi, Hur and
Shobal.
1 Chronicles 4:1

Father, Your son Jesus would come to earth through the line of
Judah and Perez. It is wonderful to know that Your plan of
giving mankind a way to You was being worked out in the lives
of Judah and Perez 1500 years before Jesus would be born on
this earth. We can live this day knowing that Your plans are
perfect and are always on time. May Your will be done this day
in our lives.

They were helped in fighting them, and God delivered the Hagrites and all their allies into their hands, because they cried out to him during the battle. He answered their prayers, because they trusted in him.
1 Chronicles 5:20

Father, the Reubenites, the Gadites and the half-tribe of Manasseh had 44,760 men ready for military service but the battle was Yours. May we trust in You this day as they did. Our hope is in You our Lord and God.

These are the men David put in charge of the music in the house of the Lord after the ark came to rest there.
1 Chronicles 6:31

Father, may our lips sing praises from our hearts this morning for what You have done by showing us Your great love for us through Your words and deeds. Just as David sang in Your house let us sing a joyful noise that pleases You. We will enter Your gates with thanksgiving in our hearts we will enter Your courts with praise.

All these were descendants of Asher-heads of families, choice men, brave warriors and outstanding leaders. The number of men ready for battle, as listed in their genealogy, was 26,000.
1 Chronicles 7:40

Father, may our family be as the family of Asher, May we follow You and not be led away by satan. Let us use the tools of prayer, Your word in the Bible, and the Holy Spirit's guidance to be spiritual warriors this day. Go before us Father and set the path that You would have our steps to take.

Ner was the father of Kish, Kish the father of Saul, and Saul the father of Jonathan, Malki-Shua, Abinadab and Esh-Baal.
1 Chronicles 8:33

Father, from Benjamin's lineage came King Saul. You tried to tell Your chosen people the Israelites to obey Your laws and follow only You but they would one day call on a king to lead them like the other nations around them. May we go this day and learn from the past and base this day on Your Word in the Bible. May we follow only You. The Alpha and Omega.

They and their descendants were in charge of guarding the gates of the house of the Lord-the house called the tent of meeting.
1 Chronicles 9:23

Father, just as You once met with Your chosen people the Israelites at the tent of meeting, now the Holy Spirit lives with Your children that have accepted Your Son Jesus Christ as their savior. May we guard our hearts with the same responsibility as did the gatekeepers of old.

Saul died because he was unfaithful to the Lord; he did not keep the word of the Lord and even consulted a medium for guidance.
1 Chronicles 10:13

Father, may we be faithful to You and love and live for You this day with all our hearts, mind, and actions. May we be guided by the Holy Spirit. Oh how sweet to trust in Jesus.

And David became more and more powerful, because the Lord
Almighty was with him.
1 Chronicles 11:9

Father, our strength comes from You. Just as David was a man
after Your own heart, may we learn from his life and have no
other god before You. You are the creator of all and nothing is
more important in our lives than our relationship with You.

These were the men who came to David at Ziklag, while he was
banished from the presence of Saul son of Kish (they were
among the warriors who helped him in battle).
1 Chronicles 12:1

Father, may we come to You as these men to prepare for
spiritual battle today. Shield us Father with Your shield and
spear. We can face the enemy only with Your strength and
protection. May we keep our focus on the prize of hearing well
done my good and faithful servant.

David and all the Israelites were celebrating with all their might before God, with songs and with harps, lyres, timbrels, cymbals and trumpets.
1 Chronicles 13:8

Father, David was bringing the ark back from Abinadab's house. The ark is where Your presence dwelt. Now the Holy Spirit resides in us Your children that have accepted Jesus. Jesus, Your perfect Son who came and died for our sins on the Cross of Calvary. Let us rejoice this day as David and all Israel

As soon as you hear the sound of marching in the tops of the poplar trees, move out to battle, because that will mean God has gone out in front of you to strike the Philistine army.
1 Chronicles 14:15

Father, go before us this day. Knowing that You go before us gives us the peace and strength to face this day Thank You Father for Your promises that are always kept.

It was because you, the Levites, did not bring it up the first time that the Lord our God broke out in anger against us. We did not inquire of him about how to do it in the prescribed way.
1 Chronicles 15:13

Father, You had told the children of Israel how You wanted the Levites to carry the ark on poles on their shoulders. They did not obey and Uzzah was struck down and died when he touched the ark that had slid on the new cart when the oxen stumbled. You expected obedience. May we obey Your Word today and live in obedience to You.

Let the heavens rejoice, let the earth be glad; let them say among the nations, "The Lord reigns!
1 Chronicles 16:31

Father, one day every knee will bow and tongue confess that You are the one true God. Thank You for the opportunity to have forgiveness of our sins and have a relationship with You through Jesus. The heavens and creation are wonders of Your greatness and Jesus is proof of Your love. May we live today showing others our love and devotion to You. Our God Reigns.

Now then, tell my servant David, 'This is what the Lord Almighty says: I took you from the pasture, from tending the flock, and appointed you ruler over my people Israel.
1 Chronicles 17:7

Father, You took a shepherd and made Him a king. You knew David. David knew that You alone were His God. From the lineage of David one day Jesus would be born. May we go this day and live for You with the same love and devotion as Your son Jesus. Not our will but Yours be done this day.

David reigned over all Israel, doing what was just and right for all his people.
1 Chronicles 18:14

Father, may we do what is just and right according to You this day. With our families, our friends, and the ones we come in contact let us shine Your love that is inside us through the Holy Spirit. Thank You Jesus for showing us the true meaning of love.

Be strong, and let us fight bravely for our people and the cities of our God. The Lord will do what is good in his sight.
1 Chronicles 19:13

Father, may we go bravely into this fallen world today and do our best to live for You. May we fight the good fight. Lead us not into temptation but deliver us from evil. Do what is good in Your sight.

These were descendants of Rapha in Gath, and they fell at the hands of David and his men.
1 Chronicles 20:8

Father, David and his men, through You going before them, defeated the giants of the world in battle. They had strength and courage that came from You.
David had faced the giant Goliath as a young boy and went to face Goliath with assurance You would be with him just as You were with him when he was out in the pastures protecting the sheep from wild animals. Thank You for Your words in the Bible that let us know You will be with us this day. You will never leave us or forsake us as Your children.

Satan rose up against Israel and incited David to take a census
of Israel
1 Chronicles 21:1

Father, through pride David would count Your chosen people.
Even David made a bad choice and his action resulted in 70,000
Israelites being killed by a plague. Our sins affect not only us
but others. Satan still roams this earth seeking to destroy. May
we stand firm in Your word and make choices this day that are
pleasing to You.

Then you will have success if you are careful to observe the
decrees and laws that the Lord gave Moses for Israel. Be strong
and courageous. Do not be afraid or discouraged.
1 Chronicles 22:13

Father, Solomon took the place of his Father David as King
over Israel. David would prepare for the building of a temple
for you with 3,700 tons of gold, 37,500 tons of silver, and
quantities of bronze and iron too great to be weighed, and wood
and stone. How humbling to know now that the ones on earth
that accept Jesus as their savior are temples to the Holy Spirit.
How costly is each soul that accepts You Father. May we live
today as You as wish: as a temple for You observing Your laws
and decrees and worshiping only You. Praise the Lord Praise
the Lord let the earth hear His voice.

They were also to stand every morning to thank and praise the Lord. They were to do the same in the evening.
1 Chronicles 23:30

Father, let praise and song come from our lips and hearts all through the day. May we let the joy deep in our souls bring forth a sweet incense to Your throne room. Our lips will praise you for You are holy.

They divided them impartially by casting lots, for there were officials of the sanctuary and officials of God among the descendants of both Eleazar and Ithamar.
1 Chronicles 24:5

Father, there is no need for casting lots for the Holy Spirit has been sent to guide and direct our paths while on this earth. Thank You for Your Word contained in the Bible inspired by You for us to live by and know Your love for us Your children. My hope is built on nothing less than Jesus blood and righteousness.

David, together with the commanders of the army, set apart some of the sons of Asaph, Heman and Jeduthun for the ministry of prophesying, accompanied by harps, lyres and cymbals. Here is the list of the men who performed this service:

1 Chronicles 25:1

Father, You would talk through Your prophets to Your chosen people the Israelites. Today You talk to us Your children that have accepted Jesus through Your completed Word in the Bible and through the Holy Spirit who is our Advocate and who Jesus told would teach us all things. We are able to talk to You through Jesus who sits at Your right hand. May we have a little talk with Jesus.

⊢━━━━━━━━━━━━━━⊣

Shubael, a descendant of Gershom son of Moses, was the official in charge of the treasuries.

1 Chronicles 26:24

Father, Moses spent 40 years in the wilderness after running away from Egypt. He went from living with Kings to living in a wilderness. He began a home and a family and You came to him to lead Your children from the bondage of slavery. You saw in Moses a leader just like You saw in David and Gideon and others You used through the Bible. Their strength came from You. Moses tried to tell You of his feeling of inadequacy but eventually followed You to the task. You equipped and were so patient with Moses. Now we see that his descendent Shubael is following You. Shubael is in charge of the treasuries. May we follow You this day and our children's children and future generations make the choice to follow You. May they accept Jesus as their Savior and Lord and marry the spouse that You have for them.

Joab son of Zeruiah began to count the men but did not finish. God's wrath came on Israel on account of this numbering, and the number v.las not entered in the book of the annals of King David.
1 Chronicles 27:24

Father, may we learn from our mistakes. Just as David learned from his mistake that resulted in the death of thousands of Israelites, may we also not repeat our mistakes. May we listen and learn from Your word what is pleasing to You.
When temptations come today let us look and turn toward Jesus who gives us the ability to withstand.

David also said to Solomon his son, "Be strong and courageous, and do the work. Do not be afraid or discouraged, for the Lord God, my God, is with you. He will not fail you or forsake you until all the work for the service of the temple of the Lord is finished.
1 Chronicles 28:20

Father, may we be strong and courageous today to carry out the tasks before us. Let us not be afraid or discouraged. This is made possible knowing that You are with us and will not fail us or forsake us.

Yours, Lord, is the greatness and the power and the glory and the majesty and the splendor, for everything in heaven and earth is yours. Yours, Lord, is the kingdom; you are exalted as head over all.
1 Chronicles 29:11

Father, we come to worship only You. May You be first in all we think and do this day. May we serve and do Your will today and the rest of the days we walk on this earth.

God said to Solomon, "Since this is your heart's desire and you have not asked for wealth,possessions or honor, nor for the death of your enemies, and since you have not asked for a long life but for wisdom and knowledge to govern my people over whom I have made you king."
2 Chronicles 1:11

Father, may we lead as Solomon. Solomon knew You as His God. He needed You to lead the Israelites. May we rely on You and not ourselves. We choose to give You our best this day.

But who is able to build a temple for him, since the heavens, even the highest heavens, cannot contain him?Who then am I to build a temple for him, except as a place to burn sacrifices before him?
2 Chronicles 2:6

Father, Solomon set out to build Your temple. A temporary temple that the Israelites would come and burn fragrant incense and burn offerings. Praise the name of Jesus who came and died for mankind as the sacrificial Lamb. Ones that accept Jesus as their savior become a temple for God where the Holy Spirit resides. A temple made possible by the blood of the Lamb Jesus Christ. May many come and get the free gift of forgiveness of sins this day.

He adorned the temple with precious stones. And the gold he used was gold of Parvaim.
2 Chronicles 3:6

Father, just as the very best was put into the building of Your temple by Solomon, may we give our best to You this day. Let our steps lead to You and our words reflect our love and desire to please You.

The Sea stood on twelve bulls, three facing north, three facing west, three facing south and three facing east. The Sea rested on top of them, and their hindquarters were toward the center.
2 Chronicles 4:4

Father, the Sea in the temple was to be used by the priests for washing. Thank You Father for Your love, thank You Jesus for washing the ones that ask sins away, and thank You Holy Spirit for walking each step with the ones that ask for forgiveness through Jesus. What peace in knowing that Jesus is now the High Priest. Mankind must come to Him for the forgiveness of sins. We no longer are required to go to a temple or building to offer sacrifices. Jesus was the sacrifice and only through Him is the forgiveness of sins. On Christ the solid rock I stand all other ground is sinking sand.

And the priests could not perform their service because of the cloud, for the glory of the Lord filled the temple of God.
2 Chronicles 5:14
Father, what magnificent sights and sounds must have occurred on the day the Levites brought up the ark and the tent of meeting and all the sacred furnishings in it. What a moment when the glory of the Lord filled the temple Solomon and the workers built for You. Accompanied by trumpets, cymbals and other instruments, the singers raised their voices in praise to the Lord and sang: "He is good; His love endures forever." We lift our voices and sing again and again this day: "He is good; His love endures forever."

He said: "Lord, the God of Israel, there is no God like You in heaven or on earth - You who keep Your covenant of love with your servants who continue wholeheartedly in Your way.
2 Chronicles 6:14

Father, we come to You today just as Solomon did as he dedicated the temple marveling at Your greatness and love for us. Your temple was built by Solomon in Jerusalem but is now each man, woman, and child that had accepted Jesus as their Lord and Savior. Just as Solomon knelt down with outstretched arms before the whole assembly, we come this day thanking You for keeping your covenant of love found in Your word. May we serve you wholeheartedly this day.

If my people, who are called by my name, will humble themselves and pray and seek my face and turn from their wicked ways, then I will hear from heaven, and I will forgive their sin and will heal their land.
2 Chronicles 7:14

Father, may we live humble, pray, and seek Your face this day. This pleases You today just as it did in Solomon's time some 2,400 years ago. Let us run from wickedness and choose goodness. Let us look to Jesus and the Cross. We lay our fears, disappointments, worries, and shortcomings at the Cross. Only through the blood of Jesus are we able to live the life that You intended. A life of peace and joy in all circumstances.

Solomon brought Pharaoh's daughter up from the City of David to the palace he had built for her, for he said, "My wife must not live in the palace of David king of Israel, because the places the ark of the Lord has entered are holy."
2 Chronicles 8:11

Father, Solomon had married a pagan wife. Marriage is an institution that You started and the one a person marries should be a fellow believer in You and have accepted Jesus Christ as their Lord and Savior. Jesus is the bridegroom. The church shall be His bride. Solomon's marriage to these pagan wives eventually caused tragic events. Thank You Father for the guidance of who we should marry while on this earth.

All the kings of the earth sought audience with Solomon to hear the wisdom God had put in his heart.
2 Chronicles 9:23

Father, the Queen of Sheba came to see for herself the riches and wisdom of Solomon. She left with more than she came and saw for herself how You had blessed Solomon. I am sure it left an impression for the rest of her life. You had put the wisdom in Solomon's heart and he reigned for 40 years. May our hearts be as receptive as Solomon's this day to Your will.

So Israel has been in rebellion against the house of David to this day.
2 Chronicles 10:19

Father, Your chosen people the Israelites had trouble getting along and fought against each other. May we strive today to have peace and not malice or hatred. Thank You Jesus for showing us how to love our neighbor.

"This is what the Lord says: Do not go up to fight against your fellow Israelites. Go home, every one of you, for this is my doing.'" So they obeyed the words of the Lord and turned back from marching against Jeroboam.
2 Chronicles 11:4

Father, may we obey Your word as Rehoboam and the 180,000 men obeyed and did not march to war against Jeroboam. May Your plans not ours be done this day.

Because Rehoboam humbled himself, the Lord's anger turned from him, and he was not totally destroyed. Indeed, there was some good in Judah.
2 Chronicles 12:12

Father, Rehoboam and all Israel had abandoned You and after 5 years Shishak King of Egypt attacked them because of their unfaithfulness. Because of their repentance, they were not destroyed but were made subjects to Shishak and the gold and other items were carried from the temple Solomon had built. Because Rehoboam humbled himself, Your anger turned from him and there was some good in Judah. Rehoboam did evil because he had not set his heart on seeking You. May we learn from Rehoboam and seek and worship You this day. May You be first in our thoughts, deeds, and actions. May we be willing servants of the one true God.

As for us, the Lord is our God, and we have not forsaken him. The priests who serve the Lord are sons of Aaron, and the Levites assist them.
2 Chronicles 13: 10

Father, it is sad to read that this war was between Your chosen people. A war that in this battle alone, 500,000 Israelites fell before Judah. May we strive to live in peace today with our fellow Christians.

Then Asa called to the Lord his God and said, "Lord, there is no one like you to help the powerless against the mighty. Help us, Lord our God, for we rely on you, and in your name we have come against this vast army. Lord, you are our God; do not let mere mortals prevail against you."
2 Chronicles 14:11

Father, Asa knew who could help him when he needed help the most. He called on You and You answered. We come this day in war against satan and his followers. We rely on You to go before us. May we be less like us and more like You.

For a long time Israel was without the true God, without a priest to teach and without the law.
2 Chronicles 15:3

Father, King Asa did so much good during his time as King of Judah even deposing his grandmother for her worship of asherah. Asa's heart was fully committed to You for all his life. When Your Son Jesus came to this earth He is now the High Priest forevermore. He came and fulfilled the law. Mankind has been given the gift to accept fellowship with You through the forgiveness of their sins by acceptance of Your Son Jesus. Jesus is the King of Kings and Lord of Lords. May many come to You this day. Let us who have accepted Jesus as our Savior look to Your Son this day and obey and do Your will.

For the eyes of the Lord range throughout the earth to strengthen those whose hearts are fully committed to him. You have done a foolish thing, and from now on you will be at war."
2 Chronicles 16:9

Father, Asa relied on the king of Aram and not on You. The army of the king of Aram had escaped from Asa's hands. For whatever reason, Asa has turned to the world and not wholly on You. You had went before and crushed armies that outnumbered his but now he turned to others for help. Father, may we never forget the God You are and that our help comes from You.

His heart was devoted to the ways of the Lord; furthermore, he removed the high places and the Asherah poles from Judah.
2 Chronicles 17:6

Father, Jehoshaphat took the place of Asa as King of Judah. He did not consult the Baals but followed You the God of his father and followed Your commands rather than the practices of Israel. May we do the same this day. Father thank you for Your love, Thank You Jesus for coming to earth and dying for our sins on the Cross of Calvary and giving us a way back to our Father through the forgiveness of sins that only comes through You. Thank You Holy Spirit for walking each step of the day with the ones who have accepted Jesus as Lord and Savior of their lives. Go before us this day Father and may Your will be done on earth as it is in heaven.

But Jehoshaphat also said to the king of Israel, "First seek the counsel of the Lord."
2 Chronicles 18:4

Father, 400 prophets told King Arab of Israel that he would be successful in war against Ramoth Gilied. However, Jehoshaphat the king of Judah asked, "Is there no longer a prophet of the Lord here whom we can inquire of?" May we rely on Your Word and the guiding of the Holy Spirit this day. May we follow the steps You wish us to take and bring honor and glory to Your name.

Now let the fear of the Lord be on you. Judge carefully, for with the Lord our God there is no injustice or partiality or bribery."
2 Chronicles 19:7

Father, as Your children we come to worship You this day. It is wonderful to know that You are always correct and there is never a mistake in Your judgments. You know what each person does and no one can hide anything from You. You even know the thoughts of everyone at every moment. People can hide things from the world but nothing is hidden from You. Thank You Jesus for allowing us to be free from condemnation and the wrath of judgment and to live in a life of forgiveness and joy. We go this day singing and giving praise to our Savior and Redeemer.

He said: "Listen, King Jehoshaphat and all who live in Judah and Jerusalem! This is what the Lord says to you: 'Do not be afraid or discouraged because of this vast army. For the battle is not yours, but God's.
2 Chronicles 20:15

Father, we put our battles before You. We stand behind You and watch as You bring down attacks and assaults from the enemy. This is how we fight our battles. We wear your armor. Thank You Father for being our protector.

Jehoram was thirty-two years old when he became king, and he reigned in Jerusalem eight years. He passed away, to no one's regret, and was buried in the City of David, but not in the tombs of the kings.
2 Chronicles 21:20

Father, may we learn from Jehoram who was King of Judah. He made terrible choices that were displeasing to You. Let us live for You today and our choices be pleasing to You. Our focus is on serving and living according to Your Word.

He did evil in the eyes of the Lord, as the house of Ahab had done, for after his father's death they became his advisers, to his undoing.
2 Chronicles 22:4

Father, so Ahaziah son of Jehoram king of Judah began to reign. He allowed his mother to encourage him to act wickedly. He also allowed the house of Ahab to become his advisors. Thank You Jesus for coming to earth and giving us a direct path to our Father that goes through You. Thank You Holy Spirit for guiding and leading us as we go through this day. May we surround ourselves with children of God who help us make decisions that will keep us in Your perfect will Father. May we hold fast to Your Word.

All the people of the land rejoiced, and the city was calm, because Athaliah had been slain with the sword.
2 Chronicles 23;21

Father, one day Jesus will come to this earth again not to bring peace but judgment. He will shield the sword of righteousness. You are a Holy and righteous God and sins that displease You will be no more. May many come to know You this day while we live in the period of mercy and grace brought forth through the blood of Jesus.

Joash did what was right in the eyes of the Lord all the years of
Jehoiada the priest.
2 Chronicles 24:2

Father, what a man Jehoiada was for You. He lived for 130
years and was buried with the kings in the City of David. While
he was high priest the temple was put back in order. All the
people and officials gladly gave. Jehoiada's son was later
martyred for Your name by the order of Joash. May we go this
day and stand firm on love and devotion to You Father and not
turn from You like Joash, Judah, and Jerusalem. May we stand
on Your Word.

He did what was right in the eyes of the Lord, but not
wholeheartedly.
2 Chronicles 25:2

Father, Amaziah was King of Judah and listened to someone
You had sent to him about not paying for men of Israel to go
fight with his army. However, Amaziah brought back from
battle the idols from the people of Seir and bowed down and
burned sacrifices to them. May we serve You wholeheartedly
this day and bow down to no one or nothing but to You Father.
Our worship is to You.

But after Uzziah became powerful, his pride led to his downfall. He was unfaithful to the Lord his God, and entered the temple of the Lord to burn incense on the altar of incense.
2 Chronicles 26:16

Father, Uzziah became king of Judah and did so much good like his Father Amaziah had done. He lived during the time of Zechariah and sought You. He loved the soil and had people out working the fertile soil. He built towers, walls, cisterns to help the people of Judah. However, after he became powerful, his pride led to his downfall. He was unfaithful to You and went into the temple to burn incense on the altar of incense. This was a job You had given to the priests who were descendants of Aaron. He was struck with leprosy and banned from the temple and palace. His son Jotham then became in charge of the palace and governed the people. Father, may we learn from King Uzziah and never be prideful. May we humble ourselves this day and know that You provide all we have and to You is all power and glory.

Jotham grew powerful because he walked steadfastly before the Lord his God.
2 Chronicles 27:6

Father, may we walk unwavering before You this day

In his time of trouble King Ahaz became even more unfaithful
to the Lord.
2 Chronicles 28:22

Father, let us turn to You in our times of trouble. You love us so much and are always willing to provide protection and comfort when asked. There is no better place to go than to Your throne room. Thank You Father for Your great love and faithfulness for Your children.

├─────────────────┤

The priests then slaughtered the goats and presented their blood on the altar for a sin offering to atone for all Israel, because the king had ordered the burnt offering and the sin offering for all Israel.
2 Chronicles 29:24

Father, King Hezekiah did what was right in Your eyes and led in the ways that pleased You. He and the people gave a sin offering for all Israel. Thank You Jesus for coming to this earth and providing a way from sin not only for Israel but for all nations and people. Praise the name of Jesus today and forevermore.

The priests and the Levites stood to bless the people, and God heard them, for their prayer reached heaven, his holy dwelling place.
2 Chronicles 30:27

Father, the prayers lifted by the priests and Levites reached You in heaven 2300 years ago on behalf of Your chosen people. We offer our prayers today through the High Priest Jesus Christ who sits at Your right hand in Your holy dwelling place in heaven. What assurance in knowing that every word we lift to You is heard by our Creator. May all we do and say today bring a sweet incense to You.

This is what Hezekiah did throughout Judah, doing what was good and right and faithful before the Lord his God.
2 Chronicles 31:20

Father, just as Hezekiah, may we do what is good and right and faithful before You this day. May we seek You and work wholeheartedly for Your kingdom.

With him is only the arm of flesh, but with us is the Lord our God to help us and to fight our battles." And the people gained confidence from what Hezekiah the king of Judah said.
2 Chronicles 32:8

Father, King Hezekiah knew to be strong and courageous knowing that You went before them. We have assurance as Your children in knowing that all that happens today goes before Your throne room. You have total control. Just as You sent an angel to wipe out the Assyria army of king Sennacherib, we have confidence in Your protection of us this day. May Your will be done Father.

And when he prayed to Him, the Lord was moved by his entreaty and listened to his plea; so He brought him back to Jerusalem and to his kingdom. Then Manasseh knew that the Lord is God.
2 Chronicles 33:13

Father, unlike King Hezekiah, his son King Manasseh did much evil in Your sight including sacrificing his children in the fire in the Valley of Ben Hinnom, practicing divination and witchcraft, sought omens, and consulted mediums and spiritists. He was humbled when taken captive with a ring in his nose and bronze shackles by the Assyrians and taken to Babylon. He turned to You and was restored. May we learn from King Manasseh and always turn to You Father. Let today be our best day of worship and devotion to You.

The king stood by his pillar and renewed the covenant in the presence of the Lord-to follow the Lord and keep his commands, statutes and decrees with all his heart and all his soul, and to obey the words of the covenant written in this book.
2 Chronicles 34:31

Father, the Book of the Law was found in the temple by the priest Hilkiah and given to King Josiah. During his reign, he had purged in Judah and Jerusalem of high places, Asherah poles and idols. May we also be as Josiah and do what pleases you this day with all our heart and soul. May our actions be pleasing to You Father.

Josiah, however, would not turn away from him, but disguised himself to engage him in battle. He would not listen to what Necho had said at God's command but went to fight him on the plain of Megiddo.
2 Chronicles 35:22

Father, Josiah would not listen and take head to Your warning. One day at Megiddo the Battle of Armageddon will take place. May all that have not listened and accepted the gift of salvation through Jesus make that choice this day. Thank You Jesus for the final victory that comes through You.

The Lord, the God of their ancestors, sent word to them through his messengers again and again, because he had pity on his people and on his dwelling place.
2 Chronicles 36:15

Father, how You love Your children. You love us when we are walking in Your will. You love us when we are walking away. Your love never stops. May many come to know Your love today by accepting Your son Jesus who showed Your love on the Cross of Calvary.

In the first year of Cyrus king of Persia, in order to fulfill the word of the Lord spoken by Jeremiah, the Lord moved the heart of Cyrus king of Persia to make a proclamation throughout his realm and also to put it in writing.
Ezra 1:1

Father, Your children had been overtaken by the Assyrians and Babylonians because of their choice to reject You and turn to foreign gods. Israel and Judah were scattered throughout the Assyrian empire for 70 years just as Jeremiah had told it would happen 100 years earlier. When You tell something will happen it happens. Now You have used Cyrus King of Persia to overtake Babylon and bring Your children back to their home according to Your word in Ezra and Nehemiah. How wonderful to know that Your plans are always fulfilled. How we anticipate Your plan of one day having all Your children that have accepted Your son Jesus as their savior with You for eternity in heaven. May many come to Jesus this day

When they arrived at the house of the Lord in Jerusalem, some of the heads of the families gave freewill offerings toward the rebuilding of the house of God on its
site.
Ezra 2:68

Father, how proper when Your children arrived back home from 70 years of oppression and captivity that they wanted to build a house of worship to You. Let us go this day and sing songs of praise to Your name. Go before us this day Father and may Your will be done.

With praise and thanksgiving they sang to the Lord:
"He is good; his love toward Israel endures forever." And all the people gave a great shout of praise to the Lord, because the foundation of the house of the Lord was laid.
Ezra 3:11

Father, how excited the people were to see the foundation of the temple completed. May we celebrate the same way this day knowing that You are the foundation that we reply. All we are is built on the life and death and resurrection of Your Son Jesus Christ the Messiah. Our hope is built on nothing less than Jesus blood and righteousness.

Then the peoples around them set out to discourage the people of Judah and make them afraid to go on building.
Ezra 4:4

Father, when opposition comes today let us look unto You. May we stand firm in Your word and do nothing to cause dishonor to Your Holy name. May we use discernment to make the right choices and use scripture to fight off temptations.

Then Zerubbabel son of Shealtiel and Joshua son of Jozadak set to work to rebuild the house of God in Jerusalem. And the prophets of God were with them, supporting them.
Ezra 5:2

Father, around 520 B.C., two of Your prophets Haggai and Zechariah prophesied to the Jews in Judah and Jerusalem that You had told them to finish rebuilding the temple. After 16 years, the temple was not completed and the people had been putting their own priorities above You. Your house still laid in ruins while they ran to their own houses. May we put You first this day and choose to help build Your kingdom while we walk our steps this day. Supporting and encouraging our fellow brothers and sisters in Christ. Bringing others to the doors of heaven through the name of Jesus.

The temple was completed on the third day of the month of Adar, in the sixth year of the reign of King Darius.
Ezra 6:15

Father, man was created to worship You. All of Your creation testifies to Your greatness. We come this day to worship You just as the Israelites came and worshiped at the completion of the temple. Thank You God for Your love. Thank You Jesus for coming to earth and dying for our sins on the Cross of Calvary and Your resurrection that enabled us to accept You as our Savior from our sins. Thank You Holy Spirit for living inside us and guiding each step while we walk on this earth.

———————————

For Ezra had devoted himself to the study and observance of the Law of the Lord, and to teaching its decrees and laws in Israel.
Ezra 7:10

Father, may we like Ezra commit our lives to the study and observance of the things that are pleasing to You. Thank You Holy Spirit for bringing the scripture back to us when we are tempted by evil to do acts that are not in line with the Word of God. Let today be a day that we do good and love as You Father.

There, by the Ahava Canal, I proclaimed a fast, so that we might humble ourselves before our God and ask him for a safe journey for us and our children, with all our possessions.
Ezra 8:21

Father, Ezra was protected by Your hand from enemies and bandits along the way. Protect us this day Father and go before us. May we travel the path You have for us this day. Lord, the God of Israel, you are righteous! We are left this day as a remnant. Here we are before you in our guilt, though because of it not one of us can stand in your presence.

Lord, the God of Israel, You are righteous! We are left this day as a remnant. Here we are before You in our guilt, though because of it not one of us can stand in Your presence.
Ezra 9:15

Father, Ezra was appalled when he found that the Israelites had disobeyed God and married into nations that God had told them not to mingle with in their detestable practices. Just as the Israelites, all people stand in guilt before You Father. Thank You Jesus for providing a way from our guilt and Your offer of grace and mercy. It is only through Jesus, that we can have freedom from the guilt and bondage of sin. Let us go this day singing praises of joy and thanksgiving of how Jesus set us free and letting others know how to receive the gift that comes from the acceptance of Jesus as our Savior

Then Shekaniah son of Jehiel, one of the descendants of Elam, said to Ezra, "We have been unfaithful to our God by marrying foreign women from the peoples around us. But in spite of this, there is still hope for Israel.
Ezra 10:2

Father, our hope is found in You. Just as the Israelites confessed their sins, may we confess our sins and be in a right relationship with You Father. May Your will be done. Tis so sweet to trust in Jesus.

"They are your servants and your people, whom you redeemed by your great strength and your mighty hand!'
Nehemiah 1:10

Father, we also are redeemed and can now come before You with adoration and praise. Thank You Father for allowing us to dwell on this earth knowing You as our Father. We marvel at Your creation and love.

I also told them about what the king had said to me. They replied, "Let us start rebuilding." So they began this good work.
Nehemiah 2:18

Father, You allowed Nehemiah who was the cupbearer to King Artaxerxes of Persia to go to Jerusalem and rebuild. May we also go this day and help build up Your kingdom. Let us build goodwill and speak kindly to the ones You send our way. May we overcome evil with good.

The next section was repaired by the men of Tekoa, but their nobles would not put their shoulders to the work under their supervisors.
Nehemiah 3:5

Father, how wonderful it is to see how the people came together to rebuild the walls of Jerusalem. May we choose to be like the ones that worked together as one to do Your work. Let us not be like the nobles of Tekoa with their laziness and wealth did not work. Let us choose this day to work till Jesus comes

So we rebuilt the wall till all of it reached half its
height, for the people worked with
all their heart,
Nehemiah 4:6

Father, may we work this day as Nehemiah and the workers did
on the wall of Jerusalem. Through the insults and constant
threats of others, they did their part. Let us work with all our
hearts for You.

I pondered them in my mind and then accused the nobles and
officials. I told them, "You are charging your own people
interest!"
Nehemiah 5:7

Father, Nehemiah heard the outcry of the people and went
before the ones that were taking advantage of the poor. May we
treat all men with integrity and honor. For man was created by
You in Your image.

But I prayed, "Now strengthen my hands."
Nehemiah 6:9

Father, Nehemiah, and the ones that chose to complete the wall persevered through constant opposition and threats. The wall of Jerusalem was completed in 52 days. Father, strengthen our hands this day to help build Your kingdom while we are here on this earth. May we work with the same diligence that Nehemiah and the others that chose to help him.

I put in charge of Jerusalem my brother Hanani, along with Hananiah the commander of the citadel, because he was a man of integrity and feared God more than most people do.
Nehemiah 7:2

Father, let us go this day with a clear heart. May we turn from anything that is sin and repent as soon as the Holy Spirit convicts. Let us live in integrity as Hananiah and fear Your Holy Name. Living in reverence and love to You Father.

Nehemiah said, "Go and enjoy choice food and sweet drinks, send some to those who have nothing prepared. This is holy to our Lord. Do not grieve, for the joy of the Lord is your strength."
Nehemiah 8:10

Father, the people came together and listened to the Book of the Law of Moses being read by Ezra who was the teacher of the Law. He read it aloud from daybreak till noon as he faced the square before the Water Gate and all the people listened attentively to the Book of the Law. Ezra stood on a platform and when he praised God the people raised their hands and declared Amen! Amen! The Levites also read from the Book of the Law of God, making it clear and giving the meaning so that the people understood what was being read. May we go this day with the strength from Your Word and also proclaim Amen! Amen! knowing we are Your children Father by the acceptance of Your Son Jesus and will have an eternity to worship You.

But in your great mercy you did not put an end to them or abandon them, for you are a gracious and merciful God.
Nehemiah 9:31

Father, by your Spirit you had warned Your chosen people through your prophets. They became stiff-necked in their abundance and themselves. May we learn from them and listen and obey Your will this day. Thank You Father for being a gracious and merciful Father that loves so much that He gave His only begotten Son Jesus. Praise the name of Jesus for offering to mankind the gift of salvation from sins. May many accept forgiveness of their sins today.

All these now join their fellow Israelites the nobles, and bind themselves with a curse and an oath to follow the Law of God given through Moses the servant of God and to obey carefully all the commands, regulations and decrees of the Lord our Lord.
Nehemiah 10:29

Father, Jesus did not come to abolish the law but to fulfill the Law. As children of Yours that have accepted Jesus, let us go this day living by Your Laws and please You. Thank You for the Bible that allows us to understand what is pleasing to You. Thank You Jesus for allowing us to see our Father through Your time on earth. Thank You Holy Spirit for showing us the Father through Your constant presence in our lives. Hope is found in Jesus.

Now the leaders of the people settled in Jerusalem. The rest of the people cast lots to bring one out of every ten of them to live in Jerusalem, the holy city, while the remaining nine were to stay in their own towns.
Nehemiah 11:1

Father, what a special place Jerusalem has been through the history of mankind. The site when Kings lived and Jesus our King was crucified for our sins. You tell us that one day Jesus will come back to earth and rule in New Jerusalem sent down from heaven. What a day that will be. Come Lord Jesus. May we work to bring others to You this day.

When the priests and Levites had purified themselves
ceremonially, they purified the people, the gates and the wall.
Nehemiah 12:30

Father, thank You for Your great love in sending Your Son Jesus
that whosoever would believe in Him should not perish but
have eternal life. Through the blood of Jesus, we are purified.
Let us go this day and proclaim the name of Jesus: the Root and
Offspring of David, the Bright and Morning Star.

So I rebuked the officials and asked them, "Why is the house of
God neglected?" Then I called them together and stationed
them at their posts.
Nehemiah 13:11

Father, while Nehemiah was gone from Jerusalem, the people
turned from You and sinned. When Nehemiah returned, he
purified the priests and Levites and assigned them duties.
Nehemiah held to Your commands and what pleased You. May
we do the same today and do Your will. May our choices be
pleasing to You Father.

But when the attendants delivered the king's command, Queen Vashti refused to come. Then the king became furious and burned with anger.
Esther 1:12

Father, may we treat the ones around us with dignity and respect. King Xerxes was in high spirits from wine and had ordered his wife to be brought to be seen by the people and nobles. Let us go this day with a clear mind and make choices that are pleasing to You. Choices that build up rather than tear down.

But Mordecai found out about the plot and told Queen Esther, who in turn reported it to the king, giving credit to Mordecai.
Esther 2:22

Father, Esther was a wise and beautiful young lady that made good choices and tried to do what was right. When she was taken to be possibly chosen to become Queen, she did all she could to get prepared and was humble to ask advice before going in front of King Xerxes. May we go this day and do our best for You Father

Dispatches were sent by couriers to all the king's provinces with the order to destroy, kill and annihilate all the Jews-young and old, women and children-on a single day, the thirteenth day of the twelfth month, the month of Adar, and to plunder their goods.
Esther 3:13

Father, king Xerxes had given Haman a seat of honor higher than all the nobles. But Mordecai would not kneel down or pay him honor. As a result, Haman plotted to annihilate all the Jews on the thirteenth day of the twelfth month. Haman's pride had caused him to give an order to have every man, woman, and child that was a Jew to be killed and to plunder their goods. Father, may we go this day with humility and a desire to build up and not tear down.

For if you remain silent at this time, relief and deliverance for the Jews will arise from another place, but you and your father's family will perish. And who knows but that you have come to your royal position for such a time as this?"
Esther 4:14

Father, thank You for having us where we are right now during our time on earth. May we show Your love to the ones that stand in front of us this day. May we like Esther seek guidance and direction from You.

Haman boasted to them about his vast wealth, his many sons,and all the ways the king had honored him and how he had elevated him above the other nobles and officials.
Esther 5:11

Father, in Proverbs it says that You hate a proud look. May we forever be humble in Your blessings. All we have is from You. Just as Job learned long ago, we will leave this earth just with what we came into it. Let us go this day with thanksgiving in our heart knowing we have the greatest gift You could give us.

The gift of Your Son Jesus Christ as our Redeemer and Savior. Afterward Mordecai returned to the king's gate. But Haman rushed home, with his head covered in grief.
Esther 6:12

Father, Your perfect timing is once again displayed in the life of Mordecai. Haman left his house expecting to have Mordecai executed but now is returning home in grief. His evil plans did not work out and now he will pay the price. May many turn to You today Father before it is too late to be forgiven for sins. Thank You Father for this time of mercy and grace allowed by the sacrifice of Jesus.

Esther said, "An adversary and enemy! This vile Haman!" Then Haman was terrified before the king and queen.
Esther 7:6

Father, thank You for another day of life to seek justice and do what is right in Your sight. May we have the courage of Esther to stand against evil.

For the Jews it was a time of happiness and joy, gladness and honor.
Esther 8:16
Father, the Jews were saved from the plans of Haman and their hearts were filled with joy. We Your children come this day with singing in our hearts from freedom of our sins. We will forever be Your children and worship Your Holy name. We can go this day with peace and assurance. Thank You Father for Your great love.

"If it pleases the king," Esther answered, "give the Jews in Susa permission to carry out this day's edict tomorrow also, and let Haman's ten sons be impaled on poles."
Esther 9:13

Father, Haman and ten of his sons were impaled on poles because of their wickedness and hatred toward Mordecai and the Jews. There will come a day where mankind will be judged. The ones that have not accepted Jesus and their names not found in the Book of Life will be cast into hell for eternity. May many turn from hate and evil today and ask forgiveness of their sins through the atoning blood of Jesus. Today is the day of salvation.

Mordecai the Jew was second in rank to King Xerxes, preeminent among the Jews, and held in high esteem by his many fellow Jews, because he worked for the good of his people and spoke up for the welfare of all the Jews.
Esther 10:3

Father, one can see how Your hand was on Mordecai and Esther. Your chosen people will never be erased from the earth as so many have tried and tried. Mordecai made good choices and worked to build Your kingdom. May go this day and do the same

In the land of Uz there lived a man whose name was Job. This man was blameless and upright; he feared God and shunned evil.
Job 1:1

Father, what a great man that loved You was Job. He was the greatest man in all the East. He was blameless and upright and shunned evil. Satan came to You from roaming back and forth on earth and asked to test Job. Everything Job had was in satans power but satan was not allowed on Job himself to lay a finger. Job lost his sons, daughters, servants, and possessions. Job still praised You. Job said "Naked I came from my mother's womb, and naked I will depart. The Lord gave and the Lord has taken away; may the name of the Lord be praised!' Job did not sin by charging You with wrongdoing. May we learn from Job and live today praising You Father in the good and the bad.

"All right, do with him as you please," the Lord said to Satan." But spare his life."
Job 2:6

Father, Job was now being attacked by satan with boils. It was so painful that he was taking pieces of pottery and scraping the boils. Even his wife told him to curse You and die. In all this, Job said nothing wrong. May we go this day in the same attitude as Job

I have no peace, no quietness; I have no rest, but only turmoil.
Job 3:25

Father, when trouble comes may we trust in You. Job was so so low. May we look to You for strength when we are in our valleys. We know that Your rod and Your staff protect and comfort this day as with David.

As I have observed, those who plow evil and those who sow trouble reap it,
Job 4:8

Father, Eliphaz the Temanite replied to Job with words that did not encourage or speak truth. When others we come across are going through trials, may we remember to not be like Eliphaz. May Your will be done Father.

I myself have seen a fool taking root, but suddenly his house was cursed.
Job 5:3

Job's friend Eliphaz is giving what he thinks are good words to Job. Father, we know that we will have hills and valleys in this life. We may spend the rest of our days in a valley but it might not be that we have turned from You. May we live each day knowing that You are watching over us during all our circumstances. Let this day be a day of praise to Your love, goodness, and mercy. In knowing You are with us is all we need.

Oh, that I might have my request, that God would grant what I hope for, that God would be willing to crush me, to let loose his hand and cut off my life!
Job 6:8-9

Father, You promise us You will never allow more upon us than we can bear. What is impossible for us is possible through strength in You. May we serve You this day with all our might.

"What is mankind that You make so much of them,
that You give them so much attention."
Job 7:17

Father, we are created to worship You. We have the ability to
communicate with You and through Jesus have the choice to
spend eternity with You. The Holy Spirit now dwells in each
person that accepts Jesus. Unlike before Jesus, when the Holy
Spirit would come and go among mankind, now the Holy Spirit
always goes with us and is our helper and guide. Thank You
Father for loving us so much and paying us so much attention.

Surely God does not reject one who is blameless or strengthen
the hands of evildoers.
Job 8 :20

Now Bildad the Shuhite is giving words to Job. In Job's misery,
Bildad comes and tells Job his suffering is the result of his and
his children's actions against You Father. In the Old Testament,
You did reign down judgment from Your throne. At Mount
Sinai, when the Law was given, there was thunder and lightning
and voices. Through Jesus, now we are living in the age of
grace. One day You will tell Jesus to come get Your children
and in a twinkling of an eye the ones that have accepted Jesus
will be taken to heaven. After this, Your judgment will come
again from Your throne. Job had done nothing wrong but his
friends kept coming and adding to his pain. May we approach
people this day not in judgment but with grace

He performs wonders that cannot be fathomed, miracles that cannot be counted.
Job 9:10

Father, each day is amazing to see and walk through Your creation. From the sunrise to the sunset Your light shines upon this earth and life abounds. At night, more of Your creation starts their movements. The heavens are all aligned and follow Your Word told ages ago. It is hard to fathom just how vast and wonderful Your creation is. Each day is a miracle just to walk, breathe, and live in Your works. May we go this day and enjoy.

You gave me life and showed me kindness, and in your providence watched over my spirit.
Job 10:12

Father, You are the giver of life. Because of sin there came death. All Your children will one day be with you in heaven where there is no sun. You will be the light and no more darkness will exist. You will forever watch over Your children with love. Let us go this day in anticipation of that glorious day.

"Can you fathom the mysteries of God? Can you probe the limits of the Almighty?
Job 11:7

Father, there are some mysteries that You have not revealed to mankind. In Zophar the Naamathite reply to Job, he also is telling Job his misery and circumstances are the result of his sins. We may have afflictions that may or may not be the result of our choices and decisions. Some may be due to spiritual warfare while others could be because of our own doing. Father, help us with our battles that are both within and out of our control. Thank You for Your promise that You will never leave us or forsake us. We trust You this day and for eternity to come.

"To God belong wisdom and power; counsel and understanding are His!'
Job 12:13

Father, all we need this day is found in You. Let us not get caught up in the snares of this world and satan. May we be content in knowing as we live for You and follow Your Word that our souls can be in peace. Peace that passes all understanding.

But I desire to speak to the Almighty and to argue my case with God.
Job 13:3

Father, You alone know what is best for Your children. We stand before You in humbleness and trust in You. Thank You Jesus for allowing our prayers to enter the throne room of our Father. May we have peace in knowing that all the answers we receive this day come from our Father.

Mortals, born of woman, are of few days and full of trouble.
Job 14:1

Father, we are born into a sinful world and born sinners. We that have accepted Jesus as our Savior rely on Your Word. We do have hardships and troubles while on this short time on earth. We know from Your Word that we will have trials and tribulations. We also know that You will never leave us or forsake us. All that we go through this day, the Holy Spirit is our Comforter, Counselor, and Advocate. Your Son is at Your right hand and carries our prayers to You. We have all we need to make it through this day. Not on our strength but on the strength that comes from You. May our few days on this earth build Your kingdom

What do you know that we do not know? What insights
do you have that we do not have?
Job 15:9

Father, this day will be filled with the opportunity to live and
make choices that please You. We know that as Your children
You desire us to seek You and make choices that are pleasing to
You. You are total goodness and love. We read in the 66 books
of the Bible that You gave us that You will be with us and
nothing will ever separate Your love from us. As the sun rises
today, may our praise and song rise to You Father.

Even now my witness is in heaven; my advocate is on high.
Job 16:19

Father, You know from day to dusk out thoughts and actions.
When we are falsely accused, all that matters is our hearts are
clear before You. Our Savior Jesus sits at Your right hand and
brings our prayers to Your throne. The Holy Spirit is our
Advocate as we walk each day on this earth. What peace in
knowing that we are so precious in Your sight. We trust in Your
abounding love

My eyes have grown dim with grief; my whole frame is
but a shadow.
Job 17:7

Father, when we are in the depths of grief, You are with us. You
are our comfort and peace in the storms of life. One day, we
will be in our heavenly home that You tell will never again have
sorrow or tears. You are our shelter from the storm.

"Surely such is the dwelling of an evil man; such is the place of
one who does not know God."
Job 18:21

Bildad is telling Job that he must be an evil man for all the
death, destruction, and loss of health that has happened to him.
In fact, the opposite is true. Father, thank You for showing us
that You are with us during the good and bad we experience
while on earth. Thank You Jesus that we saw Your great love
for us by coming to earth and dying for our sins that we might
have life through You. Thank You Holy Spirit for dwelling
within us each step. May we look to Jesus when we make our
choices today

I know that my redeemer lives, and that in the end He will stand
on the earth.
Job 19:25

Job, the earliest book written in the Bible, we read of the
Redeemer. Job had faith that one day his and our Redeemer
would stand on this earth. Fast forward, and we know our
Redeemer was born and lived a sinless life doing the Will of
our Father. We know He died for our sins on a Cross. We know
that three days later He arose from the grave. Mankind that
have accepted Jesus' free gift of salvation know that one day we
will stand with Him before our Father. Father, may many come
to know Jesus this day.

"Such is the fate God allots the wicked, the heritage appointed
for them by God."
Job 20:29

Father, at Your command, Your Son Jesus will come to this
earth and get Your children that have accepted Him as their
Lord and Savior. They will join the others from ages past that
had turned to You. How wonderful heaven will be for eternity
to be with You. The wicked will not enter heaven but will one
day spend eternity in hell. Hell is for satan, the fallen angels,
and the ones that chose not to follow You. May many turn from
their wicked ways that displease You and choose You this day.
Holy Spirit help us this day to make the right choices and
decisions that are pleasing to our Father.

Why do the wicked live on, growing old and increasing in
power?
Job 21:7

Father, Job is questioning why the ones that continue to live
lives that displease You are allowed to go on sinning and
nothing bad seems to happen to them. He had been living for
You and his children, servants, home, and crops had been taken
from him and destroyed. As we go this day and see that the
same may be happening, let us trust in You. We will worship
You in the highs and lows of life. This is the only way when
there seems to be no way. Jesus is the way. We know that
through acceptance of Jesus that at the resurrection we as
believers in Jesus will stand before the Judgment Seat of Christ
not for judgment but for rewards of crowns that in turn will be
laid at our Savior's feet. We also know through Your Word that
one day at the Great White Throne Judgment after the
millennium reign of Jesus that unbelievers will be judged and
then thrown into hell for eternal separation from You. May we
go this day and live our best for You.

Accept instruction from His mouth and lay up His words in
your heart.
Job 22:22

Father, when You speak angels stand ready to do Your will. You
have spoken the heavens into existence and gave mankind
breath. You have provided mankind the Bible to help us know
about how great You are and Your love for us. Through Your
guidance, man wrote the words down that are in the 66 books of
the Bible. May we hide these Words in our hearts that we might
not sin against You this day

I have not departed from the commands of His lips; I have treasured the words of His mouth more than daily bread.
Job 23:12

Father, we are satisfied as we read the Bible. You have given us the bread of life through Your Son Jesus. May we feed on Your Word and bring honor and glory to Your Holy name as we walk our steps this day.

"Why does the Almighty not set times for judgment? Why must those who know Him look in vain for such days?"
Job 24:1

Father, as Your Word tells us there will be a time of judgment on the earth. You alone know when that will be. As we look around, we see flooding, fires, earthquakes, famines, wickedness as You are aware. Holy Spirit help us go this day and bring good and not be overcome with evil. Let us trust in You and Your timing. We know that justice will be delivered one day at The Great White Throne Judgement Day. May many accept You this day and their sins be laid at the Cross of Calvary. Thank You Jesus for the forgiveness of our sins. A debt only You could pay.

"Dominion and awe belong to God; He establishes order
in the heights of heaven."
Job 25:2

Father, how in awe we are of Your greatness. From the smallest
of Your creation to the heavens, Your glory is displayed. May
we never take a day for granted to give You praise and honor.

"And these are but the outer fringe of His works; how faint the
whisper we hear of Him! Who then can understand the thunder
of His power?"
Job 26:14

Father, as we marvel at Your creation it helps us to understand
Your might and holiness. Your creation cries out to bring You
glory in its splendor. The wind through the leaves sing a song
that has rang through the beginning of creation. The roar of the
ocean waves never stops reminding us of Your control of Your
creation. You alone Father are worthy of praise.

My lips will not say anything wicked, and my tongue will not utter lies.
Job 27:4

Father, today is the day You have made, let us rejoice and be glad in it. Let us not fall into temptation and sin and use words to harm and hurt. May we speak truth and live this day with honesty. Let us build up and not tear down. May our lips forever praise You.

And He said to the human race, "The fear of the Lord-that is wisdom, and to shun evil is understanding."
Job 28:28

Father, we come to You in reverence and fall to our knees at Your greatness. May we seek wisdom today that comes from You alone.

"How I long for the months gone by, for the days when God watched over me."
Job 29:2

Father, thank You for the assurance that we are never out of Your sight. There is never a moment that You are not keeping watch over Your children. We can go this day and have peace and comfort.

"But now they mock me, men younger than I, whose fathers I would have disdained to put with my sheep dogs."
Job 30:1

Father, You alone are to be worshiped and bow down too. When others mock us and show cruelty, may we look to Jesus and the life He lived. Jesus was mocked and cruelly treated while on this earth. Your very creation chose to kill Your Son. We were all once sinners but by the blood of Jesus we no longer are bound by the clutches of sin. May mockers and sinners choose the new life that comes only through Your Son Jesus. A life of building up rather than tearing down.

Does He not see my ways and count my every step?
Job 31:4

There is not a step we take today that the Holy Spirit is not with
the ones that have accepted Jesus as their personal Savior. We
never need to feel alone, for the Holy Spirit is our Comforter.
Thank You Father for providing for our every need.

I must speak and find relief; I must open my lips and reply.
Job 32:20

Father, our words can cut like a knife. Let us think before we let
words come from our mouth that can never be taken back. May
our words build up and not destroy. Let our words forever bring
honor to You

The Spirit of God has made me; the breath of the Almighty gives me life.
Job 33:4

In the beginning Father, You created the heavens and the earth. On the sixth day, one of the things You created was man and You said it was very good. You formed man from the dust You had created earlier and breathed life into Your creation. How wonderful it is to know that life and breath came from Your hands and Your breath.

He repays everyone for what they have done; He brings on them what their conduct deserves.
Job 34:11

Father, as born sinners our conduct deserved death and hell. Eternal separation from You. You are a just God and we could not pay for the debt of our sins. Hope came from heaven to earth two thousand years ago in the precious name of Jesus. How wonderful and what peace in knowing that through Jesus we will not be punished for our sins. Through the acceptance of Jesus as our Savior, Your children have been forgiven for the things we have done that displease You. Jesus came to earth and lived a perfect, sinless life and carried our sins to the cross of Calvary. We are free of guilt and sin by the blood of Jesus. Let us go this day and live free and sing praises to our Redeemer

Look up at the heavens and see; gaze at the clouds so high above you.
Job 35:5

Father, each day is a miracle and a blessing from You. We are allowed to see Your creation and bow to Your holiness. You allow us to make choices that are only for mankind. The ones that have accepted Jesus as their Savior have made the most important choice while on earth. That decision cost Your Son to take on the sins of all mankind. As we look up toward heaven today, let us never forget the cost it took for our free gift of freedom from the bondage of sin. May many come to You this day as we did and accept Jesus as their personal Savior.

Be assured that my words are not false; one who has perfect knowledge is with you.
Job 36:4

Elihu had come to Job to let him know of the source of Job's afflictions. He had come to give advice. Father, may we use discernment when mankind comes to talk with us this day. We know as Your children, You alone are the source of knowledge and we are to follow Your will. May we choose this day to follow Your ways and turn from the advice of the world just as Job

God's voice thunders in marvelous ways; He does great things beyond our understanding.
Job 37:5

Father, how great and mighty you are. We live this day because of You. You are the maker of life and in Your hands we find comfort and peace. You have angels awaiting Your command to do Your will. Thank You for Your protection and love that You alone can provide.

Brace yourself like a man; I will question you, and you shall answer me.
Job 38:3

Father, how low Job must have felt as You questioned him. How his head must have hung low and his body limp when he realized how wrong he was. All through his pain and suffering You had never left him. May we go this day and be assured that You will also never leave us.

"Does the hawk take flight by your wisdom and spread its
wings toward the south?'
Job 39:26

Father, You put all instincts in creation. The birds know when to
migrate to have their young. The bear knows when to hibernate.
Mankind was born with an emptiness that can only be filled by
the acceptance of Jesus. May many come to You this day.

"I am unworthy-how can I reply to you?"
Job 40:4

Father, Job was ashamed as You spoke to him out of the storm.
Let us learn from Job and know that You are in control at all
times. During the good and bad while on this earth You are in
control. When our prayers seem to go unanswered You are in
control. When awards and recognitions come You are in
control. When sickness and death come You are in control. Our
peace lies in You Father You are in control.

Who has a claim against Me that I must pay? Everything
under heaven belongs to Me.
Job 41:11

we breathe is from You. We thank You in knowing that we
belong to You. You provide all we need to live this day. To be
Your children and to know Your love for us is our comfort.

Then Job replied to the Lord: "I know that you can do all
things; no purpose of yours can be thwarted."
Job 42:1

Father, You restored Job. You told his friends to carry a burnt
offering and let Job pray for them. You accepted Job's prayer on
behalf of his friends. After Job prayed for his friends, You
restored his fortunes with twice as much as he had before. Jobs'
brothers, sisters, and ones who had known him before came and
ate with him in his house. As we find in Your scriptures, You
offer acceptance, restoration, and forgiveness. Job lived a full
life and saw his children's children to the fourth generation.
May we learn from Job and live and trust in You. Knowing that
You can do all things

For the Lord watches over the way of the righteous, but the way of the wicked leads to destruction.
Psalm 1:6

Father, what a blessing to have assurance that we are children. We are washed by the blood of Jesus and our prayers reach Your throne. We stand righteous in Your sight not by what we have done but because of the acceptance of Your Son Jesus Christ. We are Your children and You are our Father. May we go this day rejoicing.

"I have installed My king on Zion, My holy mountain."
Psalm 2:6

Father, one day Jesus will come to this earth again and sit and rule in Jerusalem. He first came to earth as a servant but when He comes again He will be served. King of Kings and Lord of Lords. One day all will bow at the feet of Jesus and proclaim Jessus as Your son. The savior of the world. May many accept Jesus this day and begin their eternal worship to our King

From the Lord comes deliverance. May Your blessing be
on Your people.
Psalm 3:8

Father, thank You for Your deliverance through Your son Jesus
Christ; that whosoever would believe in Him should not perish
but have eternal life. Life free from the bondage and shame of
sins that are displeasing to You. Our hope is built on nothing
less than Jesus blood and righteousness. May we go this day
free, free indeed.

Answer me when I call to You, my righteous God. Give me
relief from my distress; have mercy on me and hear my prayer.
Psalm 4:1

Father, how wonderful to know that You love us and hear our
prayers. May we rest in knowing You will answer all our
prayers in Your righteousness. You offer mercy and grace to
each sinner. Let us go this day in assurance that You watch over
Your children

In the morning, Lord, you hear my voice; in the morning I lay my requests before You and wait expectantly.
Psalm 5:3

Father, we lay our requests before You this morning. May Your will be done. Take our requests and answer them according to Your plans and not our own. For Your ways are for the best.

Have mercy on me, LORD, for I am faint; heal me, LORD, for my bones are in agony.
Psalm 6:2

Father, our bodies are susceptible to pain and disease. We live in a world of viruses and germs. The world ecosystem could not balance without bacteria. We know during our sickness and pain that You watch over us just like a mother over her infant. When we hurt, You hurt. One day Your children will be safe in Your arms where no pain or heartache will exist. What a glorious day that will be.

My shield is God Most High, who saves the upright in heart.
Psalm 7:10

Father, shield us this day from the arrows and attacks of the enemy. The one who cunningly deceived Adam and Eve in the Garden of Eden. Throughout the history of mankind, he has roamed the earth causing confusion and death. Millions upon millions have chosen not to accept You and will one day be cast in eternal hell with Lucifer. May our hearts be pure, our eyes focused on Jesus, and with the guidance of the Holy Spirit go this day with assurance You shield us each step we take.

Lord, our Lord, how majestic is Your name in all the earth! You have set Your glory in the heavens.
Psalm 8:1

Father, Your name is above every name. There is none greater than You. In all we do today, may it be for the honor and glory of Your name. Let us give our very best to You this day.

I will give thanks to You, Lord, with all my heart; I will tell of
all Your wonderful deeds.
Psalm 9:1

With all our hearts we sing praise and honor to You Father.
From the beautiful sunrise to the moonlight tonight our lips sing
of Your majesty. You bless us with each breath and watch our
every step. Nothing we do or think today You do not know.
How wonderful it is to have a Father that loves us so. May we
go and share that love today.

But you, God, see the trouble of the afflicted; You consider
their grief and take it in hand. The victims commit themselves
to You; You are the helper of the fatherless.
Psalm 10:14

Father, let us go this day and see as You see. May the ones we
come in contact see Your love through Your children.

For the Lord is righteous, He loves justice; the upright will see His face.
Psalm 11:7

Father, one day we will stand before You. We will be allowed to enter Your presence through being washed in the blood of Jesus. How glorious it will be to see our blessed Jesus and spend eternity. Let us go in anxious anticipation of that day and do what we can to tell others about the love of Jesus.

And the words of the Lord are flawless, like silver purified in a crucible, like gold refined seven times.
Psalm 12:6

Father, thank You for Your words that You have given us in the Bible. All we need this day is found in You. You are our creator and Your greatness can be seen in Your creation. May we look to You this day for guidance and follow Your will.

But I trust in Your unfailing love; my heart rejoices in Your
salvation.
Psalm 13:5

Salvation comes from the Lord Jesus Christ who gave His life
that we might live. Father, our trust and hope resides in the
blood of Jesus. Let our hearts rejoice for the love You have for
us and the cleansing of our sins through Jesus.

The Lord looks down from heaven on all mankind
to see if there are any who understand, any who seek God.
Psalm 14:2

Father, how wonderful to know that You are watching over us.
Thank You Holy Spirit for walking each step with us today.
May we go this day in obedience to Your will.

Lord, who may dwell in Your sacred tent? Who may live on
Your holy mountain?
Psalm 15:1

Father, all mankind has been offered a dwelling place with You.
Through the blood of Jesus, mankind has the opportunity to be
washed of their sins and enter heaven one day. Thank You
Father for allowing us to have eternal dwelling with You. May
many come to know Jesus this day.

Lord, You alone are my portion and my cup; You make my lot
secure.
Psalm 16:5

Father, what a wonderful feeling to know we are secure in Your
hands. You are enough and all we have to offer is Yours. We
honor and praise Your name.

I call on You, my God, for You will answer me; turn Your ear to me and hear my prayer.
Psalm 17:6

Father, what a wonderful day to rise and start this day with You. You are our Father and we want to please You. You have given us another day of life to worship and live for You. May our choices be reflective of our love and devotion for You. Go before us this day Father just as You did David, Joshua, Ruth, Stephen, Mary, Lazarus and others who are now with You in heaven.

The Lord is my rock, my fortress and my deliverer; my God is my rock, in whom I take refuge, my shield and the horn of my salvation, my stronghold.
Psalm 18:2

Father, when we are apprehensive or in distress let us remember the words of David: You are our rock. You have never been and never will be shaken or moved. We can always rely on Your strength and guidance that is always good. Your stronghold withstands the arrows and destruction of satan. We rest in Your arms.

The heavens declare the glory of God; the skies proclaim the work of His hands.
Psalm 19:1

Father, each day the sun and moon reminds us of Your constant presence over Your creation. Just as there is never a doubt that the sun will rise each morning, there is never a doubt that You are watching over us. Thank You for letting us witness the works of Your hand.

Some trust in chariots and some in horses, but we trust in the name of the Lord our God.
Psalm 20:7

Father, we trust in You alone. You are our foundation that stands strong.

Be exalted in Your strength, Lord; we will sing and praise Your might.
Psalm 21:13

Father, when we are weak, You are strong. Our strength comes from reliance on You. You move mountains and the seas obey Your command. All of the cycles of nature and the planets orbits are set in place at Your command. You are a sovereign God. What a blessing to be Your children.

My God, my God, why have You forsaken me? Why are You so far from saving me, so far from my cries of anguish?
Psalm 22:1

Father, David said these words as he was in anguish. 1,000 years later, our Messiah Jesus, would say these words before He let out a loud cry and breathed His last on the Cross of Calvary. The centurion watched how Jesus died and said surely this was the Son of God. Jesus and David are now with You in heaven.
Thank You Father for always being with us during each moment of each day. May we gain strength through how Jesus and David relied on You during their darkest days.

The Lord is my shepherd, I lack nothing.
Psalm 23:1

Father, what a special Psalm that David wrote to You. It has been recited millions upon millions of times during mankind's time on earth. Your children are assured that we lack nothing because You are the Good Shepherd. You care for us Your sheep. May we lie down in green pastures knowing that Your eyes are never off watching over us.

The earth is the Lord's, and everything in it, the world, and all who live in it.
Psalm 24:1

Father, what a beautiful and wonderful world You created. From the mountains to the seas, Your creation declares Your greatness. One day Your children will enter heaven, our eternal home. Our imaginations cannot comprehend in Your Word how magnificent that day will be. Thank You Father for allowing us to witness Your love and power

Guide me in Your truth and teach me, for You are God my
Savior, and my hope is in You all day long.
Psalm 25:5

Father, all day long we seek Your guidance and truth. As the
greatest teacher, Your Son Jesus came and taught Your love for
mankind. As we go through this day and all our days on this
earth, our hope is found only in You. We are and have nothing
but an empty existence without You. May we walk the path You
have for us and Your will be done.

Lord, I love the house where You live, the place where Your
glory dwells.
Psalms 26:8

Father, Your glory is seen all around. The heavens declare Your
glory, the Bible declares Your glory, the earth declares Your
glory, all creation declares Your glory, and Your Son Jesus
declared Your glory while on earth. How wonderful heaven will
be when we witness Your glory that will be the light of heaven.
May we go this day rejoicing in Your glory.

One thing I ask from the Lord, this only do I seek: that I may dwell in the house of the Lord all the days of my life, to gaze on the beauty of the Lord and to seek Him in His temple.
Psalm 27:4

Father, through acceptance of Your Son Jesus as our personal Savior, we will be able to be with You for eternity. How wonderful to know You are with us now and nothing will ever separate Your love for us. Let us live this day in service for Your kingdom and telling and showing about Your great love.

The Lord is my strength and my shield; my heart trusts in Him, and He helps me. My heart leaps for joy, and with my song I praise Him.
Psalm 28:7

Father, we are so thankful for allowing us another day to live on this earth with our families and friends. From the beautiful sunrise to the stars at night, Your glory is displayed. Thank You for allowing us a choice to accept Your Son Jesus as our personal Savior. We rejoice in knowing that we Your children will not perish but have eternal life with You in heaven. For this we are most thankful.

The Lord gives strength to His people; the Lord blesses His people with peace.
Psalm 29:11

Father, what peace in knowing that through Your Son Jesus we have become heirs in Your kingdom. One day, there will be no distinctions of race or wealth. We will be in our glorified perfect bodies. We are made perfect through the atoning blood of Jesus. What strength and peace come from knowing we are Yours this day and forever will be.

Sing the praises of the Lord, you His faithful people; praise His holy name.
Psalm 30:4

Father, we come today singing praises as the sun rises. Another day we are blessed to lift our hearts with honor and glory to You. May we be faithful unto You today and make choices that reflect our love and devotion to You. Go before us this day and lead each step

Into Your hands I commit my spirit; deliver me, Lord, my
faithful God.
Psalm 31:5

As Jesus Christ was on the Cross of Calvary, He uttered the
same words David had said 1,000 years before while he was in
anguish: "into Your hands I commit my spirit." Many others
such as Stephen and Martin Luther have also found peace in
these words as they prepared to enter heaven. Father, in Your
hands we commit our spirits. We trust wholly in You.

Then I acknowledged my sin to You and did not cover up my
iniquity. I said, "I will confess my transgressions to the Lord."
And You forgave the guilt of my sin.
Psalm 32:5

Father, through the forgiveness of our sins through Jesus, we no
longer have to live with shame or guilt. Our sins have been
forgotten by You. They have been washed away and we are
white as snow. We sing praises to Jesus this morning and
forevermore.

Blessed is the nation whose God is the Lord, the people He chose for His inheritance.
Psalm 33:12

Father, Israel was chosen by you with Abraham as the people that would one day bring forth Your Son Jesus. They have played a part all throughout human history and will one day play a part when Jesus returns. We ask that You bless the United States of America and its leaders. You tell us to pray for authority and we ask that this morning. May decisions be made that reflect justice and help the poor. Let leaders come forth not for selfish reasons and greed but to serve for the good of mankind and to honor and glorify Your will. May freedom ring so that many can freely choose Your Son Jesus this morning as their Savior.

The Lord is close to the brokenhearted and saves those who are crushed in spirit.
Psalm 34:18

Father, when we hurt and are afraid You are close at all times. You comfort us in our affliction. How wonderful is Your love.

My tongue will proclaim Your righteousness, Your praises all day long.
Psalm 35:28

Father, from sunrise to sunset You are worthy of praise and honor and glory. Hallowed be Your name. As the birds awake this morning chirping and singing to a new day so will we sing praises all day long. As the oceans never cease to crash on the beach with their beautiful roar so will we never cease to proclaim Your righteousness. Forever our lips will praise You.

Your love, Lord, reaches to the heavens, your faithfulness to the skies.
Psalm 36:5

Father, how You love us. You show Your love each day. We never have to worry about You having a bad day and taking out Your anger on us. You are forever Holy and never changing. You are constant in Your love. We are in the protective arms of a loving Father. In that we find peace and comfort.
The law of their God is in their hearts; their feet do not slip.

The law of their God is in their hearts; their feet do not slip.
Psalm 37:31

Father, Your word is truth and life. Your Son Jesus came to earth not to abolish Your laws but to fulfill them. Righteousness is found through Jesus. We stand firm in Jesus.

Lord, I wait for You; You will answer, Lord my God.
Psalm 38:15

Father, go before us this day. As we lift up prayers to You this morning, we know that You will hear each one. Thank You for answering them as a Holy all knowing God. You alone know what is best. May Your kingdom come, Your will be done on earth as it is heaven

"But now, Lord, what do I look for? My hope is in You.
Psalm 39:7

Father, we put our hope in You. You have extended grace to mankind. Grace that was the greatest gift offered to mankind through Jesus. We have accepted Your grace and now can go this day knowing we have eternal life with You. We no longer need to look for we have found Jesus.

He lifted me out of the slimy pit, out of the mud and mire;
He set my feet on a rock and gave me a firm place to stand.
Psalm 40:2

Father, thank You for lifting us out of the slimy pit of sin and shame. Through Jesus, we walk freely and are not filthy with the guilt of sin. We are now Your temples and Your Spirit lives in us. We stand firm and secure out of the mud and mire on a rock. You Father, are our rock.

Even my close friend, someone I trusted, one who shared my bread, has turned against me.
Psalm 41:9

Father, even when our closest friends and family turn against us we always have You. You never have and never will take Your eyes off Your children. We are in Your constant care. We can trust in You.

By day the Lord directs His love, at night His song is with me-a prayer to the God of my life.
Psalm 42:8

Father, whether it be day or night You are with us. Through sickness and health, You are by our side. Nothing will separate Your children from Your love

Then I will go to the altar of God, to God, my joy and my delight. I will praise you with the lyre, 0 God, my God.
Psalm 43:4

Father, we come with joy and thanksgiving this day. No matter what our circumstance, You are God Almighty and we will praise You. Our joy and hope is found in You.

I put no trust in my bow, my sword does not bring me victory.
Psalm 44:6

Father, may we not look to no one or anything but put our trust in You. Victory comes through the Cross of Calvary. Nation upon nation throughout the history of mankind have fallen because of their pride and reluctance to bow and surrender to You. Power is not in the bow, sword, or nuclear weapons but in You. May we and our leaders turn to You.

Your throne, O God, will last for ever and ever; a scepter of justice will be the scepter of your kingdom.
Psalm 45:6

Father, the earth will pass away one day and the new heaven will come down for Your children to live with You for ever and ever. Once we accepted Jesus as our Savior and Lord, our eternal destinations became heaven instead of hell. May many come to Jesus this day and receive the gift of salvation that He came to earth over 2000 years ago to provide.

There is a river whose streams make glad the city of God, the holy place where the Most High dwells.
Psalm 46:4

Father, how beautiful heaven must be. Thank You for another day to witness the earth and the heavens until we one day walk along the river of the water of life, as clear as crystal, flowing from Your throne and of the Lamb. Thank You for our homes and health. Thank You for our church and freedom to worship You freely in the United States. Thank You for our families. Thank You for our employment and providing for our needs. Thank You for sending the Holy Spirit to help as our Advocate. Thank You most of all for Jesus and Your love for mankind. We have so much to be thankful.

Sing praises to God, sing praises; sing praises to our King, sing praises.
Psalm 47:6

Father, we come to you today singing praises:
There is coming a day when we'll be taken away to our home up in the sky
The trumpet shall sound and in a twinkling of an eye we will enter the pearly gates
Chorus
Come, come Lord Jesus, Come in Your majesty
Let the heavens split wide open , Come get Your redeemed

Jesus will take us by the hand and lead us to the promised land where our home shall ever be
Our Father will be there and our loved ones we will see and we'll worship for eternity
Chorus
Let us go this day and proclaim Jesus name to the ones that's never heard
May they join us there in hallelujah square as we offer our crowns at Jesus feet
Chorus
Our Father will be there and our loved ones we shall see and we'll worship for eternity
Lyrics by Dr. Lance Boyd

Great is the Lord, and most worthy of praise, in the city of our
God, His holy mountain.
Psalm 48:1

Father, You are worthy of praise.

I love the Lord Jesus with all my heart and soul.
He is the one I turn to when I'm feeling all alone
He'll never forsake me because it's written so
Trust me my son and I'll lead you to your home
Chorus
How glorious it will be, How glorious it will be
To sit with my Father and see my family
How glorious it will be, How glorious it will be
To sit and talk with Jesus for all eternity

I love the Lord Jesus, How can I tell the ways
He's there shining the light when I have lost my way
I'll sing songs of praises unto the one I speak
And one day I'll be at home with Him
How glorious it will be.
Chorus
Lyrics by Dr. Lance Boyd

But God will redeem me from the realm of the dead; He will surely take me to Himself.
Psalm 49:15

Father, we are assured of our future home in heaven with You through Your word. Thank You in Your goodness to allow us the Bible that lets us know our eternal home that will be in heaven through the acceptance of Your Son Jesus. We have been redeemed by the blood of the Lamb.

I know every bird in the mountains, and the insects in the fields are mine.
Psalm 50:11

Father, it is beyond my understanding that You know every bird that will awake today and sing their songs. Songs that speak of the greatness of Your creation. You watch over all of mankind and know our every move. What peace in knowing Your love for Your children.

My sacrifice, O God, is a broken spirit; a broken and contrite heart You, God, will not despise.
Psalm 51:17

Father, just as David we have all sinned and fell short of Your glory. May we come to You like David when we transgress against You and bring a broken spirit. Thank You for loving us even when we do things that are displeasing to You. May Your will be done.

For what You have done I will always praise You in the presence of Your faithful people. And I will hope in Your name, for Your name is good.
Psalm 52:9

Father, in Your name is goodness and hope. Our lips will sing and lift praise for Your mercy and grace. Thank You Jesus for coming to this earth and being born in a manger, living a perfect sinless life, and dying on the Cross of Calvary so that we might have a way to our Father by the forgiveness of our sins. You took on the sins of the world and defeated death. Through the blood that Jesus shed at Calvary, our sins can be forgiven by believing in Jesus. May many come to You today Father through the Cross and not perish but have eternal life.

God looks down from heaven on all mankind to see if there are any who understand, any who seek God.
Psalm 53:2

Father, in Your love You look at mankind and want us to come unto You. You know what is best for mankind and that is a relationship with You through Your Son Jesus Christ. "Heaven came down and glory filled my soul" are wonderful words in a song describing Jesus coming to earth to offer forgiveness of our sins. May many find You today Father and their "night be turned to day."

Surely God is my help; the Lord is the one who sustains me.
Psalm 54:4

Father, without You we are but sheep among wolves on this earth. You guide and protect us and show us the path to take. When trouble comes we trust in You and Your Word. When good times come we praise Your Holy name. In the good and the bad we will keep our eyes on You.

Evening, morning and noon I cry out in distress, and He hears my voice.
Psalm 55:17

Father, You never tire or sleep. You constantly watch over mankind and nothing happens without You knowing. You hear every word that is spoken. You know every thought. You are sovereign and can do what You want, when You want, and how You want. The laws of nature and science were created by You and can be changed at Your command. What a mighty God we serve.

When I am afraid, I put my trust in you.
Psalm 56:3

Father, just as when the Philistines had seized David in Gath we will put our trust in You. What else can we cling to when we have nowhere else to go but You Father. Through Jesus, You look upon us and all power resides through You. When we can't; You can and do. Your name is wonderful.

Awake, my soul! Awake, harp and lyre! I will awaken the dawn.
Psalm 57:8

Father, thank You for another day as we awaken to see a
sunrise. Another day to breathe in air and smell Your creation.
Another day to feel the leaves. Another day to hear the water as
it passes over rocks in the creek. Another day to walk in the
woods with the ones we love. Another day to eat apples,
oranges, and pecans. Another day to read Your Word and how
much You love us. Another day to hold the hand of the one we
love as we offer prayer and praise to You. May we enjoy this
day to its fullest.

Then people will say, "Surely the righteous still are rewarded;
surely there is a God who judges the earth."
Psalm 58:11

Father, one day every knee will bow and confess that You are
God. Every person that has been born will acknowledge that
Jesus was the Messiah. All mankind will stand before You and
be judged. Ones that have accepted Jesus have had their sins
forgiven through the Cross of Calvary. But woe to the ones that
never accepted the gift of salvation that resulted from Your son
Jesus that was born on this earth to do Your will and give
mankind a way back to You from their sins. Praise the Holy
Name of Jesus.

But I will sing of Your strength, in the morning I will sing of Your love; for You are my fortress, my refuge in times of trouble.
Psalm 59:16

Father, what a wonderful new day to live free from sin and the bondage of guilt. We go behind You and take shelter in Your fortress. When troubles come we are reminded of Your works of Jericho and walls that seem impenetrable came crashing down. Thank You Jesus for coming and being born in a manger and growing to show us the nature of God. The ultimate show of love by dying for our sins on the Cross of Calvary that we might have life. We sing in knowing we have eternal life with You.

With God we will gain the victory, and He will trample down our enemies.
Psalm 60:12

Father, victory has come through Jesus. A victory that only could be won by Him alone. Our enemy, Satan and his followers are the losers and will one day spend eternity in hell. May many come to Jesus today.

Then I will ever sing in praise of Your name and fulfill my
vows day after day.
Psalm 61:8

Father, we have been blessed with another day to sing and
worship Your Holy name. Thank You for our health and ability
to be able to glorify You through our steps today. May we sing
in praise of You wanting and allowing us to have a relationship
with You. We are Yours and our hearts sing for joy.

Truly my soul finds rest in God; my salvation comes from him.
Psalm 62:1

Father, when we surrender our souls to You is when we have
peace and contentment. Once we have heard of Jesus and the
Holy Spirit stirs our hearts, our souls and in most being is
stirred like a roaring river until we submit to Your calling. Satan
tries to make one feel salvation is by works and is much too
hard to obtain but Jesus is the way to You. Only through Jesus
is salvation possible. All mankind is asked to do is surrender
their soul to Jesus and then the roaring river becomes a gentle
stream. No more doubt, confusion, or works are needed. Our
souls find rest at the Cross of Calvary.

You, God, are my God,
earnestly I seek You; I thirst for You, my whole being longs for
You, in a dry and parched land where there is no water.
Psalm 63:1

Father, You created mankind to need water and food to survive.
Just as we need nourishment for our bodies to function, we are
also born to have a relationship with You. We are born to
worship and serve You for eternity. May we feed from Your
Word today and have fellowship with You throughout the day.
Let us come to Your table and feast of Your goodness and
grace.

The righteous will rejoice in the Lord and take refuge in Him;
all the upright in heart will glory in Him!
Psalm 64:10

Father, we have found You through Jesus. We were sinners that
had no hope. Once we believed in Your Son, we were born
again. As we confessed with our mouth that Jesus is Lord and
believed in our heart that You raised Him from the dead our sins
were forgiven. How our hearts rejoice knowing that we are
forever Yours.

You who answer prayer, to You all people will come.
Psalm 65:2

Father, it is so assuring to know that You hear Your children as we talk and lift up prayer to You. Through acceptance of Jesus, we have access to Your throne room in heaven. Our prayers are lifted and You hear each one. What is also wonderful is knowing that You answer each one according to Your will being done. May our praise and prayers be sweet incense to You this day. Thank You for Your love Father.

Shout for joy to God, all the earth!
Psalm 66:1

Father, we come to You with shouts of joy for what You have done and what You will do. You have created all that we see, hear, smell, and touch. When You spoke life into existence, each breath of every creature was known by You. Just as the birds sing this morning, we lift up our voices to You. What a mighty God we serve.

May God be gracious to us and bless us and make his face shine on us–so that Your ways may be known on earth, Your salvation among all nations.
Psalm 67:1-2

Father, when mankind looks upon Your children may they see a peculiar people. A people that does not do as the world but follows Your will that is written in the Bible. May they see Your children love and show love among their fellow man. May Your children shine in a dark world.

You, God, are awesome in Your sanctuary; the God of Israel gives power and strength to His people. Praise be to God!
Psalm 68:35

Father, thank You for the strength to go this day and live for You. May we make choices that help build Your kingdom by the people we come in contact. Thank You Holy Spirit for revealing temptation and the power to resist through the name above all names our Lord and Savior Jesus Christ.

They put gall in my food and gave me vinegar for my thirst.
Psalm 69:21

Father, David is telling us that in his suffering all that is offered him is vinegar and gall. As Jesus was near death on the Cross of Calvary, the soldiers offered Him vinegar mixed with gall. Jesus refused the gall and vinegar so He could keep a clear mind. The gall would have dulled His senses. Father, may we keep our bodies pure and clean so as to have a clear mind so to always at all times be in fellowship with You. May we not allow satan and his demons a crack in our spiritual armor.

Hasten, O God, to save me; come quickly, Lord, to help me.
Psalm 70:1

Father, in our times of distress, You are our comfort. If it be Your will, come quickly Father. May we walk with You today and allow the Holy Spirit to direct our steps. May we grow through our hard times to learn to rely on You. May we celebrate our good times. Let us always strive to be in the right relationship with You. May we be at the right place, at the right time, doing the right thing.

For You have been my hope, Sovereign Lord, my confidence
since my youth.
Psalm 71:5

Father, we were shameful sinners before we accepted Jesus as
our Savior and were born again into fellowship with You. We
now have assurance and confidence in You. In Your Word is
found wisdom and goodness. The fruit of the Spirit is love, joy,
peace, forbearance, kindness, goodness, faithfulness, gentleness
and self-control. Our hope is found in You.

Praise be to the Lord God, the God of Israel, who alone does
marvelous deeds.
Psalm 72:18

Father, You alone do marvelous deeds. You have created all that
exists. You have allowed mankind to have the choice to spend
eternal fellowship with You. How marvelous are Your deeds.
May we praise and worship You Father throughout this day and
forevermore through eternity.

But as for me, it is good to be near God. I have made the Sovereign Lord my refuge; I will tell of all Your deeds.
Psalm 73:28

Father, You have made it possible for mankind to be near Your Holiness. We should never worry that we might lose our salvation and spend eternity away from You. Jesus paid it all so we could have our transgressions against You forgiven. May we go this day and tell others of the Gospel of Jesus Christ and the wonderful gift of salvation.

But God is my King from long ago; He brings salvation on the earth.
Psalms 74:12

Father, You are the creator of time. Time as we know with the sun and revolving planets were Your design. You are King over all. You have offered mankind salvation from their sins through Jesus. May many receive the calling from the Holy Spirit today and know You as their Father. A Father who is love.

As for me, I will declare this forever; I will sing praise to the
God of Jacob.
Psalm 75:9

Father, we call to You now. We call to the God of Jacob for
guidance and direction this day to do Your will. May our steps
be led by Your divine guidance. Let Your hand hold ours each
step we take. Provide our needs and may we be content in Your
many blessings. We sing praise to You our God.

At your rebuke, God of Jacob, both horse and chariot lie still.
Psalm 76:6

Father, we seek You when faced with fears and anxiety. At Your
command horses and chariots of war are crushed by the waters.
What have we to fear when in Your will. Fear was abolished at
the Cross of Calvary along with our sins and inability to follow
the law. Jesus came not to abolish the law but to fulfill the law.
We have accepted Jesus and have been set free from the law.
We are not to feel shame or the fear of death. Nations rise and
fall as You are in control. We trust in You Father. Only in You is
found peace and contentment

I will remember the deeds of the Lord; yes, I will remember
Your miracles of long ago.
Psalm 77:11

Father, thank You for telling us about miracles You have
performed. You have parted the sea; withheld rain; called up
men to heaven, rescued men from furnaces of fire, brought
down quail, brought forth water from a rock, and miracle after
miracle that only You can do. Your creation is beyond
comprehension. Thank You for the miracle of raising Your son
Jesus from the grace that gave mankind a choice to receive
forgiveness from their sins and be brought back into fellowship
with You. We look forward to another day to witness miracle
after miracle this day. Open our eyes that we may see.

And David shepherded them with integrity of heart; with
skillful hands he led them.
Psalm 78:72

Father, may we serve You today with integrity of heart. Let all
sin be left at the Cross of Calvary and pure hearts rejoice of
Your goodness.

Then we Your people, the sheep of Your pasture, will praise
You forever; from generation to generation
we will proclaim Your praise.
Psalm 79:13

Father, we are as sheep dependent on Your protection and
guidance. Shepherd us today with Your staff and strength. May
we follow Your perfect will and praise You for eternity.

Restore us, 0 God; make Your face shine on us, that we may be
saved.
Psalm 80:3

Father, how we need You. You are the source of this dark sinful
world that satan roams. Only Your light penetrates the darkness.
Your children spread Your light with their words and actions.
May we go this day and be a light to a dying world that has no
hope but to be restored and saved from their sins and
wretchedness through the blood of Jesus Christ. Our Savior and
Lord.

"But my people would not listen to me; Israel would not submit to me."
Psalm 81:11

Father, may we listen to You today from Your Word and through the Holy Spirit. May we be submissive to Your will. Let us follow You as Jesus did and Your will and not ours be Let us follow You as Jesus did and Your will and not ours be done.

Rise up, O God, judge the earth, for all the nations are Your inheritance.
Psalm 82:8

Father, all is under Your control. We live in a time of mercy and grace. Mankind is allowed to choose You or satan. One day, all mankind will acknowledge that Jesus is King of Kings and Lord of Lords. For the ones that did not choose Jesus while on earth it will be too late to ask for salvation. May many come to You today through the blood of Jesus and stand before You at the Judgement Seat of Christ where the redeemed will receive our rewards. The ones that have not accepted Jesus will stand before the Great White Throne Judgement and their names will not be written in the Book of Life. They will be thrown into the lake of fire. May many accept You today Father and choose heaven rather than eternal separation from You. Today is the day of salvation

Let them know that You, whose name is the Lord–that You
alone are the Most High over all the earth.
Psalm 83:18

Father, You have made known that You are the Most High.
From the heavens and stars that are each bigger than the earth to
the depths of the seas, You have declared Your glory and
splendor. You sent Your only begotten Son Jesus to show us
how You love mankind and want to have an eternal relationship
with each of us. You are our Lord and may we be in Your will
this day.

Lord Almighty, blessed is the one who trusts in You.
Psalm 84:12

Father, as rains fall like Your blessings, we will trust in You. As
Your children, we look to You for assurance. Assurance that
You are with us today and for eternity. We know You are in
control and every step we take the Holy Spirit is with us. We
are blessed to know that our sins have been forgiven through
the acceptance of Jesus. Jesus will one day judge all mankind
and He will know us that have asked for the forgiveness of our
sins and submitted our lives to Him. We shall dwell in heaven
with You for eternity. Blessed assurance Jesus is ours.

Righteousness goes before Him and prepares the way for His steps.
Psalm 85:13

Father, go before us this day. As we face the obstacles that come before us today, we know that You never put more than we can endure. We rely on You Father and may Your will be done. Guide us Holy Spirit and show us the way of our Father. How we need You Father each second of each day.

You, Lord, are forgiving and good, abounding in love to all who call to You.
Psalm 86:5

Father, thank You for forgiveness for the ones that call to have their trespasses against You forgiven. In Your great love, You allow our sins to be wiped clean and never held against us. You are so so good Father. We are not worthy but through Your Son Jesus we are made white as snow. Praise the name of Jesus our Savior and Advocate. We can call upon You at anytime since we are now Your temple as the Holy Spirit resides in us just as You once resided in the tabernacle and temple in the Holy of Holies. What peace in knowing You are always with us.

The Lord loves the gates of Zion more than all the other dwellings of Jacob.
Psalm 87:2

Father, Your chosen people that came from Abraham will once again have their home with You in Zion (Jerusalem). The piece of ground has been fought over for millennium has been attacked 52 times, captured and recaptured 44 times, besieged 23 times, and destroyed twice. It is one of the oldest cities in the world and will one day be where Jesus reigns on earth for 1,000 years after the tribulation. It is no wonder why satan has enticed war on the ground for thousands of years. We look forward to the peace that will one day come.

But I cry to You for help, Lord; in the morning my prayer comes before You.
Psalm 88:13

Father, we come before You with joy in our hearts. We have another day to see Your beautiful wonders. We have another day to hold our families. We have another day to show the ones we are in contact with how much You have done for us. We have another day to talk with in prayer throughout our day. Our hearts are filled with joy.

I will declare that Your love stands firm forever, that You have established Your faithfulness in heaven itself.
Psalm 89:2

Father, Your love stands the rest of time. We feel Your love as we hold our new born babies, look up into the heavens, walk the beaches, hear the wind blowing through the leaves, and listen to the waters rolling over the rocks. Thank You Father for loving the world so much that You gave Your only begotten Son. Thank You Jesus for loving mankind so much that You died for our sins on the Cross of Calvary. Your love Father has been before the earth began and will always remain through eternity. Thank You Father for displaying Your love to Your children. A love that stands forever.

Before the mountains were born or You brought forth the whole world, from everlasting to everlasting You are God.
Psalm 90:2

Father, we come this morning bowing before You. We acknowledge You are God. You have always been and forever will be. You have created the world and heavens. How wonderful to know You are our Father. Yes, we bow and honor You Father.

"Because he loves Me," says the Lord, "I will rescue him; I will protect him, for he acknowledges My name.
Psalm 91:14

Father, we Your children acknowledge You as the one true God. We bow and serve You. May Your will and not ours be done for You know what is best and have a perfect plan.

But you, Lord, are forever exalted.
Psalm 92:8

Father, we sing praises to You this morning. As the day goes by, we will praise Your name. When we lay down to sleep, we will close our eyes in praise to You. May You alone be exalted today and forevermore.

Your statutes, Lord, stand firm; holiness adorns Your house
for endless days.
Psalm 93:5

Father, Your Word stands firm. Satan used scripture in a
deceptive way to tempt Jesus in the wilderness. Jesus used
scripture in a correct way to resist satan and his evil. May we
use scripture as You intended and use discernment as we search
through Your Holy Bible. The inspired Word that helps us know
You and Your nature. We stand firm in You.

But the Lord has become my fortress, and my God the rock in
whom I take refuge.
Psalm 94:22

Father, in who can we trust but You. You are our rock and on
Your Word Your children who have accepted Jesus as their
Savior stand. All other ground is sinking sand, All other ground
is sinking sand. May we go this day and forevermore walking
on the sure foundation of Jesus Christ our Lord and Savior.

Come, let us bow down in worship, let us kneel before the Lord
our Maker.
Psalm 95:6

Father, we will bow before You this day and worship You. We
were created to have a relationship with You. Life is abundant
with joy once we believe in Jesus and have our sins removed by
His blood. We are born again and start our eternal relationship
with You; the Lord our Maker. Nothing will ever remove the
joy in knowing our eternal state. We are forever Yours.

Let all creation rejoice before the Lord, for He comes, He
comes to judge the earth. He will judge the world in
righteousness and the peoples in His faithfulness.
Psalm 96:13

Father, thank You for allowing Jesus to come and take the
punishment for our sins. Jesus showed how much He loves
mankind by coming to this earth and suffering on the Cross of
Calvary. Our sins were left at the foot of the Cross. Praise the
name of Jesus.

The Lord reigns, let the earth be glad; let the distant shores
rejoice.
Psalm 97:1

Father, from the beginning You have reigned and You reign
today and You will reign through eternity. You watch and never
take Your hand off Your children that have believed in Jesus as
their Savior. We rejoice in knowing You reign. Our God reigns.

He has remembered His love and His faithfulness to Israel;
all the ends of the earth have seen the salvation of our God.
Psalm 98:3

Father, ever since You started Your chosen people out of the
line of Abraham, You have had a plan. You have always been
faithful but they could not keep their end of the covenant. You
sent Your Son Jesus not just that Israel might have a way to You
through forgiveness of their sins but also to the rest of the
world.
Salvation is a free gift for all mankind. Thank You Father for
Your love, mercy, and grace.

The Lord reigns, let the nations tremble; He sits enthroned
between the cherubim, let the earth shake.
Psalm 99:1

Father, in the tabernacle in The Holy of Holies was the Ark of
the Covenant that had the two cherubim on each end facing
each other. Your presence was in the place. In heaven the angels
are continually lifting praise to Your holiness. You are the light
and at the center of all worship in heaven. We offer that same
praise and bow unto You Father. Let all creation lift praise and
honor and glory to the one true God.

For the Lord is good and His love endures forever; His
faithfulness continues through all generations.
Psalm 100:5

Father, you are goodness and love. In Your wisdom, You gave
mankind a soul and the ability to experience love. You offer
love to mankind through Jesus. Your love never ends through
eternity. Thank You Father for Your endless love.

I will sing of Your love and justice; to You, Lord, I will sing
praise.
Psalm 101:1

Father, only You are worthy of praise. May we have joyful
hearts in knowing we have a friend in Jesus. We have assurance
that the Holy Spirit dwells inside us. We can never describe the
peace that transcends all understanding.

But You remain the same, and Your years will never end.
Psalms 102:27

Father, it is hard to imagine how You have never changed. You
have always been. Creation was made by You. In the world You
created; man dies, plants die, and the seasons change. You
never change and remain the same. All of creation is in balance
through You. May we go this day in awe of Your greatness

Praise the Lord, all His works everywhere in His dominion.
Praise the Lord, my soul.
Psalm 103:22

Father, as we wake to another day and wait for the sunrise, we praise You. From the depths of our soul, we sing and lift up joyful words of Your deeds. You are alone our passion to go this day and live life. May each step be pleasing to You. May each word that leaves our mouth be pleasing to You. May our lives be pleasing to You. In the precious name of Jesus we pray, amen.

I will sing to the Lord all my life: I will sing praise to my God as long as I live.
Psalm 104:33

Father, we sing songs and lift praise to You this morning. Thank You for another day to worship You on this earth as there is constant worship in heaven. I pray we bring honor to Your name in all we do.

Look to the Lord and His strength; seek His face always.
Psalm 105:4

Father, where can we go but to You. This world is hard to walk.
Wars, earthquakes, starvation, disease, and death. We know it
was not intended but is a result of satan and sin. You have
blessed the United States beyond measure and so many choose
to follow You in our country. We call on Your strength this day
and thank You for freedom of worship and food in our mouths.
You are our God and we praise You,

Praise be to the Lord, the God of Israel, from everlasting to
everlasting. Let all the people say, "Amen!" Praise the Lord.
Psalm 106:48

Father, we will praise you today and forevermore. You are
worthy of all worship. You created all things for good. Let us go
this day and sing with joyful hearts.

He brought them out of darkness, the utter darkness, and broke away their chains.
Psalm 107:14

Father, we were chained by our sins but Jesus came and broke our chains. We were set free from the bondage of sin. We are now free and able to have fellowship with You. Praise the name of Jesus.

With God we will gain the victory, and He will trample down our enemies.
Psalm 108:13

Father, the victory is Yours. You are the creator of all and nothing is out of Your control. Thank You for allowing mankind to have a relationship with You. As Your children, nothing can happen to us that is not permitted by You. How wonderful to know we are always in Your care

Help me, lord my God; save me according to Your
unfailing love.
Psalm 109:26

Father, thank You for always watching over us and Your
protection. There is never a moment satan is not on Your leash.
May we go this day and show love like Jesus showed
while here on earth. A love that is unfailing.

The Lord says to my Lord: "Sit at My right hand until I make
Your enemies a footstool for Your feet."
Psalm 110:1

Father, You revealed that one day Jesus would come and He
would be a priest forever, in the order of Melchizedek. Your
plans are perfect and come in Your timing. Thank You for
allowing us to know what the future holds in store through Your
Word. We are overcomers through faith in Jesus.

Great are the works of the Lord; they are pondered by all who delight in them.
Psalm 111:2

Father, being able to get up in the mornings and hear the birds sing and the sun come up is such a blessing. To be able to work and have interaction with our fellow man is such a blessing. To have family that love us and friends is such a blessing. To know we have Jesus as our Savior and we will spend eternity with You is the greatest blessing. We delight in knowing that all this is possible because of You. Great are Your works. Great is Your love.

Even in darkness light dawns for the upright, for those who are gracious and compassionate and righteous.
Psalm 112:4

Father, in our deepest sorrow You are our light. When mountains stand before us, You are our light. When we can't see to take our next step, You are our light. Through it all, You are our light.

From the rising of the sun to the place where it sets, the name of
the Lord is to be praised.
Psalm 113:3

Father, as the sun rises we will praise You. When the sun is
above we will praise You. When the sun sets we will praise
You. You will be praised at night as we await the sun to rise
again and start a new day. Each day we shall praise Your name.

Tremble, earth, at the presence of the Lord, at the presence of
the God of Jacob.
Psalm 114:7

Father, we bow in submission to You this morning. Thank You
for another day of life. A day to worship and praise Your name.
Our hearts rejoice in knowing You first loved us. We desire to
bring a sweet incense of worship to You today and pour our
love to You. Thank You Father for allowing us to experience
true love through the acceptance of Jesus as our Savior. We now
are promised to be loved for eternity. Praise the name of Jesus

Not to us, Lord, not to us but to Your name be the glory,
because of Your love and faithfulness.
Psalm 115:1

Father, may all honor and glory go to Your Holy name this day
and forever more. All we do is for Your kingdom. We wish to
please You through our works today. Thank You for loving us
and Your hand of protection.

I love the Lord, for He heard my voice; He heard my cry for
mercy.
Psalm 116:1

Father, we have called upon the name of Jesus to come and
forgive us of our sins. We could not be reconciled on our works
but only through the blood of Jesus. Your mercy and grace is
sufficient. We thank You for redemption and live to serve You.
May we lift our voices with praise and our hearts to You this
day. We love You Father

For great is His love toward us, and the faithfulness of the Lord endures forever. Praise the Lord.
Psalm 117:2

Father, thank You for Your love. Your love will never leave Your children. We go this day knowing forever and ever we are in Your arms of love.

You are my God, and I will praise You; You are my God, and I will exalt You.
Psalm 118:28

Father, we love You. Thank You for the health to get up out of bed this morning. Thank You for being able to breathe the fresh air. Thank You for being able to walk. Thank You for the ability to communicate with the ones we love. May we go this day and praise and worship You for these many blessings

I have hidden Your word in my heart that I might not sin against You.
Psalm 119:11

Father, we love and want to live our lives in honor and glory to Your name. Thank You Holy Spirit for indwelling in us to show us the way to please our Father. Thank You Father for Your Holy Word that helps us know what pleases You. May we go this day and live for You. Let us use discernment as we face decisions and may they be pleasing to You. Thank You Jesus for Your teachings that show us the nature of our Father.

I call on the Lord in my distress, and He answers me.
Psalm 120:1

Father, we know You hear our every word that is spoken. You watch our every move. At all times we are never out of Your watchful eye. You know what is best for us and may we trust in Your infinite wisdom as You answer our prayers today.

My help comes from the Lord, the Maker of heaven and earth.
Psalm 121:2

Father, we know that You will be with us each step of this day. We have assurance through Your Word. Obstacles will come our way but You are our shield. Just as so many of Your children have been persecuted through the years, we too face the onslaught of the enemy in these days. We thank You for America and the ones who sacrificed so much that we might worship You in freedom. May many come to Jesus today and start living a life of eternal freedom. I pray for our leaders that they will look to You for wisdom. Our help comes from You.

I rejoiced with those who said to me, "Let us go to the house of the Lord."
Psalm 122:1

Father, thank You for our churches that we attend that help us learn more about You. Thank You for our pastors that bring us sermons. Thank You for our fellow Christian brothers and sisters that encourage us as we study and walk this journey on earth. One day, Your children will be gathered in Your house for eternity. What a wonderful homecoming that will be.

I lift up my eyes to You, to You who sit enthroned in heaven.
Psalm 123:1

Father, through the heavens You sit enthroned in majesty. You Son Jesus left this earth and ascended upward to sit at Your right hand in heaven where he awaits His return to rapture Your church. We look to You this day for wisdom that only comes from You. Thank You Holy Spirit for helping us discern right from wrong. We want to do what pleases You Father. We want to be faithful servants of our Lord Jesus Christ. May our minds be clear in Your Word. May we grow closer to You this day.

Our help is in the name of the Lord, the Maker of heaven and earth.
Psalm 124:8

Father, we run to You. Where is better than in Your protective arms. May our hearts be pure and what we say, do, and think be pleasing to You. How wonderful You are.

As the mountains surround Jerusalem, so the Lord surrounds
His people both now and forevermore.
Psalm 125:2

Father, we are surrounded by Your presence. There is never a
moment You are not with us. How wonderful to know You will
never be out of our presence for the rest of eternity.

The Lord has done great things for us, and we are filled with
joy.
Psalm 126:3

Father, You have done more than we deserve. We were sinners
with no hope and You sent Your Son Jesus for atonement for
our sins. We were as filthy as rags but through the blood of
Jesus we are now washed white as snow. Our hearts are filled
with joy. Your mercy, grace , and love are offered to all
mankind. May many repent of their sins and accept Jesus as
Lord this day.

Unless the Lord builds the house, the builders labor in vain. Unless the Lord watches over the city, the guards stand watch in vain.
Psalm 127:1

Father, thank You for the blueprint You gave us for raising our families. Mothers play such an instrumental part in creating an atmosphere of learning and loving. Thank You for giving them the opportunity to look to You for guidance. May mothers be blessed today and evermore.

Blessed are all who fear the Lord, who walk in obedience to Him. You will eat the fruit of your labor; blessings and prosperity will be yours. Your wife will be like a fruitful vine within your house; your children will be like olive shoots around your table. Yes, this will be the blessing for the man who fears the Lord.
Psalm 128:1-4

Thank You Father for Your blessings

"But the Lord is righteous; He has cut me free from the cords of the wicked."
Psalm 129:4

Father, we are no longer bound by the bondage of sin. Jesus took on the sins of the world at the Cross of Calvary. After three days, He defeated death and arose from the grave. Through acceptance of Jesus, we too can have abundant life through the forgiveness of our sins. Praise Jesus for cutting the cords of sin and making us free to run to Your arms.

Out of the depths I cry to you, Lord; Lord, hear my voice. Let your ears be attentive to my cry for mercy.
Psalm 130:1-2

Father, there is no depth of pain that Jesus did not feel. There is no rejection that Jesus did not endure. Jesus can relate to our deepest sorrow and despair. Jesus relied on You and so will we. Thank You Father for Your strength that enables us to go through hardships and struggles of this world.
My heart is not proud, Lord, my eyes are not haughty; I do not concern myself with great matters or things too wonderful for me.

My heart is not proud, Lord, my eyes are not haughty;
I do not concern myself with great matters or things too
wonderful for me.
Psalm 131:1

Father, who are we to have pride, arrogance, and haughtiness.
We are Your creation to serve You. All we have and are is
because of You. Thank You Father for Your love. We bow and
worship You this day and all the days to come. Then we will
bow and worship You in heaven forever and ever. What joy and
peace in knowing You are in control.

For the Lord has chosen Zion, He has desired it for his
dwelling, saying, "This is my resting place for ever and ever;
here I will sit enthroned, for I have desired it.
Psalm 132:13-14

Father, one day this heaven and earth will pass away and there
will be no more sea. There will be a new heaven and a new
earth. Then a New Jerusalem will come down from heaven
from You. You will dwell with Your children forever.
What a day that will be Father.

How good and pleasant it is when God's people live together in unity!
Psalm 133:1

Father, may we live a life that does not bring trouble unto others. Let us do unto others as we would have them do upon us. Let us love our neighbors and turn the other cheek. May we be slow to speak and patient to listen. May the world see unity in Your children. A unity of following Your Word and not being led astray by false teachings. May we use discernment and obey Your Word. Holy Spirit keep us on the narrow path this day.

Lift up your hands in the sanctuary and praise the Lord.
Psalm 134:2

Father, we praise You this morning. You have offered mankind a way back to You through Your Son Jesus Christ. The ones that accept Jesus as their Savior are no longer bound by the guilt of their sins. We are free and are Your children. How blessed we are to go this day and know we are Yours.

The Lord does whatever pleases Him, in the heavens and on the earth, in the seas and all their depths.
Psalm 135:6

Father, You do whatever pleases You. May we be used this day to please You. Our choice to choose and believe in Jesus pleased You. When we obey and follow Your Word pleases You. When we stop and tell of Your goodness and mercy to others pleases You. When we put You above all pleases You. We know these things please You from Your Word. We look forward to another sunrise to go and help. Do it again Father. Bring another day so we may go and show our love for You.

With a mighty hand and outstretched arm; His love endures forever.
Psalm 136:12

Father, Your love endures forever. Hold us in Your hands today as we walk this earth. Embrace us with Your love as only You can. Thank You Jesus for outstretched arms as You hung on the Cross of Calvary. We lay our sins at the foot of the Cross. How wonderful to know our sins are forgiven and one day we will run to You Father with outstretched arms as we enter heaven.

By the rivers of Babylon we sat and wept when we remembered
Zion.
Psalm 137:1

Father, You allowed John in Revelation to see that one day
Babylon will be destroyed and a New Jerusalem will come
down from heaven. You will be the light and we will be with
You forever. In this world we have tears but one day You will
wipe our tears away and none will ever be shed again
throughout eternity. Praise Your Holy name.

Though the Lord is exalted, He looks kindly on the lowly;
though lofty, He sees them from afar.
Psalm 138:6

Father, thank You for having mercy on us. We were lowly born
sinners that had no hope. Once hopeless, but now with the
opportunity to ask Jesus for forgiveness from our sins. Once
only concerned with self, now we honor and serve You. Once
lowly, now through acceptance of Jesus as our Lord we will one
day rise to meet You in heaven

You know when I sit and when I rise; You perceive my thoughts from afar.
Psalm 139:2

Father, You are all knowing. Nothing is hidden from You. May our thoughts be pure and our actions bring honor to Your Holy name.

I know that the Lord secures justice for the poor and upholds the cause of the needy.
Psalm 140:12

Father, You look at the heart of man and not material wealth. You look at the heart and not power. You look at the heart. You gave Your only begotten Son for all mankind so they might accept Jesus into their heart. Thank You Father for Your love

May my prayer be set before You like incense; may the lifting up of my hands be like the evening sacrifice.
Psalm 141:2

Father, help us this day as we walk this earth. You have given us all we need to resist the evil one. You have sent Jesus to have forgiveness of our sins that we can be born again and be Your child whose name is written in the Lambs Book of Life. You have given us the Holy Spirit that resides in each of Your children that have accepted Jesus. Your angels do Your will. We still have the free will to make decisions. May our walk be straight to You Father. May our thoughts, actions, and decisions bring honor to Your name. May we please You in all we say, do, and think.

I cry aloud to the Lord; I lift up my voice to the Lord for mercy.
Psalm 142:1

Father, how wonderful to know that You hear our cries for mercy. You do not punish us for the sins we do. It took Your Son Jesus to take the sins of the world. They were left at the Cross of Calvary. We deserved death but through the blood of Jesus we have life. You answer our prayers in the plans You have for us. How our hearts sing for joy knowing of the grace we received when we accepted Jesus.

Let the morning bring me word of Your unfailing love, for I have put my trust in You. Show me the way I should go, for to You I entrust my life.
Psalm 143:8

Father, each morning we shall arise and praise Your Holy name. As the sun rises, we remember the promises that are found in Your Word. We shall read the Bible and search this day so we can be the child You would have us to be. Through the blood of Jesus, You see us as not what we were but as Your children. We desire to live our lives to please You. Our trust is in You.

Praise be to the Lord my Rock, who trains my hands for war, my fingers for battle.
Psalm 144:1

Father, as we go this day into this world let us take Your assurance that we can never be separated from You. The enemy destroys and pillages but You build and love. May we put on the full armor of Your Word and fight evil with Your goodness. Go before us Father as our shield. We follow You

Great is the Lord and most worthy of praise; His greatness no one can fathom.
Psalm 145:3

Father, we marvel at the heavens. The planets are in perfect orbit and the stars all bigger than the earth. Galaxies upon galaxies extend through space. The smallness of an atom and the 30 trillion cells in our bodies cannot be seen but through a microscope. Your works are amazing. Thank You for allowing us to have the ability to enjoy Your creation and for loving us.

I will praise the Lord all my life; I will sing praise to my God as long as I live.
Psalm 146:2

Father, what a wonderful day to praise Your Holy name. All days are for us to worship You. Rainy days we will worship You. Sunny days we will worship You. May we proclaim the name of Jesus each and every day as our Lord and Savior with a joyful heart.

He determines the number of the stars and calls them each
by name
Psalm 147:4

Father, when we look up at night into our Milky Way galaxy
and see the over 300 billion stars in the sky, You know each one
by name. You know all the other stars of the galaxies in the
entire universe by name that man cannot comprehend. You also
know the heart of each of the 8 billion 22 million people on
earth right this second. May each one accept Jesus as their
savior and be filled with the peace in knowing they will spend
eternity within Your arms.

Praise the Lord. Praise the Lord from the heavens; praise Him
in the heights above.
Psalm 148:1

Father, angels praise You in heaven and we will praise You on
earth. You are our God and worthy of all praise. May we go this
wonderful day You have made and enjoy fellowship with You.

For the Lord takes delight in His people; He crowns the humble with victory.
Psalm 149:4

Father, our relationship with You is possible through the acceptance of Jesus. We are servants to Your will for our lives. We humbly bow before You this day and submit to the one true God. You are our Father and we will worship You through eternity.

Let everything that has breath praise the Lord. Praise the Lord.
Psalm 150:6

Father, we praise You this day. As long as we have breath, we will praise You in the morning, afternoon, and night. Praise will continually flow from our hearts to You for eternity.

The fear of the Lord is the beginning of knowledge, but fools despise wisdom and instruction.
Proverbs 1:7

Father, You are the source of wisdom and truth. May we look to You this day for direction that is pleasing to You.

For the Lord gives wisdom; from His mouth come knowledge and understanding.
Proverbs 2:6

Father, we look to You today for wisdom, knowledge, and understanding. May we seek truth that is found in reading the Bible. May we hold to the teachings of Jesus. Help us Holy Spirit this day as we step into another day to walk the path our Father has before us.

Trust in the Lord with all your heart and lean not on your own understanding; in all your ways submit to Him, and He will make your paths straight.
Proverbs 3:5-6

Father, in You we put our trust. We know that your ways are best for us for eternity. May we follow the straight and narrow path.

Above all else, guard your heart, for everything you do flows from it.
Proverbs 4:23

Father, by accepting Jesus as our personal Savior, we have given our hearts to You. Out of our hearts flow praise and worship to You this morning. May many accept Your Son this day and begin living for You, the one true God.

For your ways are in full view of the Lord, and He examines all
your paths.
Proverbs 5:21

Father, how good to know that each step we take today You are
watching. There is no door or wall that we are hidden from You
Go before us Father and may we follow Your will.

When you walk, they will guide you; when you sleep, they will
watch over you; when you awake, they will speak to you.
Proverbs 6:22

Father, thank You for seeing us through Jesus. Once we
accepted Jesus, You no longer see us as we were. Now we are
made clean and spotless from our sins through Jesus. We will
hide Your Word in our hearts so we might not sin against You.
We wish to please You Father just as Jesus did while on earth.
May we go this day rejoicing that we go not alone but You are
with us always.

Keep my commands and you will live; guard my teachings as
the apple of your eye.
Proverbs 7:2

Father, to live is to follow You. We live on this earth just a short
time compared to after we die and enter heaven for eternity.
Accepting Jesus, we no longer are dead in our sins but are
living life as You intended. A life with a relationship with You
through Jesus. May we keep Your Word and Jesus teachings
close to our heart today and live life abundantly in Your will.

To fear the Lord is to hate evil; I hate pride and arrogance,
evil behavior and perverse speech.
Proverbs 8:13

Father, may the words that we speak bring honor and glory to
Your name. May our actions show the love that Jesus taught
while on earth. May we be humble and not boastful. May we
hate evil and overcome evil with good. Go before us this day
Father and let us follow You.

The fear of the Lord is the beginning of wisdom, and
knowledge of the Holy One is understanding.
Proverbs 9:10

Father, as we read our Bible today, help us understand Your
Word. How wonderful to read what You knew we needed as we
walk upon this earth. How wonderful to know You loved us so
much that You sent Jesus. How wonderful to know You sent the
Holy Spirit. How wonderful to know our eternal destination.

How wonderful to read Your Word and find peace.
Hatred stirs up conflict, but love covers over all wrongs.
Proverbs 10:12

Father, the greatest show of love that has and will ever be
known is You giving Your Son Jesus. Jesus who came to earth
to die for mankind so they could have their sins forgiven. The
meaning of love can be found at the Cross of Calvary.

The Lord detests those whose hearts are perverse, but He delights in those whose ways are blameless.
Proverbs 11:20

Father, how wonderful that You know our hearts and our love For You. We will one day stand blameless before You through the blood of Jesus whom we asked to wash our sins away. Praise the one who paid our debt and raised our life up from the dead.

From the fruit of their lips people are filled with good things, and the work of their hands brings them reward.
Proverbs 12:14

Father, thank You for the health to work. The ability to go and build up and not tear down. We desire that our work brings good and helps bring others to You.

Those who guard their lips preserve their lives, but those who speak rashly will come to ruin.
Proverbs 13:3

Father, may we speak as Jesus with love and compassion for our fellow man. Let us think and contemplate before we speak. Let our words be pleasing to You.

The simple believe anything, but the prudent give thought to their steps.
Proverbs 14:15

Father, let us look to You for guidance and direction. Let us use our words carefully and think about what would please You before we speak. Let the places we go bring honor and glory to Your name. Thank You Father for Your great love.

The eyes of the Lord are everywhere, keeping watch on the wicked and the good.
Proverbs 15:3

Father, all of mankind's deeds are watched by You. You see the good and the bad; hate and love; humility and pride. May our deeds be pleasing to You.

Commit to the Lord whatever you do, and He will establish your plans.
Proverbs 16:3

Father, not our will be done but Yours. May our lives be lived for Your honor and glory. Just as Jesus came to this earth to accomplish Your will for mankind, let us please You this day. May we hear the words well done my good and faithful servant.

A friend loves at all times, and a brother is born for a time of adversity.
Proverbs 17:17

Father, just as Jesus is a friend of sinners may we be the same Jesus did not come into the world for the healthy but for the sick with sin. We are all born sinners but through the blood of Jesus we can be washed from our sins. May we help each other and be friends through the good and bad times on this earth as we do Your will.

The words of the mouth are deep waters, but the fountain of wisdom is a rushing stream.
Proverbs 18:4

Father, let singing and praise rush like waters from our mouth this day and forever to You our God. All our hope is found at the Cross of Calvary where our sins were laid and remembered no more. Just as Jesus was resurrected after the third day and defeated death, we will one day be taken to heaven to spend eternity. Yes, our lips will praise You.

Many are the plans in a person's heart, but it is the Lord's purpose that prevails.
Proverbs 19:21

Father, guide our way and open and close doors in what You would have us do for Your kingdom. Let us not go down a path that would lead away from Your perfect will. We want to live the life that pleases You.

Who can say, "I have kept my heart pure; I am clean and without sin"?
Proverbs 20:9

Father, we were born sinners on this earth. It is only through believing and asking Your son Jesus that we have had our sins forgiven by You. We love You Father and with the Holy Sprit within us this day will go and make choices that reflect our love and devotion for You

There is no wisdom, no insight, no plan that can succeed
against the Lord.
Proverbs 21:30

Father, as we start this day let us look to Your will. May we
seek Your counsel and walk in the way You desire. Let Your
living Word speak to our hearts and may we joyfully obey Your
commands. For Your ways are good.

A good name is more desirable than great riches; to be
esteemed is better than silver or gold.
Proverbs 22:1

Father, may we go this day and not ruin our name. We have
been given a new name once we accepted You through Jesus.
We have been given a name that is more precious than any
other: Your child. May we not do any misdeed that could cause
shame to You Father. May our choices and actions be pleasing
to You.

Apply your heart to instruction and your ears to words of knowledge.
Proverbs 23:12

Father, thank You for Your Word in the Bible. It is so refreshing to read and study what You would have us to know. Help us Holy Spirit to recall scripture when we are tempted today. May our choices reflect obedience to Your Word Father.

If you falter in a time of trouble, how small is your strength!
Proverbs 24:10

Father, today is another day on this earth to sing and worship You our God. May we grow in wisdom and knowledge of Your Word to help us overcome our trials and temptations. May we behave as Jesus taught His disciples.

Like a city whose walls are broken through is a person who lacks self-control.
Proverbs 25:28

Father, as we go this day may we use self-control and not indulge in the ways of the world. Let us use constraint when we are tempted to fall away from the commands You have told in Your word. May we choose to make choices as Jesus taught and our walls stand tall and strong.

Like one who grabs a stray dog by the ears is someone who rushes into a quarrel not their own.
Proverbs 26:17

Father, thank You for wisdom that comes from Your word. May we go this morning not following the world's ways but Your way.

As iron sharpens iron, so one person sharpens another.
Proverbs 27:17

Father, may we build and encourage the ones we come in contact with today. Just as Jesus sent His disciples in groups of two so not to be alone as they carried the message to others, may we strengthen and help sharpen the people You place before us.

The wicked flee though no one pursues, but the righteous are as bold as a lion.
Proverbs 28:1

Father, we are weak but You are strong. We are sheep and You are our shepherd. As we go today, may we not stand in the way of Your will. We are but vessels to go and tell others of Your glory and splendor. May we trust in You.

An angry person stirs up conflict, and a hot-tempered person
commits many sins.
Proverbs 29:22

Father, thank You for showing us in scripture that we are living
in a period of mercy and grace. Your Word also says that a day
of judgment will come where all mankind will stand before You
and receive the punishment for their sins. For the ones that have
accepted Jesus as their Savior, our sins were pardoned at the
Cross. Thank You Jesus for showing us how we should conduct
ourselves while on this earth as Your followers. May we reflect
Your love and compassion while You were on this earth. Help
us this day Holy Spirit to resist anger and hot- temperedness.
Help us grow and mature and bring honor and glory to our
Fathers name.

Every word of God is flawless; He is a shield to those who take
refuge in Him.
Proverbs 30:5

Father, how we need You this morning and every morning.
Knowing that You watch over us provides comfort and peace as
we journey out into another day. May we cling to Your flawless
Word and promises. You are our shield and refuge. Thank You
for Your protection.

Her children arise and call her blessed; her husband also, and he praises her.
Proverbs 31:28

Father, may mothers that live for You have blessings poured down upon them this day. The love that mothers pour into their families is so special. To watch them care for a newborn baby, reading books to children at night, attending church, caring for a sick child, telling Bible stories, fixing cupcakes, putting on band-aids, praying, teaching Sunday School and Vacation Bible School, preparing meals, attending events, reading her Bible, and the list goes on is a momma. Yes, a wife and momma of noble character is a rare jewel.

"Meaningless! Meaningless!" says the Teacher. "Utterly meaningless! Everything is meaningless."
Ecclesiastes 1:2

Father, after David died his son Solomon was now king over Israel and You came to him in a dream at Gibeon and asked him for whatever he wanted You to give him. Solomon asked You to give him, your servant, a discerning heart to govern your people and to distinguish between right and wrong as he was king. You were pleased with his answer and provided his request. Through wisdom, he found that nothing is meaningful apart from You. May we learn from the life of Solomon what is and is not meaningful.

I became greater by far than anyone in Jerusalem before me. In all this my wisdom stayed with me.
Ecclesiastes 2:9

Father, Solomon had amassed fortune and fame but he found it to be meaningless. What the world says is meaningful, Solomon says is meaningless. May we learn from Solomon and put our desire to love You. May we build rewards that will be given in heaven at the Judgement Seat of Christ that moth and rust do not destroy and where thieves do not break in and steal. There is a time for everything, and a season for every activity under the heavens.

Ecclesiastes 3:1

Father, as we go this day we rely on You. May we do our best in all we do for You. Thank You Father for our health to get up and help build Your kingdom. May we be a light to the ones we come in contact and love as Jesus. This is the season of mercy and grace in the history of mankind. May many accept Jesus today.

Though one may be overpowered, two can defend themselves.
A cord of three strands is not quickly broken.
Ecclesiastes 4:12

Father, thank You for family and friends who help strengthen
and encourage us while on earth. As Your children we look to
You, Jesus, and the Holy Spirit and know that nothing can break
Your love for us. We can go this day knowing your love is
infinitely stronger than a cord of three strands.

They seldom reflect on the days of their life, because God keeps
them occupied with gladness of heart.
Ecclesiastes 5:20

Father, thank You for the many blessings You have given us
while on earth. All things come from You and through You. Our
hearts rejoice in knowing that You care and love us so much.

Even if he lives a thousand years twice over but fails to enjoy
his prosperity. Do not all go to the same place?
Ecclesiastes 6:6

Father, thank You for the beautiful creation You have given
mankind to enjoy. From the mountains to the prairies to the
beaches and in between is wonders that only Your hands could
shape into existence. We are so blessed and one day to be able
to enter beautiful heaven and our mansions and golden streets
and gates of pearls is beyond our comprehension. How great
You are Father.

This only have I found: God created mankind upright, but they
have gone in search of many schemes.
Ecclesiastes 7:29

Father, thank You for Your love and patience for mankind.
Thank You for Jesus who came to this earth to die for our sins.
May we stay focused on You this day and not follow the
temptations and schemes of evil. Help us Holy Spirit as we step
into another day. Let it be a day of devotion and service to You
Father.

Then I saw all that God has done. No one can comprehend what goes on under the sun. Despite all their efforts to search it out, no one can discover its meaning. Even if the wise claim they know, they cannot really comprehend it.
Ecclesiastes 8:17

Father, how great You are. Your heavens and earth declare Your glory. We stand in awe of Your creation. May Your name be magnified and sung from east to west. May we sing songs of praise to our Redeemer as the sun rises until it sits. Praise the name of our Lord Jesus Christ.

The quiet words of the wise are more to be heeded than the shouts of a ruler of fools.
Ecclesiastes 9:17

Father, we seek wisdom and knowledge from You. Holy Spirit help us this day recall and lead us in the path of righteousness. May our choices and decisions be acceptable and bring honor to Your name Father. May we not choose convenience or an easy way out if it is not in Your will. May our courage and strength be strong and our resolve sure. We ask these things in the name of Jesus Christ Your Son.

If the ax is dull and its edge unsharpened, more strength is
needed, but skill will bring success.
Ecclesiastes 10:10

Father, may we work this day to sharpen our skills and talents
You have given us. Help us Holy Spirit to discern and make
wise choices. Thank You Father for allowing us another day to
have strength and breath to go and help build Your kingdom.
What a blessing to be Your child and have Your love for us as
we step into another day.

As you do not know the path of the wind, or how the body is
formed in a mother's womb, so you cannot understand the work
of God, the Maker of all things.
Ecclesiastes 11:5

Father, You have no beginning or end. You are the alpha and
omega. Your works tell of Your power and majesty. You knew
that we would be conceived and know when our last breath will
be on this earth. Jesus said Your will is that everyone who looks
to Jesus and believes in Him shall have eternal life, and Jesus
would raise them up at the last day. Thank You for creating man
to have eternal life and may many turn from their sins and
follow Your will this day

Now all has been heard; here is the conclusion of the matter:
Fear God and keep his commandments, for this is the duty of all
mankind.
Ecclesiastes 12:13

Father, the conclusion is for mankind to have You first in our
life and live as You intended. Let us go this day and live and
serve You. May we stay clear of false gods that are here today
and gone tomorrow and are not pleasing to You. Let us hold to
Your Word and love. May we store up treasures that are eternal

How beautiful you are, my darling! Oh, how beautiful! Your
eyes are doves.
Song of Songs 1:15

Father, thank you for letting mankind experience love and
friendship. Thank you for marriage and the special love
between a husband and wife. We look forward to one day when
Jesus comes to get His bride, the church. No greater love is
there than Your love Father.

Like a lily among thorns is my darling among the young women.
Song of Songs 2:2

Father, You created Eve to be a helper and companion for Adam. You saw it was not good for Adam to be alone on the earth. Thank You for our spouses and how we work together on this earth to bring honor to Your name as we raise our children in a Godly home. May many choose a Christian spouse today and choose to live their lives together the way You intended.

Come out, and look, you daughters of Zion. Look on King Solomon wearing a crown, the crown with which his mother crowned him on the day of his wedding, the day his heart rejoiced.
Song of Songs 3:11

Father, how joyful hearts rejoice at the day of a wedding. The bride adorned in white, family and friends in attendance celebrating the union of a man and woman making vows to live and enjoy life together as You ordained while they journey on this earth. We look forward to one day when Jesus comes and gets His bride. May we be ready when that glorious day happens.

You are a garden fountain, well of flowing water streaming down from Lebanon.
Song of Songs 4:15

Father, Your flowing water of love will never end. We can have peace that Your love is streaming continuously and will never run dry. We are refreshed through prayer and reading Your Word. May many come this day to drink of the living water that was provided through Jesus and never thirst again.

His mouth is sweetness itself; he is altogether lovely. This is my beloved, this is my friend, daughters of Jerusalem.
Song of Songs 5:16

Father, out of Jesus mouth came words that were sweet to You but bitter to the world. Jesus was perfect in every way. There was no flaw or sin that Jesus ever committed. Thank You Jesus, our Savior, for loving us and being a friend to sinners. Help us Holy Spirit as we go this day to do our Fathers will. Strengthen us Father each step.

My beloved has gone down to his garden, to the beds of spices
to browse in the gardens and to gather lilies.
Song of Songs 6:2

Father, how wonderful Your creation. The smallest of seeds that
grow into a beautiful flower. Fruits, vegetables, and herbs that
are pleasing to the taste. The fragile baby chicks that grow and
produce eggs for our nourishment. Mankind who is born into
sin and has the opportunity to accept Jesus and one day enter
heaven. How wonderful Your creation.

I belong to my beloved, and his desire is for me.
Song of Songs 7:10

Father, how our hearts rejoice in knowing we belong to You.
Jesus is preparing a place for Your children in heaven for us to
spend eternity. You desire to be with us. Thank You for
revealing these wonderful promises.

Daughters of Jerusalem, I charge you: Do not arouse or awaken love until it so desires.
Song of Songs 8:4

Father, today is the day of salvation. You allowed Jesus to come to this earth and show mankind true love. May we return Your love today by going and proclaiming Your Word and making choices that are pleasing to You.

"Come now, let us settle the matter," says the Lord. "Though your sins are like scarlet, they shall be as white as snow; though they are red as crimson, they shall be like wool.
Isaiah 1:18

Father, Your chosen people Israel had turned from Your ways. You told them, through Your prophet Isaiah, that their offerings had become detestable to You. You no longer listened to their prayers. You told them they had become a burden to You and to turn from their wicked ways and wash and make themselves clean. The ones that would turn back to You with penitent hearts will be returned to You but the ones that chose to keep on with their sins would be broken and perish. Father, may we go this day and learn from the Book of Isaiah and never do as they did by worshiping idols and not having You first in our heart. May we be pleasing in Your sight Father.

He will judge between the nations and will settle disputes for many peoples. They will beat their swords into plowshares and their spears into pruning hooks. Nation will not take up sword against nation, nor will they train for war anymore.
Isaiah 2:4

Father, one day after the church has been taken to heaven and the seven year tribulation period is over Jesus will come to this earth and spend 1,000 years on His throne in Jerusalem. It will be a time of peace and swords will be turned to plowshares and spears into pruning hooks. Deserts will be lush with vegetation, lions will sleep with lambs, worship will abound, people that are 200 years old will be as age 20, mankind will have the deep joy in having Jesus reigning over the earth. How wonderful to know that we will be with Jesus during that time.

The look on their faces testifies against them; they parade their sin like Sodom; they do not hide it. Woe to them! They have brought disaster upon themselves.
Isaiah 3:9

Father, Israel had turned from You. They had become haughty and worshiped other idols. We come humbly before You this morning and praise Your holy name. Thank You for Your many blessings and Your love for us. What joy we have in knowing we are Your children.

t will be a shelter and shade from the heat of the day, and a
refuge and hiding place from the storm and rain.
Isaiah 4:6

Father, when storms come You are our shelter. We can take
comfort in knowing that your hand is upon us at all times.
Thank you Father for Your love.

But the Lord Almighty will be exalted by his justice, and the
holy God will be proved holy by his righteous acts.
Isaiah 5:16

Father, how wonderful and gracious You are to Your children.
Thank You for Your love and protection. May we go this day
and make choices that are pleasing to You.

Then I heard the voice of the Lord saying, "Whom shall I send? And who will go for us?" And I said, "Here am I. Send me!"
Isaiah 6:8

Father, just as Isaiah answered, we also answer. May we go this day and do Your will. May we speak Your name and tell of Your greatness. How wonderful it is Father to tell of Your love for us and the joy we have in the assurance of our salvation. Just as the coal was taken from the altar of the temple by tongs by the seraphim and touched Isaiah's lips and his guilt was taken away and his sins atoned for, our sins have been removed by the blood of Jesus. We go this day free from guilt and shame. Here we are Father, send us.

Therefore the Lord himself will give you a sign: The virgin will conceive and give birth to a son, and will call him Immanuel.
Isaiah 7:14

Father, just as Isaiah told that Ephraim would be shattered as a people in 65 years, You told Isaiah that Jesus would be born on this earth 700 years before Jesus was born to Mary. You are all knowing and nothing is a surprise to You. How wonderful to know that we are in Your care. May we stand firm in our faith or we can not stand at all.

Consult God's instruction and the testimony of warning. If anyone does not speak according to this word, they have no light of dawn.
Isaiah 8:20

Father, may we go to Your Word today and obey. Thank You for Your living Word that speaks wisdom and truth. May we have no idols that are more important than You in our lives. Let us love and not hate. May we spend more time with You and not allow this world to consume us with the unnecessary. May we use Your Word to separate truth from the evil one.

For to us a child is born, to us a Son is given, and the government will be on His shoulders. And He will be called Wonderful Counselor, Mighty God, Everlasting Father, Prince of Peace.
Isaiah 9:6

Father, Your Son Jesus did come many centuries after Isaiah made this prophecy. Before the beginning of time, You knew that Jesus would need to come to this earth for mankind and provide a way to You from our sin. Jesus is all these names as Isaiah wrote and our Savior. Praise the name of Jesus.

In that day the remnant of Israel, the survivors of Jacob
will no longer rely on him who struck them down but will truly
rely on the Lord, the Holy One of Israel.
Isaiah 10:20

Father, we rely on You this morning. As we go into another day,
may we walk toward You and not the world. Go before us this
day that we might serve in the places You place us and the
people we come in contact. May we love mankind as Jesus.
May many come to You this day and truly rely on You.

A shoot will come up from the stump of Jesse; from his roots a
Branch will bear fruit.
Isaiah 11:1

Father, Jesus did come to this earth from the line of Jesse just as
You said through Isaiah. The spirit of wisdom, council, and
knowledge came with Jesus. Righteousness was his belt and
faithfulness was the sash around His waist.
One day Jesus will come again and the wolf will live with the
lamb. May we live today in anticipation of You coming Jesus.
May You be pleased with our choices and decisions today.
Father, in Your perfect time Jesus will come again. Come Lord
Jesus.

"Surely God is my salvation; I will trust and not be afraid. The Lord, the Lord himself, is my strength and my defense; He has become my salvation."
Isaiah 12:2

Father, we come to You this morning because we need You. We need You for our strength. We need You to protect our families. We need You so we can face trials without fear. We can do all things through Christ that gives us strength.
We come to You Father.

I will punish the world for its evil, the wicked for their sins. I will put an end to the arrogance of the haughty and will humble the pride of the ruthless.
Isaiah 13:11

Father, thank you for allowing mankind to choose to accept Jesus as their Savior. We live today in the period of mercy and grace. Today is the day of salvation. May many who are living in a way that displeases You choose to follow You. You have made the way through Jesus but it is mankind's choice to accept the gift. Thank You for Your love Father.

What answer shall be given to the envoys of that nation? "The Lord has established Zion, and in her His afflicted people will find refuge."
Isaiah 14:32

Father, the poor and afflicted run to You. Sinners run to You. Where can we go to find peace but into Your loving arms. This morning, we run to You.

A prophecy against Moab: Ar in Moab is ruined, destroyed in a night! Kirin Moab is ruined, destroyed in a night!
Isaiah 15:1

Father, in a short time what took years and years to build, You can destroy. What pride and arrogance the Moabites developed and Your wrath came down on them. There is no one that has ever lived that will not one day stand before Your judgment and give an account for each second and choices made while on earth. May we learn from the Moabites that You are a just God. May we choose Your ways.

In love a throne will be established; in faithfulness a man will sit on it-one from the house of David-one who in judging seeks justice and speeds the cause of righteousness.
Isaiah 16:5

Father, Jesus will one day come after the tribulation period and through love and righteousness reign from His throne in Jerusalem. How wonderful to know that we will be part of that glorious day.

In that day people will look to their Maker and turn their eyes to the Holy One of Israel.
Isaiah 17:7

Father, You are the Holy One of mankind. We drop to our knees in worship to You this morning. All that we have is Yours. May we go this day and have our eyes focused solely on You.

At that time gifts will be brought to the Lord Almighty
from a people tall and smooth-skinned, from a people feared far
and wide, an aggressive nation of strange speech, whose land is
divided by rivers-the gifts will be brought to Mount Zion, the
place of the Name of the Lord Almighty.
Isaiah 18:7

Father, what a special place Jerusalem. Your Son Jesus walked
the streets and one day will return to Jerusalem (Mount Zion)
and establish His throne for 1,000 years. After the 1,000 year
reign, the New Jerusalem will come down from the heavens
with the shape of a cube measuring 1,500 miles on each side
with an area of 2,250,000 square miles and a volume of
3,375,000,000 cubic miles. The foundation walls will be 72
yards with 12 layers of precious stones: jasper, sapphire,
chalcedony, emerald, sardonyx, sardius, chrysolite, beryl, topaz,
chrysoprase, jacinth, and amethyst. The streets will be of
translucent gold. Your glory will illuminate the city and the
Lamb is its light. All whose names are written in the Lambs
Book of Life will dwell forever with You. How wonderful and
beautiful heaven will be.

The Lord has poured into them a spirit of dizziness; they make
Egypt stagger in all that she does, as a drunkard staggers around
in his vomit.
Isaiah 19:14

Father, may we go this day and live in a way that pleases You.
Just as a daddy and momma disciplines their children out of
love, I pray that You will not have to discipline us. We come
and confess our sins and transgressions against You and Your
holiness this morning. Thank You for Your patience and love.

Then the Lord said, "Just as my servant Isaiah has gone stripped and barefoot for three years, as a sign and portent against Egypt and Cush.
Isaiah 20:3

Father, for three years Isaiah went around without shoes or sackcloth, just as You told him to, showing what would happen to Egypt and Cush by the Assyrians. Now the Assyrians are taking Egyptians and Cushites away into exile stripped and without shoes. Those who trusted in Cush and boasted in Egypt will now be in shame. May we learn from this history in the Bible and trust in You Father.

They set the tables, they spread the rugs, they eat, they drink!
Get up, you officers, oil the shields!
Isaiah 21:5

Father, may we always be on our guard. May we never get lazy and content. We will pray, read Your Word, and serve You until we die or Jesus comes for us in the rapture. May we keep our shields in front of us shining and ready to repel the deception and temptations of the evil one. You are our shield of protection Father. Go before us.

"In that day I will summon my servant, Eliakim son of Hilkiah."
Isaiah 22 20

Father, may we be ready like Eliakim. When You summon let us rise and do Your will. We are Your servants Father.

The Lord Almighty planned it, to bring down her pride in all her splendor and to humble all who are renowned on the earth.
Isaiah 23:9

Father, the people of Tyre had not been living for You. May we learn from them and have You as our first love. May nothing come before service and devotion to You Father.

The moon will be dismayed, the sun ashamed; for the Lord Almighty will reign on Mount Zion and in Jerusalem, and before its elders-with great glory.
Isaiah 24:23

Father, the glory of Jesus will be among Your children forevermore. We will have the Good Shepherd to watch over us for eternity. What comfort and security.

Lord, you are my God; I will exalt You and praise Your name, for in perfect faithfulness You have done wonderful things, things planned long ago.
Isaiah 25:1

Father, we praise You for our salvation. Salvation that was possible through Jesus. How wonderful to know that we are Yours. Each step we take today we are assured You are with us. Our prayers are heard by You, the maker of all things. May we go through this day with clear hearts and minds.

Trust in the Lord forever, for the Lord, the Lord Himself, is the Rock eternal.
Isaiah 26:4

Father, we have put our trust in You. You are the rock that never moves and are unshakable. We have nothing to fear knowing You are with us at all times. You watch our every move. You know our every thought. On Christ the solid rock I stand, all other ground is sinking sand.

And in that day a great trumpet will sound. Those who were perishing in Assyria and those who were exiled in Egypt will come and worship the Lord on the holy mountain in Jerusalem.
Isaiah 27:13

Father, one day the trumpet will sound and Your people will meet on the mountain of Jerusalem. What a special day that will be of worship and praise to You. We will be marching to Zion, beautiful, beautiful Zion, we will be marching to Zion, the beautiful city of God.

All this also comes from the Lord Almighty, whose plan is wonderful, whose wisdom is magnificent.
Isaiah 28:29

Father, we come to You this morning and desire to please and honor You. Help us to follow the plan You have for us. Go before us and may we follow Your steps.

The Lord says: "These people come near to me with their mouth and honor me with their lips, but their hearts are far from me. Their worship of me is based on merely human rules they have been taught.
Isaiah 29:13

Father, may we obey Your Word and not add or take away. The Jewish scholars added thousands of subcategories to the original 10 Commandments You gave Moses. The Pharisees became legalistic, only being concerned with the outward appearance of keeping the laws rather than the inward Spirit of the laws. Jesus sees the heart of man. Jesus told the Pharisees on the outside they looked righteous but on the inside their hearts were filled with hypocrisy and lawlessness. May we go today living in the true meaning of the law.

Yet the Lord longs to be gracious to you; therefore He will rise up to show you compassion. For the Lord is a God of justice. Blessed are all who wait for Him!
Isaiah 30:18

Father, thank You for Your compassion for mankind. Even though we are born sinners, You love us. Your grace and mercy has been offered and many have received forgiveness through Your Son Jesus Christ. May many come to You this day. We wait eagerly for Jesus return.

Woe to those who go down to Egypt for help, who rely on horses, who trust in the multitude of their chariots and in the great strength of their horsemen, but do not look to the Holy One of Israel, or seek help from the Lord.
Isaiah 31:1

Father, our strength comes from You. We are weak but You are strong. We are inadequate but You are adequate to meet every need. May we not look to ourselves but only to You.

Then the eyes of those who see will no longer be closed, and the ears of those who hear will listen.
Isaiah 32:3

Father, may we be alert and live today with our eyes open. Open to Your goodness, mercy, and love. Closed to sin and temptations. Let our ears hear the sounds of Your creation and music that pleases You. Let them be closed to gossip, slander, and hate.

Lord, be gracious to us; we long for You. Be our strength every morning, our salvation in time of distress.
Isaiah 33:2

Father, we can turn to You any place and at any time. We will turn to You in the good times and the bad. No one cheers us on more than You and no one can hold us in hurt closer than You. Thank You for Your everlasting love.

Come near, you nations, and listen; pay attention, you peoples! Let the earth hear, and all that is in it, the world, and all that comes out of it!
Isaiah 34:1

Father, thank You for blessing us with Your Word. May we read it today, tomorrow, and as long as we have breath on this earth. Let us not just read but internalize in our hearts and draw near to You. How wonderful that You created mankind to be able to comprehend Your Words. You, Jesus, and the Holy Spirit's love and compassion for us is found from Genesis to Revelation. May we search and find what You have for us this day.

And a highway will be there; it will be called the Way of Holiness; it will be for those who walk on that Way. The unclean will not journey on it; wicked fools will not go about on it.
Isaiah 35:8

Father, may we walk the straight and narrow path this day not swerving to the right or to the left. Let us not get distracted by exit signs of sin. May we follow the Way of Holiness that is found through Jesus Christ Your Son.

Come now, make a bargain with my master, the king of Assyria: I will give you two thousand horses-if you can put riders on them!
Isaiah 36:8

Father, let us not fall into temptation with what the world offers. The Assyrian king Sennacherib sent his field commander to Jerusalem to get the people of Judah to surrender to him. May we serve You Father and never bargain with the world.

Then the angel of the Lord went out and put to death a hundred and eighty-five thousand in the Assyrian camp. When the people got up the next morning there were all the dead bodies!
Isaiah 37:36

Father, King Hezekiah of Judah was in distress as the Assyrian King Sennacherib was threatening to attack. King Hezekiah tore his clothes, put on sackcloth and went to the temple of the Lord. He sent messengers also in sackcloth to ask the Prophet Isaiah to inquire to the Lord. You told them You would have Sennacherib cut down. May we seek You this day Father. You are all we need.

"I will make the shadow cast by the sun go back the ten steps it has gone down on the stairway of Ahaz." So the sunlight went back the ten steps it had gone down.
Isaiah 38:8

Father, King Hezekiah was sick and you had Isaiah tell him he was going to die. King Hezekiah prayed and wept bitterly and asked that you spare his life. You told Isaiah to tell him he would live 15 more years and You would deliver him and the people from the King of Assyria. You would defend the city. As a sign, You caused the sun's shadow to go back 10 steps on the stairs of Ahaz. You are an amazing God. How powerful is prayer and a relationship with You.

The prophet asked, "What did they see in your palace?" "They saw everything in my palace," Hezekiah said. "There is nothing among my treasures that I did not show them."
Isaiah 39:4

Father, You know our heart. Hezekiah showed the visitors from Babylon all that was in the storehouses and all the kingdom. It was not his but Yours. Because of this, Isaiah prophesied that one day all in the storehouses would be taken to Babylon and some of King Hezekiah's descendants would be taken away and become eunuchs in the palace of the king of Babylon. May we go this day with humble hearts and proclaim all we have is Yours.

A voice of one calling: "In the wilderness prepare the way for the Lord; make straight in the desert a highway for our God."
Isaiah 40:3

Father, some 900 years after Isaiah wrote this verse, John the Baptist would be born and use this passage to introduce Your Son Jesus as Lord. John carried out Your will for his life on this earth and now is in heaven. May we also tell of Jesus as our Lord this day in the wilderness. May many make straight a path to their heart for Jesus to enter this day.

So do not fear, for I am with you; do not be dismayed, for I am your God. I will strengthen you and help you; I will uphold you with My righteous right hand.
Isaiah 41:10

Father, when we can't, You can. Help us as we walk this earth.

This is what God the Lord says-the Creator of the heavens, who stretches them out, who spreads out the earth with all that springs from it, who gives breath to its people, and life to those who walk on it.
Isaiah 42:5

Father, You are the giver of life. You shaped Adam from the dust and breathed life into him. From Adam and Eve, You allowed mankind to flourish on this earth with billions and billions being born through history to walk on this earth. Each one born with a choice to follow You or reject Your love. Praise the name of Jesus. All of mankind that will enter heaven one day is made possible through Jesus. Thank You for another day where ones on this earth may choose to accept Jesus and have their eternal destiny secured in heaven.

Everyone who is called by My name, whom I created for My glory, whom I formed and made.
Isaiah 43:7

Father, we are made for Your glory. All are called and many come to Your offer of salvation through Jesus of their sins. May we go proclaim Your love today and by the pulling of the Holy Spirit many many more choose to come to You this day.

This is what the Lord says-Israel's King and Redeemer, the Lord Almighty: I am the first and I am the last; apart from Me there is no God.
Isaiah 44:6

Father, apart from You there is no God. We bow and worship You. We sing songs of praise to Your Holy name. We meditate on the wonders of Your creation. May we go this day celebrating that You are our Father.

By myself I have sworn, My mouth has uttered in all integrity a word that will not be revoked: Before Me every knee will bow; by Me every tongue will swear.
Isaiah 45:23

Father, one day the ones that did not ask forgiveness of their sins will stand before You at the Great White Throne Judgement, every knee will bow and tongue confess that You are God and Jesus is the Messiah. Today is the day of salvation. May many come to You this day. Thank You for allowing Your children that have accepted Jesus as their Savior to spend eternity with You. May we live this day with integrity and bring honor to Your name.

Even to your old age and gray hairs I am he, I am he who will sustain you. I have made you and I will carry you; I will sustain you and I will rescue you.
Isaiah 46:4

Father, from conception, to our birth, to our youth, to our old age You are our God. There is not a time that You have taken Your eyes off of mankind. Once we accept Jesus as our Savior, we become Your child and we no longer have to carry the guilt of sin but can live free from the heavy burden that we could not remove. You rescued us Jesus from separation from our Father. Help sustain us Holy Spirit, our helper, this day as we step into another day. May we perform the plans You would have us do for You.

Our Redeemer-the Lord Almighty is His name-is the Holy One of Israel.
Isaiah 47:4

Father, You are the Lord Almighty. What have we to fear with You as our God? Through Jesus, we have been redeemed. We will not be found guilty of our sins because Jesus took our sins at the Cross of Calvary. We can walk in complete assurance that we serve the Holy One of Israel. May we go this day with joy in our hearts.

This is what the Lord says-Redeemer, the Holy One of Israel: "I am the Lord your God, who teaches you what is best for you, who directs you in the way you should go.
Isaiah 48:17

Father, thank You for showing us the way we should go and directing our path. When we don't know, You do. Go ahead of us Father and teach us what is best for us. May our steps not leave the path You have us to do this day.

And now the Lord says-He who formed me in the womb to be His servant to bring Jacob back to Him and gather Israel to Himself, for I am honored in the eyes of the Lord and my God has been my strength.
Isaiah 49:5

Father, You are our strength this day and every day. You never fail. How wonderful to have You as our Father and know that You love us even in our failures. May we honor You with our lives this day.

Who among you fears the Lord and obeys the word of His servant? Let the one who walks in the dark, who has no light, trust in the name of the Lord and rely on their God.
Isaiah 50:10

Father, on You we rely and trust. As the sun comes up bringing light from the darkness, You bring light when called upon. Jesus brought light to a fallen world and through His blood darkness from our sins could be turned to light. May we shine that light today.

For I am the Lord your God, who stirs up the sea so that its waves roar-the Lord Almighty is His name.
Isaiah 51:15

Father, how vast and mighty is the sea. The waves crash and roar time after time after time. May we offer praise, worship, and our best today time after time after time. Let the waves remind us of your greatness and might. Let the roar of the waves remind us You are constantly with us each second of every day. May the sound never leave our ears.

But you will not leave in haste or go in flight; for the Lord will go before you, the God of Israel will be your rear guard.
Isaiah 52:12

Father, you protect us from the front and back. We do not have to think about being surprised since you are watching over us. We do not have to run from danger or when life gets hard since we know that You will be with us each step of the way. May we go this day with the assurance that You guard over us.

But He was pierced for our transgressions, He was crushed for our iniquities; the punishment that brought us peace was on Him, and by His wounds we are healed.
Isaiah 53:5

Father, through Jesus we have peace. Through the wounds of Jesus, our wounds of sin have been healed. We owe eternal life to our Lord and Savior Jesus Christ. We start this day recognizing that through Jesus we have been made acceptable to You Father.

Though the mountains be shaken and the hills be removed, yet my unfailing love for you will not be shaken nor my covenant of peace be removed," says the Lord, who has compassion on you.
Isaiah 54:10

Father, thank You for Your unfailing love that will never be shaken.. A love that reaches out when we fail. A love that comforts us in times of grief. A love that forgives when we displease You. A love that cheers us on as we run to the finish line. A love that sent Jesus so we might forever be in the arms of Your love.

As the heavens are higher than the earth, so are My ways higher than your ways and My thoughts than your thoughts.
Isaiah 55:9

Father, how You love and want what is best for us. Help us Holy Spirit as we walk into another day. Father, You have provided for our needs and may we do our part and follow Your will. May we live for You today; for Your ways are better.

These I will bring to My holy mountain and give them joy in My house of prayer. Their burnt offerings and sacrifices will be accepted on My altar; for My house will be called a house of prayer for all nations.
Isaiah 56:7

Father, thank You for allowing whoever desires to come and take the water of life freely. Not just the Israelites but whoever. Your house is a house of prayer for all nations and peoples. It is wonderful to know our prayers are acceptable to You. Through Jesus, at Your right hand, You answer each prayer in Your perfect wisdom. We offer prayers of praise and worship to You this morning Father for Your faithfulness and love.

For this is what the high and exalted One says-He who lives forever, whose name is holy: "I live in a high and holy place, but also with the one who is contrite and lowly in spirit, to revive the spirit of the lowly and to revive the heart of the contrite.
Isaiah 57:15

Father, we come to be revived this morning. Fill us with Your love and compassion. As the darkness turns to light this morning, may the darkness in our hearts light for You.

Then your light will break forth like the dawn, and your healing will quickly appear; then your righteousness will go before you, and the glory of the Lord will be your rear guard.
Isaiah 58:8

Father, we ask that You go before us this day. May we choose Your ways today and be a light for You. May our conscience be clear and we have peace knowing that we have spent this day in Your will. Thank You Father for Your many blessings.

Surely the arm of the Lord is not too short to save, nor His ear too dull to hear.
Isaiah 59:1

Father, praise Your name for loving us so much. Thank You for hearing our prayers and answering each one with infinite wisdom and according to Your will for our lives. All mankind is in the reach of salvation if only they would take Your outstretched hand. You have made the way straight and it is the choice of each individual to accept Jesus. May many come to You today and ask for forgiveness of their sins

The sun will no more be your light by day, nor will the brightness of the moon shine on you, for the Lord will be your everlasting light, and your God will be your glory.
Isaiah 60:19

Father, one day the sun will not need to shine and the moon will not reflect light for You will be the light in heaven. Your glory will be experienced without end. It is beyond our thoughts to grasp how wonderful heaven will be for eternity. We know by Your Word that Jesus is preparing our mansion in heaven and one day we will be taken to spend eternity with You. May many make the choice to accept Jesus as their Lord this day so they can begin their eternal relationship with Your Son.

And provide for those who grieve in Zion-to bestow on them a crown of beauty instead of ashes, the oil of joy instead of mourning, and a garment of praise instead of a spirit of despair. They will be called oaks of righteousness, a planting of the Lord for the display of his splendor.
Isaiah 61:3

Father, the storms of life will come while on this earth. May we stand as oaks of righteousness in Your strength.

No longer will they call you Deserted, or name your land
Desolate. But you will be called Hephzibah, and your land
Beulah; for the Lord will take delight in you, and your land will
be married.
Isaiah 62:4

Father, one day we Your children will return to Your land called
Beulah. We will no longer be scattered but will be together in
sweet Beulah land.

Who is this coming from Edom,from Bozrah, with His
garments stained crimson? Who is this, robed in splendor,
striding forward in the greatness of his strength? "It is I,
proclaiming victory, mighty to save."
Isaiah 63:1

Father, from the cities of old to present day cities, mankind
needed a Savior. Our Messiah Jesus came to this earth to make
atonement for mankind's sins. Jesus is mighty to save

Yet You, Lord, are our Fattier. We are the clay, You are the potter; we are all the work of Your hand.
Isaiah 64:8

Father, we trust in You. Take us and mold us in Your perfect will for our lives. Your ways are what is best for us each day we live on this earth. Take us in Your Holy hands and shape us into jars of clay to carry the living water of Jesus. May many drink freely of the water today.

The wolf and the lamb will feed together, and the lion will eat straw like the ox, and dust will be the serpent's food. They will neither harm nor destroy on all my holy mountain,"
says the Lord.
Isaiah 65:25

Father, just as it was once in the Garden of Eden, a day will come when there will be no more bloodshed. There will be perfect harmony and sin will be no more. How wonderful it will be to live in peace and perfect tranquility with You for eternity.

Has not My hand made all these things, and so they came into being?" declares the Lord. "These are the ones I look on with favor: those who are humble and contrite in spirit, and who tremble at my word.
Isaiah 66:2

Father, may we go this day and please You. May we be humble and know that all things are made possible by You. Let the words that we read in Your Bible stay on our minds throughout the day as we are tempted by things that displease You. May we quickly run from sin and into Your arms.

Before I formed you in the womb I knew you, before you were born I set you apart; I appointed you as a prophet to the nations.
Jeremiah 1:5

Father, Your Word came to Jeremiah. Your Living Word in the Bible can be read each day by Your children. We have Your completed Bible that shows us Your love and also the judgment to come. You are all knowing and know us even before we are conceived. How important it is as Your child to read the entire Bible from Genesis to Revelation and discover truth and goodness. May a day never pass that the pages of the Bible are not read.

I had planted you like a choice vine of sound and reliable stock.
How then did you turn against Me into a corrupt, wild vine?
Jeremiah 2:21

Father, may we learn from the terrible choices of Your chosen
people Israel. You had led them from bondage and disaster
overtook their enemies. Through time, they turned to idols and
selfish pleasure. May we learn from their failures and keep our
eyes focused on Your Word. May we give thanks and praise to
Jesus this and every day for His sacrifice for our sins. We are
Your children and You alone are our God.

In those days the people of Judah will join the people of Israel,
and together they will come from a northern land to the land I
gave your ancestors as an inheritance.
Jeremiah 3:18

Father, one day Jesus will come back to this earth and reign
1,000 years. At that time, Israel and Judah will return to
Jerusalem and live and reign with Jesus.
Gentiles that have accepted Jesus as their Savior will also be
with Jesus during the 1,000 years. What an inheritance we have
for the ones that love You Father.

Jerusalem, wash the evil from your heart and be saved. How long will you harbor wicked thoughts?
Jeremiah 4:14

Father, not many years would pass until the words You gave Jeremiah that a nation that would be Babylon would come and overthrow Israel and Judah. I pray we will learn from their mistakes and our thoughts be focused on You Father and not of this world. May we seek to please You this day in goodness and love.

Go up and down the streets of Jerusalem, look around and consider, search through her squares. If you can find but one person who deals honestly and seeks the truth, I will forgive this city.
Jeremiah 5:1

Father, at one time Your chosen people looked only to You. At this time in history in the Book of Jeremiah, You were asking to find one person who dealt honestly and seeked truth. May You find many this day that seek You with their whole heart. Ones that are living for You and doing Your will.

This is what the Lord says: "Stand at the crossroads and look; ask for the ancient paths, ask where the good way is, and walk in it, and you will find rest for your souls. But you said, 'We will not walk in it.'
Jeremiah 6:16

Father, the people of Israel did not want to look to You. They did not want to follow the ways You showed through Moses and others throughout history. May many walk the path to Jesus this day. The way to You finds rest for our souls.

They have built the high places of Topheth in the Valley of Ben Hinnom to burn their sons and daughters in the fire-something I did not command, nor did it enter My mind.
Jeremiah 7:31

Father, it is hard to imagine how wicked and deprived the people of Judah had become when they did evil in Your eyes. They had set up their detestable idols in Your house that bears Your Name and had defiled it. They killed their sons and daughters. Humans that were created by You in Your image have been scarified and murdered through selfishness, envy, and greed. May we respect life this day. May we see each human as You see them: a creation with a soul that has a eternal choice to accept Jesus and live for You.

You who are my Comforter in sorrow, my heart is faint within me.
Jeremiah 8:18

Father, our comfort comes in knowing that Your loving arms are wrapped around us. Your love has defeated death and sorrow. As the sun comes up today, may it remind us that Your light has overtaken darkness.

But let the one who boasts boast about this: that they have the understanding to know Me, that I am the Lord, who exercises kindness, justice and righteousness on earth, for in these I delight," declares the Lord.
Jeremiah 9:24

Father, may we delight You by exercising kindness, justice and righteousness on earth. Thank You for allowing us to know You through the Bible, Your Son Jesus and the Holy Spirit. You are our Lord and we put You above all other.
Like a scarecrow in a cucumber field, their idols cannot speak; they must be carried because they cannot walk. Do not fear them; they can do no harm nor can they do any good.

Like a scarecrow in a cucumber field, their idols cannot speak; they must be carried because they cannot walk. Do not fear them; they can do no harm nor can they do any good.
Jeremiah 10:5

Father, You alone are the one true God. You are the creator of all. May we go this day and bow and worship You, the creator, and not the things You created.

From the time I brought your ancestors up from Egypt until today, I warned them again and again, saying, "Obey me."
Jeremiah 11:7

Father, may we go this day and obey You. Help us Holy Spirit as You are the Spirit of Truth and our Comforter.

And if they learn well the ways of my people and swear by My name, saying, 'As surely as the Lord lives'-even as they once taught My people to swear by Baal-then they will be established among My people.
Jeremiah 12:16

Father, You are great in compassion and mercy. May nations and people come and learn of Your ways. You have made the way and given a choice to follow. As surely as the Lord lives, in God we trust.

For as a belt is bound around the waist, so I bound all the people of Israel and all the people of Judah to me,' declares the Lord, 'to be my people for my renown and praise and honor. But they have not listened.'
Jeremiah 13:11

Father, thank You for allowing Your children to be bound by Your love. As we walk this day, may we hold each other up and encourage. May we listen and obey Your Word for Your renown and praise and honor.

Do any of the worthless idols of the nations bring rain? Do the skies themselves send down showers? No, it is You, Lord our God. Therefore our hope is in You, for You are the one who does all this.
Jeremiah 14:22

Father, all blessings come from You. The sunrise, air to breathe and food to eat are just a few of the blessings You provide. We thank You and praise Your name for the blessings You shower on us this day.

When Your words came, I ate them; they were my joy and my heart's delight, for I bear Your name, Lord God Almighty.
Jeremiah 15:16

Father, may we take in Your words today. Let them be joy and our hearts delight. Just as drinking water is to our bodies, reading Your word is to our heart and soul. We have communion and fellowship with You.

My eyes are on all their ways; they are not hidden from Me, nor is their sin concealed from My eyes.
Jeremiah 16:17

Father, how wonderful to know that You watch us every moment of day and night. You know the good and the bad that we do. Nothing is hidden from You. May we confess our sins that we commit and have nothing that stands between our relationship to You.

"But blessed is the one who trusts in the Lord, whose confidence is in Him. They will be like a tree planted by the water that sends out its roots by the stream. It does not fear when heat comes; its leaves are always green. It has no worries in a year of drought
and never fail to bear fruit."
Jeremiah 17:7-8

Father, as we go through this day let us trust and have confidence in Your Word. Let us stand strong and gain our strength from You. Help us Holy Spirit to stand firm when temptations come our way. May we bear fruit for Your kingdom.

He said, "Can I not do with you, Israel, as this potter does?"
declares the Lord. "Like clay in the hand of the potter, so are
you in My hand, Israel.
Jeremiah 18:6

Father, shape and mold us with Your hands. May we do our part
and not be too wet or dry as You take us and create what pleases
You. May we withstand the fire in the kiln and come out
stronger to do Your will.

They have built the high places of Baal to burn their children in
the fire as offerings to Baal-something I did not command or
mention, nor did it enter my mind.
Jeremiah 19:5

Father, when You created mankind, we had no sin. Adam and
Eve were the first that sinned and every human that has lived on
this earth since has sinned and did things that displease You.
Just as You clothed Adam and Eve after their sin, You clothe
the ones that accept Jesus in righteousness. Not because of our
works but because we were washed of our sins through the
blood of Jesus. We bow today to You Father and may our
worship and praise be pleasing to You. We give our best to You.

But the Lord is with me like a mighty warrior; so my persecutors will stumble and not prevail. They will fail and be thoroughly disgraced; their dishonor will never be forgotten.
Jeremiah 20:11

Father, Jeremiah has proclaimed Your Word and his friends and the people despise him. The priest Pasur son of Immer had Jeremiah beaten and put in the stocks at the Upper Gate of Benjamin at the Lord's temple for telling the people what You had told him too. The people did not want to hear truth and turn from their ways. Jeremiah opens his heart to You and tells how everyone ridicules and mocks him. Jeremiah knew to go to You- the mighty warrior. May we go this day and share Your Word that You have given in the Bible. Let us go and proclaim Jesus as the way to You.

┣━━━━━━━━━━━━━━━━┫

I will punish you as your deeds deserve, declares the Lord. I will kindle a fire in your forests that will consume everything around you.
Jeremiah 21:14

Father, You are about to allow Babylon and it's King Nebuchadnezzar to attack Israel. Because of their sins against You, the ones that stay in the city will die and the others who surrender to the Babylonians will live. They will be a remnant left of Your chosen people. Just as the Babylonians are going to destroy the city with fire, one day all who have not accepted Jesus will be tormented forever in the Lake of Fire. May many come to You today Father and escape the punishment our deeds deserve. May they accept salvation through Jesus who paid for mankind's sins on the Cross of Calvary.

This is what the Lord says: Do what is just and right. Rescue from the hand of the oppressor the one who has been robbed. Do no wrong or violence to the foreigner, the fatherless or the widow, and do not shed innocent blood in this place.
Jeremiah 22:3

Father, You spoke through Jeremiah and told what You expected from the Kings of Judah. May we go this day and lead in such a way. Let us go and be leaders that please You.

———————————————

But if they had stood in My council, they would have proclaimed My words to My people and would have turned them from their evil ways and from their evil deeds.
Jeremiah 23:22

Father, the false prophets of Jeremiah's time on this earth had chosen to give Your people lies. They were telling people delusions from their own minds and not Your Word. Now we have Your Word in the Bible. May we study and learn from truth today and be equipped to go this day and be fruitful for You.

I will give them a heart to know Me, that I am the Lord. They will be My people, and I will be their God, for they will return to Me with all their heart.
Jeremiah 24:7

Father, thank You for allowing Your children to have forgiveness and mercy. We strive to please You. May all our heart be devoted to You this day.

For twenty-three years-from the thirteenth year of Josiah son of Amon king of Judah until this very day-the word of the Lord has come to me and I have spoken to you again and again, but you have not listened.
Jeremiah 25:3

Father, for twenty-three years You spoke through Jeremiah to bring Your chosen people back to You from their sinful ways. For over 2,000 years, You have used Your children to spread Your Word of forgiveness through Your Son Jesus. Just as Your nation was taken into captivity for 70 years by the Babylonians, one day the ones that reject Jesus will be cast into eternal torment in hell. May many hear and receive forgiveness this day.

They brought Uriah out of Egypt and took him to King Jehoiakim, who had him struck down with a sword and his body thrown into the burial place of the common people.
Jeremiah 26:23

Father, Uriah was Your prophet and was put to death by King Jehoiakim. Through history, so many have committed their lives to You and obeyed what You would have them do while on this earth. May we go this day and do the same.

All nations will serve him and his son and his grandson until the time for his land comes; then many nations and great kings will subjugate him.
Jeremiah 27:7

Father, because of Israel's sins, You had brought Nebuchadnezzar into the pages of history. His son and grandson will also play parts in the history of Your people Israel. You had warned other nations including Israel to fall under the government of Babylon for a time until You will bring Israel back to Your chosen land Jerusalem. May we follow the plan You have for our lives and do Your will. May we not fall into the same snares of the enemy as Israel.

Then the prophet Jeremiah said to Hananiah the prophet, "Listen, Hananiah! The Lord has not sent you, yet you have persuaded this nation to trust in lies.
Jeremiah 28:15

Father, may we trust in Your Word. The false prophet Hananiah had told the people what they wanted to hear. Jeremiah had told the people only what You told him to tell the people. May we stand on Your word this day and only tell truth. May we guard our hearts from being persuaded by false teaching and lies.

For I know the plans I have for you," declares the Lord, "plans to prosper you and not to harm you, plans to give you hope and a future.
Jeremiah 29:11

Father, after 70 years, You will bring Your chosen people who have been taken to Babylon by King Nebuchadnezzar back to Jerusalem from bondage. You have told them to increase in number while in bondage. You would hear their prayers when they seek You with all their hearts. Thank You Father for hearing our prayers while in the bondage of sin. Thank You for allowing us to seek and find You Father. We were lost but now are in Your loving arms.

This is what the Lord, the God of Israel, says: Write in a book
all the words I have spoken to you.
Jeremiah 30:2

Father, Jeremiah was obedient and wrote down what You
revealed to Him. The people of Israel and Judah would be in a
season of bondage but You would bring them back to the
promised land. We too write a story each day by the choices and
obedience we make for You. May we go this day and when we
go back and read our story tonight may we have no regrets of
our choices. Let the words on the pages be pleasing to You.

I will refresh the weary and satisfy the faint.
Jeremiah 31:25

Father, refresh us this day. As we read Your Word, refresh us as
cold water running in a mountain creek. Bring life to the weary
and carry burdens that weigh down. Do what only You can do

I will rejoice in doing them good and will assuredly plant them
in this land with all my heart and soul.
Jeremiah 32:41

Father, how You wanted the people of Israel to live and worship
You. They chose differently and paid a heavy price of bondage.
You told Jeremiah to buy a field in the besieged wasteland in
that one day You would restore the land with promised
prosperity. As always Your Word came true. May we focus and
obey Your Word this day.

Call to Me and I will answer you and tell you great and
unsearchable things you do not know.
Jeremiah 33:3

Father, we call on You today. How wonderful to know that You
will answer and tell us great and unsearchable things. May we
go through this day knowing we are never alone. You are in
constant reach at all times 24/7/365.
Recently you repented and did what is right in My sight: Each

Recently you repented and did what is right in My sight: Each of you proclaimed freedom to your own people. You even made a covenant before Me in the house that bears My Name.
Jeremiah 34:15

Father, the people had not listened to You to let their fellow Hebrews go free after seven years who had sold themselves as slaves. You had given them this command when they left Egypt so long ago. You have now told them through Jeremiah to release all their slaves and they did. Not long after, they turned around and put their fellow Hebrews back in slavery. Because of their disobedience, the Babylonians who had withdrawn would return and capture King Zedekiah, his officials, and lay waste to Judah. May we go this day and do what You would have us do Father. May we learn that disobeying You has consequences that will not only harm us but the ones around us.

This is what the Lord Almighty, the God of Israel, says: Go and tell the people of Judah and those living in Jerusalem, Will you not learn a lesson and obey My words? declares the Lord.
Jeremiah 35:13

Father, may we go this day and obey Your Word. Let us go and demonstrate our love to You by loving the ones You place in front of us this day

Whenever Jehudi had read three or four columns of the scroll, the king cut them off with a scribe's knife and threw them into the firepot, until the entire scroll was burned in the fire.
Jeremiah 36:23

Father, Baruch had written on a scroll the words You had given to Your prophet Jeremiah. Jeremiah sent Baruch to the temple to read the scroll to the people in hopes they would repent and come back to You from their sinful ways. The king's officials were in fear and sent Jehudi to go and get the scroll from Baruch to read to King Jehoiakim of Judah. The king however did not fear You and burned the scroll. You said that the king's body would be thrown out and exposed to the heat by day and the frost by night. Just as the king rejected Your Word and threw the scroll into the fire, many have rejected You and will torment in the fire of hell for eternity. May many listen and accept Your Word this day and accept salvation that comes through Your Son Jesus Christ.

Jeremiah was put into a vaulted cell in a dungeon, where he remained a long time.
Jeremiah 37:16

Father, may we stand for You as Jeremiah. He had broken no law but was falsely put in prison. Just as others throughout the Bible have suffered to do Your will, Jeremiah lived in Your truth and love. Let us go this day and live in Your truth and love.

Then the officials said to the king, This man should be put to death. He is discouraging the soldiers who are left in this city, as well as all the people, by the things he is saying to them. This man is not seeking the good of these people but their ruin.
Jeremiah 38:4

Father, Jeremiah was not seeking ruin for the people but good. May we surround ourselves with wise counsel this day. Counsel that speaks truth from loving You.

I will save you; you will not fall by the sword but will escape with your life, because you trust in me, declares the Lord.
Jeremiah 39:18

Father, You had told Jeremiah while he had been confined in the courtyard of the guard to tell Ebed-Melek the Cushite that You would save him because he had put his trust in You. Nebuchadnezzar had laid siege to Jerusalem for two years and has now taken the city. The royal palace was burned, King Zedekiah had his eyes put out and his children killed, people were taken to Babylon, and the walls of Jerusalem are broken down. You did not forget the ones faithful and who trusted in Your Word. May we do the same today and trust in Your Word.

And now the Lord has brought it about; He has done just as He said He would. All this happened because you people sinned against the Lord and did not obey Him.
Jeremiah 40:3

Father, the people of Jerusalem and Judah were being carried to Babylon in chains along with Jeremiah. The captain of the guard came and released Jeremiah and freed him to go freely to Babylon or stay. Jeremiah stayed and went to Gedaliah son of Ahikam at Mizpah and stayed with him among the people who were left behind in the land. May we obey and do Your will as Jeremiah. Just as the chains were taken from the wrists of Jeremiah, our chains of sin have been removed from sin through Jesus. We are no longer slaves to sin but free in Christ.

And they went on, stopping at Geruth Kimham near Bethlehem on their way to Egypt.
Jeremiah 41:17

Father, the people of Mizpah who had survived with their lives, whom Johanan had recovered from Ishmael son of Nethaniah after Ishmael had assassinated Gedaliah son of Ahikam were now fleeing to Egypt. Our Savior Jesus also left Bethlehem where He was born as a baby with His mother Mary and daddy Joseph and went to Egypt for safety from King Herod. Egypt, who once was the nation who held Your chosen people as slaves has also been a refuge through history. May we be a haven of rest for the hurting today. May we stop and listen to one's that need Your love

Pray that the Lord your God will tell us where we should go
and what we should do.
Jeremiah 42:3

Father, a small remnant went to Jeremiah and asked him to go
to You on what they should do. After 10 days, You told
Jeremiah to tell them not to go to Egypt but to stay where they
were in Chimham, near Bethlehem. You would have
Nebuchadnezzar show compassion to the remnant. You told
them that You would relent concerning the disaster that You
inflicted on them. You told them You would build them up and
not tear them down. Father, may we do Your will this day and
build us up Father: Build us up.

When Jeremiah had finished telling the people all the words of
the Lord their God-everything the Lord had sent him to tell
them- Azariah son of Hoshaiah and Johanan son of Kareah and
all the arrogant men said to Jeremiah, "You are lying! The Lord
our God has not sent you to say, 'You must not go to Egypt to
settle there.
Jeremiah 43:1-2

Just as God sent His word to His true prophet Jeremiah, God
has also sent His word through the Bible we read each day.
These men led others from the Word of God just like others in
this world will try to lead you from God's Truth. Read God's
Word each day and meditate on it and ask the Holy Spirit to
help you understand God's meaning each time you read. God
promises if we search for Him, He will be found. True wisdom
and peace comes from God alone.

Again and again I sent my servants the prophets, who said, 'Do not do this detestable thing that I hate!
Jeremiah 44:4

God's chosen people had chosen to worship a false god. Let today be a day we bow only to our Lord in all we do.

Should you then seek great things for yourself? Do not seek them. For I will bring disaster on all people, declares the Lord, but wherever you go I will let you escape with your life.
Jeremiah 45:5

Father, may all we do this day be not for self but for You. May Your will be done and not our own. We are Your servants and wish to please You by our actions and choices.

This is the message the Lord spoke to Jeremiah the prophet about the coming of Nebuchadnezzar king of Babylon to attack Egypt.
Jeremiah 46:13

Father, You know what the future holds. You are in control of all things at all times. You are sovereign and need not explain Your will. All things work out for good from Your plans. May we not hinder Your perfect plan for our lives this day.

For the day has come to destroy all the Philistines and to remove all survivors who could help Tyre and Sidon. The Lord is about to destroy the Philistines, the remnant from the coasts of Caphtor.
Jeremiah 47:4

Father, the Philistines go back to David and Goliath. You used David and a sling to defeat a giant. A small boy had the courage and faith in You to be with him against overwhelming odds. When has impossible ever stopped You our God. May we face the world as David against the Philistines.

Moab will be destroyed as a nation because she defied the Lord.
Jeremiah 48:42

Father, thank You for the blessings You have bestowed on The United States of America. We know our future home is in heaven that is perfect with Your presence. While on earth, we thank You for allowing us to live in a country where we are free to worship Your holy name. We pray Your continued blessings on our country.

This is what the Lord says: "If those who do not deserve to drink the cup(must drink it, why should you go unpunished? You will not go unpunished, but must drink it.
Jeremiah 49:12

Father, Your Son Jesus chose to drink from the bitter cup for our sins. Jesus did not deserve to die, for he was perfect and spotless from sin. Praise the name of Jesus for shedding His blood for the atonement of our sins.

Yet their Redeemer is strong; the LORD Almighty is His name. He will vigorously defend their cause so that He may bring rest to their land, but unrest to those who live in Babylon.
Jeremiah 50:34

Father, our strength comes from You. We have peace in knowing that You defend and watch over us Your children that have accepted Jesus as our Lord and Savior. Praise the name of Jesus. Thank You Holy Spirit for guiding us as we travel on this earth.

He who is the Portion of Jacob is not like these, for He is the Maker of all things, including the people of his inheritance the Lord Almighty is His name.
Jeremiah 51:19

Father, You are the creator of all things. From the heavens to the bottom of the sea. You know each star and each microorganism. We marvel at Your greatness. Thank You for loving us so that You gave Your only begotten Son Jesus to make a way back to You from sin. May we show our love for You this day

It was because of the Lord's anger that all this happened to Jerusalem and Judah, and in the end he thrust them from his presence.
Jeremiah 52:3

Father, Your chosen people broke the covenant. It was because of their disobedience that Your anger aroused. May our actions be pleasing to You today and thank You for Your grace and mercy today.

"The Lord is righteous, yet I rebelled against his command. Listen, all you peoples; look on my suffering. My young men and young women have gone into exile.
Lamentation 1:18

Father, You are great and righteous. Thank You for forgiving us for our rebellion through the blood of Jesus. We have assurance in Your word that our sins and trespasses are remembered by You no more. Praise the name of Jesus for allowing us to have fellowship and the promise we will be with You forever.

The Lord has done what he planned; he has fulfilled his word,
which he decreed long ago.
Lamentation 2:17

Thank God for His plans and not ours. He watches over us each
day. He has angels to attend us.

Because of the Lord's great love we are not consumed, for his
compassions never fail. They are new every morning; great is
your faithfulness.
Lamentation 3:22-23

Father, thank You for a new day and the promise in knowing
Your compassions never fail and Your love is with us today.
You are our faithful Father and love Your children with a love
beyond our comprehension. We worship and sing praises to
Your name today and forevermore.

Your punishment will end, Daughter Zion; he will not prolong your exile. But he will punish your sin, Daughter Edom, and expose your wickedness.
Lamentation 4:22

Father, Your chosen people has sinned against You. They had taken up idols and broke Your laws. We now live in an age of grace and mercy through Your Son Jesus. One day, all Your children that have accepted Jesus will sit beneath Your throne in heaven and praise and worship and sing songs to Your Holy name. May we live today knowing You are with us from today until eternity.

Our ancestors sinned and are no more, and we bear their punishment.
Lamentations 5:7

Father, we have sinned against You and fall short of Your glory. Mankind that has accepted forgiveness of their sins through Jesus no longer lives under the chains of sin. We are free from our sins and no longer have to carry them. We no longer have to bear our burdens alone. The Holy Spirit goes before us in prayer to You Father. We no longer have to travel this life alone. Praise Your name.

Like the appearance of a rainbow in the clouds on a rainy day, so was the radiance around him. This was the appearance of the likeness of the glory of the Lord. When I saw it, I fell facedown, and I heard the voice of one speaking.
Ezekiel 1:28

Father, how wonderful it will be once we get to heaven and see Your glory as Ezekiel describes. We indeed will fall face down and worship Your holiness. May we honor and praise while we walk the days we are on earth. Let a day not pass unless we have given You our praise and adoration.

As he spoke, the Spirit came into me and raised me to my feet, and I heard him speaking to me.
Ezekiel 2:2

Father, You gave Your prophet Ezekiel all he needed to go to the Israelites and tell them what You had written in the scroll. May we go today and do Your will regardless of the consequences. You are our God and May all we do be pleasing to You.

Then the Spirit lifted me up, and I heard behind me a loud rumbling sound as the glory of the Lord rose from the place where it was standing.
Ezekiel 3:12

Father, what a magnificent sound it must have been for Ezekiel to hear as Your presence left. It was the sound of the wings of the living creatures brushing against each other and the sound of the wheels beside them. How great You are my Father. Your creation sings of Your greatness. From the streams to the wind through the trees. As for me, I lift my voice in praise today and forevermore.

I have assigned you the same number of days as the years of their sin. So for 390 days you will bear the sin of the people of Israel.
Ezekiel 4:5

Father, Jesus would come to earth 2,500 years after Ezekiel and bear the sins of mankind once and for all. Jesus, the name above all names, the King of Kings and Lord of Lords. Praise the name of Jesus for allowing mankind the opportunity to accept and believe in the Son of God. May we forever more praise the Lord our God

This is what the Sovereign Lord says: This is Jerusalem, which
I have set in the center of the nations, with countries all around
her.
Ezekiel 5:5

Father, Your great love for Jerusalem and the Israelites was not
met with the same devotion. Because of their wickedness and
not following Your commands, they will now feel Your wrath.
Thank You Jesus for coming and dying for our sins that we
would never have to feel the wrath of our Father. We were made
spotless by the precious blood of the Lamb of God.

And they will know that I am the Lord,
when their people lie slain among their
idols around their altars, on every high hill and on all the
mountaintops, under every spreading tree and every leafy
oak-places where they offered fragrant incense to all their idols.
Ezekiel 6:13

Father, Your chosen people that started with Abraham and
Sarah have now done detestable practices. They have taken
idols and offered fragrant incense. You alone are worthy of
man's praise. Now You will punish them for their sins. I pray
that we will learn form Your word and never bow to anything
other than You Father.

I am about to pour out my wrath on you and spend my anger against you. I will judge you according to your conduct and repay you for all your detestable practices.
Ezekiel 7:8

Father, praise the name of Jesus that we do not have to face Your wrath one day at judgment. On that day, every knee will bow and tongue confess that Jesus Christ is Lord.

And he said to me, "Son of man, do you see what they are doing-the utterly detestable things the Israelites are doing here, things that will drive me far from my sanctuary? But you will see things that are even more detestable.
Ezekiel 8:6

Father, along with other detestable practices, Your chosen people were bowing not to You but to things You had created. We are to enjoy Your creation but never worship anything but You Father. May we stay focused on You and never worship anything but You, our one true God.

And said to him, "Go throughout the city of Jerusalem and put a mark on the foreheads of those who grieve and lament over all the detestable things that are done in it.
Ezekiel 9:4

Father, one day at judgment, our sins will be covered by the blood of Jesus our savior. Just as Your judgment passed over the Israelites who had the mark on their foreheads, we will be covered by the blood of Jesus. Praise the name of Jesus who bore our sins.

The sound of the wings of the cherubim could be heard as far away as the outer court, like the voice of God Almighty when he speaks.
Ezekiel 10:5

Father, what a magnificent sound Ezekiel must have heard that day. One day we will hear Your voice in heaven. It will be the most wonderful sound that will ever be heard. We will sing praises to You Father and have fellowship for eternity. What a day that will be when our Jesus we shall see

Therefore say: 'This is what the Sovereign Lord says: I will gather you from the nations and bring you back from the countries where you have been scattered, and I will give you back the land of Israel again.' "They will return to it and remove all its vile images and detestable idols.
Ezekiel 11: 17-18

God told the prophet Ezekiel how He longed for His children Israel to look to Him. Let us today put away anything that is between our relationship to our Lord.

Whatever I say will be fulfilled, declares the Sovereign Lord.
Ezekiel 12:28

Father, thank you for being a creator that always is true. You are a Holy God that hates sin and disease. Thank you for your promise that we will live eternally in your presence in perfect peace

Son of man, prophesy against the prophets of Israel who are now prophesying. Say to those who prophesy out of their own imagination: Hear the word of the Lord!
Ezekiel 13:2

Father, false prophets had been falsely telling Your children lies. You hate lies as You tell us in Proverbs. May we look to Your word and not the world for truth. You are truth and life.

The word of the Lord came to me: "Son of man, if a country sins against me by being unfaithful and I stretch out my hand against it to cut off its food supply and send famine upon it and kill its people and their animals, even if these three men-Noah, Daniel and Job-were in it, they could save only themselves by their righteousness, declares the Sovereign Lord.
Ezekiel 14:12-14

As Jesus took His last breath He asked God to forgive man for they knew not what they do. I can find no place in the New Testament where Jesus killed but He came to heal and gave man a choice to follow Him. Thank you Father for the New Covenant of grace and mercy.
There will be a time of judgment once our Savior comes to get the Church but thank God by Jesus blood God holds back His wrath on man and sin during this present age. I pray many more will accept Him today.

I will make the land desolate because they have been
unfaithful, declares the Sovereign Lord.
Ezekiel 15:8

Father, You created the land and made it fruitful. You tell us in
Genesis that the land was created and it was good. Because of
the Israelites' sins, the land would become desolate. Our actions
and choices have consequences and may we learn from the
Israelites and never turn from You.

So I will establish My covenant with you, and you will know
that I am the Lord. Then, when I make atonement for you for all
you have done, you will remember and be ashamed and never
again open your mouth because of your humiliation, declares
the Sovereign Lord.'"
Ezekiel 16:62-63

God's chosen people had taken their eyes off of their God and
chose to do detestable acts that were against a Holy God. God
did punish but did not completely destroy. Our Savior, Jesus
Christ would come one day from this line of people. Praise God
for His love and atonement for our disobedience.

This is what the Sovereign Lord says: I myself will take a shoot from the very top of a cedar and plant it; I will break off a tender sprig from its topmost shoots and plant it on a high and lofty mountain.
Ezekiel 17:22

Thank you God for sending your Son and your future promise of planting Your Kingdom on the high hill of Zion. We anticipate and look forward to that day.

For I take no pleasure in the death of anyone, declares the Sovereign Lord. Repent and live!
Ezekiel 18:32

True life comes from You Father once man accepts your Son. Thank you for loving each individual that You have created and giving each of us a choice to accept your love by repentance of our sin nature. I pray today many more will come to You

Your mother was like a vine in your vineyard planted by the water; it was fruitful and full of branches because of abundant water.
Ezekiel 19:10

Father You are the source of strength to help us get through this day. May we be refreshed with living water that only You can provide.

I am the Lord your God.
Ezekiel 20:19

Thank you Father for choosing us as your special creation to honor and worship You. I am Your servant and I pray nothing is done today by my choices that will dishonor You. Please forgive me when I take my eyes off Your Holiness and commit sins that displease You.

The lowly will be exalted and the exalted will be brought low.
Ezekiel 21:26

Father, I pray that Your name will be exalted today by my actions. I know that all goodness comes from You and that You are the maker of all. I bow and worship You, the one True God.

I looked for someone among them who would build up the wall and stand before me in the gap on behalf of the land so I would not have to destroy it, but I found no one.
Ezekiel 22:30

Father, I thank you for the Holy Spirit that is alive is all believers. I am thankful that You will not look at Your children's sin but see pureness made possible only by the washing in Your sons blood.

You will suffer the penalty for your lewdness and bear the consequences of your sins of idolatry. Then you will know that I am the Sovereign Lord.
Ezekiel 23:49

Father, may we learn that You do not want our eyes focused on anything but You. There was never a moment Jesus was not in perfect harmony with You. I pray today for my choices and actions please You.

The next morning I did as I had been commanded.
Ezekiel 24:18

Lord, may we obey as Ezekiel.

This is what the Sovereign Lord says: Because you said "Aha!"
Ezekiel 25:3
Lord, words can be so hurtful and displeasing to You. I pray with the Holy Spirit's help my choice in speech will be more conscious of Your Holy expectations of each word that comes from my lips.

You will never be rebuilt, for I the Lord have spoken, declares
the Sovereign Lord.
Ezekiel 26:14

Let us learn from the people of Tyre that we should live lives
that are pleasing to God. Through the acceptance of Jesus, now
have the Holy Spirit that dwells in our bodies. Let us build
today instead of tear down.

Who was ever silenced like Tyre, surrounded by the sea.
Ezekiel 27:32

Father, may we shine like a lighthouse each day. Not for our
glory but for Yours.

By your great skill in trading
you have increased your wealth, and because of your wealth
your heart has grown proud.
Ezekiel 28:5

None or nothing on earth or in the heavens is worthy of worship
than You My God. May today be a day to magnify praise to
You.

You say, "The Nile belongs to me; I made it for myself."
Ezekiel 29:3

Father, let us not be as Pharaoh of Egypt but let us see creation
and everything in it as Your magnificent power and handiwork.
You alone are worthy of praise and worshiped

When I break the yoke of Egypt; there her proud strength will come to an end.
Ezekiel 30:18

Righteous Father, may there be nothing prideful in our hearts today. You used Nebuchadnezzar to break Egypt in her choices not to follow You. I pray our choices today will be pleasing to You and Your will will be done.

Which of the trees of Eden can be compared with you in splendor and majesty?
Ezekiel 31:18

As beautiful as earth is today, it is a fallen creation. How we look forward to one day seeing earth and Your creation in its perfect form without sin or blemish.

You too, Pharaoh, will be broken and will lie among the
uncircumcised, with those killed by the sword.
Ezekiel 32:28

Father, Pharaoh of Egypt will be defeated and broken. Kings
and rulers that do not worship and accept Jesus as their Lord
will one day be cast into the pits of hell to forever be separated
from You. May we go this day and spread the gospel of the
birth, life , and resurrection of Jesus. In whom alone, is the way
and the truth and the life. Salvation comes through Your
precious son Jesus.

For they hear your words but do not put them into practice.
Ezekiel 33:32

Father, let us pause and let the Holy Spirit speak to us as we
read and meditate in Your words. We worship a living God that
speaks truth and wisdom.
You

You are My sheep, the sheep of My pasture, and I am your God, declares the Sovereign Lord.
Ezekiel 34:31

Thank you Lord for watching over us each second of every day. I thank You for the mother's that look to Your Word for directions to be the momma and wife You intended. May You bless them as they tend their sheep.

You boasted against me and spoke against me without restraint, and I heard it.
Ezekiel 35:13

Father, You hear and see all things at all times. Nothing passes that You are not aware. May we remember that all we do and think is known by You. Let us live this day according to Your word.

And I will cause many people to live on you-yes, all of Israel. The towns will be inhabited and the ruins rebuilt.
Ezekiel 36:10

Father, the children of Israel would once again live in the mountains, hills, ravens, and valleys. For the sake of Your holy name, You would restore the Israelites. Thank You father for Your forgiveness for our transgressions against Your Holy name.

So I prophesied as He commanded me, and breath entered them; they came to life and stood up on their feet-a vast army.
Ezekiel 37:10

My God, how great is Your love and desire for Your people to honor and love You. You take dry bones and bring to life like you took our sin and forgot forever, giving us a new body to live with You through eternity.

And so I will show My greatness and My holiness, and I will make Myself known in the sight of many nations. Then they will know that I am the Lord.
Ezekiel 38:23

You are great and holy my God. You do what pleases You. I praise Your sovereign power. I pray blessing on our leaders this morning that they will turn to You for direction and discernment.

Therefore this is what the Sovereign Lord says: I will now restore the fortunes of Jacob and will have compassion on all the people of Israel, and I will be zealous for My holy name.
Ezekiel 39:25

Thank you Father for allowing us to have forgiveness for our sins. By the blood of Your Son we were able to have fellowship with You. Oh, how great is Your love for Your children.

These are the sons of Zadok, who are the only Levites who may draw near to the Lord to minister before Him.
Ezekiel 40:46

Father, I pray my worship today will be pleasing as sweet incense to You. You are my God and my strength. I am in awe that You allow me to draw near to You.

He said to me, "This is the Most Holy Place."
Ezekiel 41:4

Father, The inner sanctuary that you showed Ezekiel was the Most Holy Place since it was where you resided. Now, the Holy Spirit resides in Your believers. Let us use our bodies to show Honor to You.

Once the priests enter the holy precincts, they are not to go into the outer court until they leave behind the garments in which they minister, for these are holy. They are to put on other clothes before they go near the places that are for the people.
Ezekiel 42:14

Father, thank you for tearing the separation from You at the cross when the temple curtain torn into giving man the opportunity to have fellowship with You. We no longer have to have prophets or priests to give us Your words but You speak directly to our hearts by Your Spirit.

The glory of the Lord entered the temple through the gate facing east.
Ezekiel 43:4

Father, just as the sun comes up from the east each morning as You put in order, we look forward to the day that Your Son will come from the eastern sky to gather His children. Amen.

This is what the Sovereign Lord says: No foreigner uncircumcised in heart and flesh is to enter my sanctuary, not even the foreigners who live among the Israelites.
Ezekiel 44:9

Jesus, thank you for making the way for us to come to the Father. You made it possible by obeying Your Father and creating the only way by the cross. May today be a day of praise and worship to you.

"During the seven days of the festival, which begins in the seventh month on the fifteenth day, he is to make the same provision for sin offerings, burnt offerings, grain offerings and oil.
Ezekiel 45:25

Father, Your children the Israelites are to make festivals and offerings to You. You have been merciful to them for their sins. Thank You Father for also forgiving us for our sins and transgressions against Your Holy name. May we be found worthy and do all in our power to proclaim Your holy name. Holy Spirit guide us along our path today and help us to reach others with the gospel of Jesus.

He said to me, "These are the kitchens where those who minister at the temple are to cook the sacrifices of the people."
Ezekiel 46:24

Father, may my day be pleasing to You. I offer the best I have to You today and will make choices that reflect readings of Your word. I thank You for the Holy Spirit that will help me recall and know Your will.

In whatever tribe a foreigner resides, there you are to give them their inheritance," declares the Sovereign Lord.
Ezekiel 47:23

Father, it is hard to understand your love for mankind as You offer us the choice to be joint heirs one day with Your son Jesus. Let today be pleasing to You and may our choices be wise and may we use discernment in our decisions.

In the center of it will be the sanctuary of the Lord.
Ezekiel 48:10

Father, may all my actions and deeds fall in the center of Your will today. May my heart and all that is within me praise You for who You are; my Lord and God.

To these four young men God gave knowledge and understanding of all kinds of literature and learning.
Daniel 1:17

Through Daniel and his friends, You Father showed Your control over their lives. You caused the chief official to show them favor and You gave them knowledge of learning and wisdom in which they were 10 times better than the magicians in King Nebuchadnezzar's court. All things go through Your hands that pertain to Your children. May we make choices as these young men who took on new names but didn't let the names change who they believed
Daniel(Belteshazzar)
Hananiah (Shadrach)
Mishael (Meshach)
Azariah (Abednego)

He urged them to plead for mercy from the God of heaven concerning this mystery, so that he and his friends might not be executed with the rest of the wise men of Babylon.
Daniel 2:18

Father, Daniel and his friends' prayers went up to You and You answered their prayer to interpret King Nebuchadnezzar's dream. Thank You for hearing our prayers and answering as a Father answers His children.

Therefore I decree that the people of any nation or language who say anything against the God of Shadrach, Meshach and Abednego be cut into pieces and their houses be turned into piles of rubble, for no other god can save in this way.
Daniel 3:29

Father, it is not possible to understand how you saved Shadrach, Meshach 8t1d Abednego. I put my hope in You are a sovereign God that can do the impossible.

Now I, Nebuchadnezzar, praise and exalt and glorify the King of heaven, because everything He does is right and all His ways are just. And those who walk in pride He is able to humble.
Daniel 4:37

Father, You used Nebuchadnezzar to fulfill Your plans on earth. My prayer is that we will learn from His life and not let pride come between us and You. Only you are worthy of honor and to be worshiped.

I have heard that the spirit of the gods is in you and that you have insight, intelligence and outstanding wisdom.
Daniel 5:14

King Belshazzar, King Nebuchadnezzar did not learn from his fathers mistakes. I pray we will learn that You Father wants us to worship only You and recognize only You as our God. When people hear of us may they know we are Your children by our actions and obedience to You.

Daniel answered, "May the king live forever! My God sent his angel, and he shut the mouths of the lions.
Daniel 6:21

Daniel called on You Father and You sent an angel to shut the mouth of the lions. Protect us today Father from the one who roams the earth seeking to destroy and harm. Lead us not into temptation but deliver us from evil as only You can.

His kingdom will be an everlasting kingdom, and all rulers will worship and obey him.
Daniel 7:27

Daniel's dream troubled him. Not until he asked one standing in his dream did he understand that the beasts in his dream represented four kings. Four kings whose kingdoms will all pass away. There will be a day we as believers in Jesus will be in an everlasting kingdom with our God. Let us not rely on our own understanding but leak only to You Father for guidance.

Son of man, he said to me, "understand that the vision concerns
the time of the end."
Daniel 8:17

Father You sent Your angel Gabriel to interpret Daniel's vision.
Thank You for allowing us to know what the end has in store;
an eternity with You.

Lord, listen! Lord, forgive! Lord, hear and act.
Daniel 9:19

Thank you Father for always listening to Your children. Thank
You for the forgiveness that comes through Your Son. Thank
You for always answering our prayers and may we be content in
the answers.

Peace! Be strong now; be strong.
Daniel 10:19

Daniel was weak from his three weeks waiting for the meaning of a revelation that came to him. When the meaning came, he could only find strength when he was touched by the revealer. Let us stay in touch with Jesus today.

With flattery he will corrupt those who have violated the covenant, but the people who know their God will firmly resist him.
Daniel 11:32

Father, thank you for Your inspired words in the Bible that allow us if we so choose to read and find
Your nature and what pleases You. May we desire to make it just as food to nourish our body's. Let Your word nourish our souls.

But at that time your people-everyone whose name is found written in the book will be delivered.
Daniel 12:1

I worship You Father for allowing my name to be written in The Book Of Life and that I am your child. You know my every thought and my heart. I pray today I show my love to You like never before.

Yet I will show love to Judah; and I will save them-not by bow, sword or battle, or by horses and horsemen, but I, the Lord their God, will save them.
Hosea 1:7

Thank you Father for Your forgiveness. I pray that many will accept Your love, grace, mercy, and forgiveness today that You offer. May the Holy Spirit touch hearts and many come to You by the atonement of sins that could only be made by the blood of Your Son, Jesus Christ, on the Cross.

She has not acknowledged that I was the one who gave her the grain.
Hosea 2:8

All we have is a blessing of God. He is the one who provides and gives us food to eat and shelter. Thank You Father for loving us and watching over our every move.

Afterward the Israelites will return and seek the Lord their God.
Hosea 3:5

Thank You Father for never turning from your children. You are so patient and loving. I pray today we show our love to You.

How then can the Lord pasture them like lambs in a meadow?
Hosea 4:16

Father, thank You for Your every moment of protection and care. The powers of evil want to devour but You guard and guide with a mighty staff.

Israel is not hidden from Me.
Hosea 5:3

We cannot hide from You Father. You watch all the things we do that displease You. I will strive today to keep my eyes focused on You and make choices that please You.

For I desire mercy, not sacrifice, and acknowledgment of God
rather than burnt offerings.
Hosea 6:6

Father, You are the one true God. You are the Lord of my life
and I will acknowledge You in all I am and do.

None of them calls on Me.
Hosea 7:7

Father, unlike Your chosen people in Hosea time, I call on You
today. I pray that my choices today will keep me in pleasing
relation to You. You always keep Your covenant promises.

Our God, we acknowledge you!
Hosea 8:2

My God, I acknowledge that You are the one true God. Nothing in this world or the heavens is to be worshiped but You. Thank You for Jesus and the Holy Spirit and Your peace from knowing I am a child of Yours for eternity.

It will not come into the temple of the Lord.
Hosea 9:4

Holy Spirit help me not bring anything into me that is unpleasant to God. I pray with Your help and guidance, today will be a day that will bring honor to my Father.

For it is time to seek the Lord.
Hosea 10:12

My God, thank You for accepting me the way I was in my
sinful nature. I felt the Holy Spirit drawing me to You and came
and asked to be reconciled to You through Jesus Your Son. Your
Word promises those who seek shall find. I pray many are
drawn and today will be the day of their salvation.

To them I was like one who lifts
a little child to the cheek, and I bent down to feed them.
Hosea 11:4

Father, thank You for Your love toward us. May we run to You
and rest in Your open arms of love, protection, and peace.

But you must return to your God; maintain love and justice,
and wait for your God always.
Hosea 12:6

Father as Jacob was told to wait on You, I pray that we will be
in Your will for our lives. May we develop a relationship with
You where we have peace and contentment knowing we are
taking steps in the direction You chose.

When I fed them, they were satisfied; when they were satisfied,
they became proud; then they forgot Me.
Hosea 13:6

You God are mighty in power and strength. You made all and
are the beginning and end. I pray today my choices reflect my
love to You.

The ways of the Lord are right.
Hosea 14:9

Thank You for creating man in Your image. You are completely Holy and good. Through You, we as believers in Your Son know complete goodness and justice. We are taught right from wrong as we study Your Word and direction from the Holy Spirit. True wisdom comes only from You.

Tell it to your children, and let your children tell it to their children, and their children to the next generation.
Joel 1:3

How precious are families that love You Father. I pray for parents that will tell their children about You. Thank you for the plan You set forth in the Bible for a happy family that worships You.

And everyone who calls on the name of the Lord will be saved.
Joel 2:32

Thank You Father for the gift of salvation. Jesus gave His life that we might live. What a price was paid 2000 years ago for Your children. I pray that many will call on You today and believe.

But the Lord will be a refuge for His people.
Joel 3:16

No matter what we are going through, You promise to provide a refuge for us. May we seek Your shelter and find comfort in Your arms of love.

He said "The Lord roars from Zion and thunders from Jerusalem; the pastures of the shepherds dry up and the top of Carmel withers."
Amos 1:2

Father, may we do nothing today that causes Your Holy name to be tarnished. Let us tell others about Your wonderful deeds and love for mankind. May we never hear Your roar and thunders of displeasure.

This is what the Lord says: "For three sins of Judah, even for four, I will not relent. Because they have rejected the law of the Lord and have not kept his decrees, because they have been led astray by false gods, the gods their ancestors followed.
Amos 2:4

Father, You hate sin. You are a Holy Father who cannot be in the presence of sin. By the blood of Jesus we Your children are washed of our sins and will one day be allowed in Your presence. Not by our deeds but by the blood of Your son Jesus. May we this day honor Your name by receiving Your law and keeping Your decrees.

The Lion has roared-who will not fear?
Amos 3:8

Father, You displayed wrath on Your children Israel for their
wicked lifestyles. Thank you Jesus for allowing a time of grace
and mercy even as the world does the same as Israel long ago.
May many come to You today and escape the wrath that will
one day roar again as a Lion after Jesus returns.

He who forms the mountains,
who creates the wind, and who reveals His thoughts to
mankind, who turns dawn to darkness, and treads on the heights
of the earth-the Lord God Almighty is His name.
Amos 4:13

I cannot comprehend Your greatness God. When I think about
grains of sand and stars you know by name, I am in awe. Thank
You for knowing me and giving me life through Your Son. A
relationship with the One True God.

This is what the Lord says to Israel: "Seek me and live."
Amos 5:4

Since You created man Father, You have longed for him to seek You and worship only You. I worship and praise Your name today and look only to You for guidance and love that is beyond my understanding. May my steps fall in the plan that pleases You today.

"I abhor the pride of Jacob and detest his fortresses; I will deliver up the city and everything in it."
Amos 6:8

Father, I humbly confess my shortcomings this day and ask Your will be done in my life. I pray for protection from the one who seeks to destroy. I pray that I will be the servant of only You, my God.

I cried out, "Sovereign Lord, forgive! How can Jacob survive?
He is so small!" So the Lord relented.
Amos 7:5-6

The Lord relented His wrath at Amos' request and saved God's
children from famine and death. Today we anticipate Christ's
return and know that God is waiting only for others to accept
Him as their Lord.
King Jeroboam of Israel would not listen and his family died as
a result and he was sent to die in a pagan country. God is in
control at all times.

The Lord has sworn by himself, the Pride of Jacob: "I will
never forget anything they have done.
Amos 8:7

Thank You Father for sending Your begotten son Jesus in which
You now no longer see or remember my sins that are washed in
His blood.

I will plant Israel in their own land, never again to be uprooted from the land I have given them," says the Lord your God.
Amos 9:15

Father, Your chosen ones of the descendants of Jacob will one day never deal with sin again. We will be with You forever in a home that has Your Glory and Holiness. What a wonderful day that will be. I pray today many will join Your family.

Though you soar like the eagle and make your nest among the stars, from there I will bring you down," declares the Lord.
Obadiah 1:4

Father, may my thoughts and actions today only be on You. I pray I will learn from the Edomites how not to live. My choices reflect my love for You and I pray none of the choices today will bring reproach to You. Thank You for the Holy Spirit that helps me stay on course.

Now the Lord provided a huge fish to swallow Jonah, and Jonah was in the belly of the fish for three days and three nights.
Jonah 1:17

Jonah ran from the Lord and as a result a great storm arose around him. Lord, I pray that we will be sensitive to the Holy Spirit and be willing to do Your plans today. Let us recall the teachings of Your Son Jesus to help us make choices that will bring sunshine not storms.

But you, Lord my God, brought my life up from the pit.
Jonah 2:6

Jonah prayed this from inside the fish. God hears the prayers of His children at all times. We have access to our Father. Thank you Father for allowing such a relationship with the One True God.

When God saw what they did and how they turned from their evil ways, he relented and did not bring on them the destruction he had threatened.
Jonah 3:10

Father, the people of Nineveh repented and accepted You. I am so thankful that me and my family have accepted You as our Lord. My heart goes out for the world and the ones that have not accepted Your love and salvation that comes from Your Son. May today many accept You today.

And should I not have concern for the great city of Nineveh, in which there are more than a hundred and twenty thousand people who cannot tell their right hand from their left-and also many animals?"
Jonah 4:11

Father, oh how You love Your creation. We are so unworthy of Your attention and love by our actions but You continue to look upon us with a love that is beyond our understanding. I thank you for Your compassion and patience. May many like the 120,000 of Nineveh come to You today.

Look! The Lord is coming from his dwelling place.
Micah 1:3

Lord, one day You will come to earth again from heaven to gather the ones on earth that have accepted your gift of salvation. Thank you for letting us know that You will come again and we will be with You forever and ever.

I will surely gather all of you Jacob; I will surely bring together the remnant of Israel.
Micah 2:12

Father, You promise one day that Your children will all be together with You. We look forward to that day. A day that will never end.

Her leaders judge for a bribe, her priests teach for a price, and her prophets tell fortunes for money. Yet they look for the Lord's support and say, "Is not the Lord among us? No disaster will come upon us."
Micah 3:11

Just as false teachers and prophets in Micah's day were blinded by money, power, and greed, I pray we will use discernment, Your word, and be sensitive of the Holy Spirit to know Your will for our lives and not fall to the temptations of this world.

The Lord will rule over them in Mount Zion from that day and forever.
Micah 4:7

Thank You Father for letting us know Your plan for us Your children. We will one day rest with You and worship Your Holy name for eternity. Only You are to be praised and glorified today and forevermore. May my singing and praise be pleasing to You.

"But you, Bethlehem Ephrathah, though you are small among the clans of Judah, out of you will come for me one who will be ruler over Israel, whose origins are from of old, from ancient times."
Micah 5:2

Over 700 years before Your Son Jesus was born, You allowed Your people to know through Your prophet Micah Your plan for Your children. It amazes me how each second of each day You know the events of each of Your children's steps. I praise You and give honor to Your Son Jesus for coming to earth and being the sacrifice for our sins and the Holy Spirit who lives in the ones who believe in Your Son and is our great Councilor.

He has shown you, 0 mortal, what is good. And what does the Lord require of you?
To act justly and to love mercy and to walk humbly with your God. Micah 6:8

Thank You for telling Your creation what You expect from us. May we love You enough to try our best today to show our love by our choices and actions.

But as for me, I watch in hope for the Lord, I wait for God my Savior; my God will hear me.
Micah 7:7

While on earth, I anticipate the coming of Jesus. You have a mansion for Your children to spend eternity with You Father. Until then, may we find comfort in Your words and walk step by step in Your will.

The Lord is good, a refuge in times of trouble. He cares for those who trust in Him.
Nahum 1:7

Father, we know that You created man to worship and trust only in You. Worship by choice and not by force. I choose to worship and trust today, the one true God. May my singing and prayer be pleasing to You.

Guard the fortress, watch the road, brace yourselves, marshal all
your strength!
Nahum 2:1

Father, protect us today. Be our strong wall of protection. May
the Holy Spirit and Your Word keep our eyes straight on the
road that is pleasing to You.

"I am against you," declares the Lord Almighty.
Nahum 3:5

Father, Nineveh was displeasing to You. I pray for our country
and leaders that they will look to only You for guidance and
strength and our nation will seek You. I can only control my
actions and I pray that I learn from Joseph, Moses, Ruth,
Enoch, Elijah, Joshua, etc. Even with my flaws You will help
me be the daddy, pawpaw, and friend You expect me to be. I am
only as good as my relationship to You. Only goodness comes
from You.

Lord, are you not from everlasting? My God, my Holy One,
you will never die.
Habakkuk 1:12

Father Habakkuk asked 2600 years ago why the wicked are
allowed to prosper on this earth. I know You are a Sovereign
God and Holy. I accept Your will and plans. You do what You
want, when You want, and how You want. No one hates sin
more than You. I will do all I can today to be a light for You. I
pray many come to know You today.

The Lord is in His holy temple; let all the earth be silent before
Him.
Habakkuk 2:20

What a peace to know that You are on Your throne with Jesus at
Your right side. Nothing we do today will not be seen by You. I
chose to worship You today and commit this day to honor only
You Father. Let all creation be silent and know that You are
God.

The Sovereign Lord is my strength.
Habakkuk 3:19

Father, thank You for giving this day to look upon and marvel in Your creation. Thank You for the strength to walk and commune with You. To know You love me and watch all my steps gives me the determination to make this day my best for You.

Be silent before the Sovereign Lord, for the day of the Lord is near.
Zephaniah 1:7

Father, while we wait on Your return may we live lives that are pleasing to You. I pray we look only to You for direction and have faith that You know us by name and love us with a love that is beyond our understanding.

Seek righteousness, seek humility.
Zephaniah 2:3

Father, I pray that we will give our best today to live for You. I pray that we will humble ourselves to Your greatness and walk in the steps You desire for our lives. Let us look into the eyes of others and let them see Your love from ours.

The Lord within her is righteous; He does no wrong. Morning by morning He dispenses His justice, and every new day He does not fail, yet the unrighteous know no shame.
Zephaniah 3:5

Father, You never make a mistake and are consistent in Your discipline to Your children. You know our every need today. I am content with my blessings. Thank You Father for Your outpouring of love.

Then Haggai, the Lord's messenger, gave this message of the Lord to the people: "I am with you," declares the Lord.
Haggai 1:13

After returning to their land after exile in Babylonia, Your children put building their houses before building a house for You Father. After hearing Your words from Your prophet Haggai, Your children repented and started working together to rebuild Your temple. Only then did You stir up their spirits. May we also put You first today and work together to please You.

Be strong, all you people of the land,' declares the Lord, 'and work. For I am with you,' declares the Lord Almighty.
Haggai 2:4

Thank You Father for allowing Your children to work and provide for our families. I pray You will provide us the strength to be the best parents and grandparents to the next generations so they will also pass to their children Your teachings and love. They will know that if they believe in Your Son Jesus then You will forever for eternity never leave them.

Return to me,' declares the Lord Almighty, 'and I will return to you,' says the Lord Almighty.
Zechariah 1:3

Father, thank you for allowing Your children to repent and turn to You. We thank You for the Holy Spirit who dwells within us and how He uses our consciousness to turn from temptations. May we have a sensitive heart to stay in the road today that you have us to walk.

To measure Jerusalem, to find out how wide and how long it is.
Zechariah 2:2

Father, I could never measure up to dwell with You in Your Holiness. Only by accepting Jesus, You are able to look upon me. My sins are gone. Holy Spirit help me today to be pleasing to the Father and lead me not into temptation but deliver me from evil.

I am going to bring my servant, the Branch. See, the stone I
have set in front of Joshua!
Zechariah 3:8-9

Father, You fulfilled Your promise of sending Your beloved Son
Jesus. Jesus is the branch that reaches out to all mankind
offering atonement for our sins. He is the stone that will never
be moved. Thank You Father for the peace and joy I have by
accepting Your love.

He asked me, "What do you see?"
Zechariah 4:2

Father, may my eyes only look upon You today. Through Your
creation,. may I see Your greatness and love. You show us Your
ever presence through the dew for the tiniest to drink, the
sheltering wings for baby chicks, to the perfect placement of
stars and rotations of planets and the moon. You are a God of
order not chaos.

I answered, "I see a flying scroll, twenty cubits long and ten cubits wide."
Zechariah 5:2

Father, I think it is no coincidence that Your Son Jesus was a carpenter. Twenty cubits by ten cubits translates to 30 feet by 15 feet which is the same measure found in Your word as the Holy Place in Your tabernacle and also the porch size of Solomon's temple. The scroll represents the divine measure man is to be measured. I would have never measured up to Your standards Father. Praise the great carpenter Jesus who fulfilled Your blueprint of salvation for mankind.

This will happen if you diligently obey the Lord your God.
Zechariah 6:15

Father, life is not about getting and doing what 1, please but obeying and searching for Your will for my life. I love you Father and ask that Your will be done.

"'When I called, they did not listen; so when they called, I would not listen,' says the Lord Almighty.
Zachariah 7:13

Father, through the prophet Zechariah we are shown that You expect us to follow You. I pray today that we follow the teachings of Your Son Jesus and when prompted by the Holy Spirit we will listen and act. Thank You Jesus, the perfect model to follow.

"Let us go with you, because we have heard that God is with you.'"
Zechariah 8:23

Father, Israel was the nation chosen by You to be Your people. Now through the blood of Jesus, all mankind is able to share in Your inheritance. Now You dwell in us through the Holy Spirit who made the choice to accept and believe in Jesus. May others want what believers have today and join Your family.

Rejoice greatly, Daughter Zion! Shout, Daughter Jerusalem!
See, your king comes to you, righteous and victorious,
lowly and riding on a donkey, on a colt, the foal of a donkey.
Zechariah 9:9

Your Son indeed came Father. Not with a sword but in peace, offering salvation to a fallen world. May many accept Your gift today and Christians rejoice and reflect Your love to the world.

I will strengthen them in the Lord and in his name they will live securely, declares the Lord.
Zechariah 10:12

Father, thank You for Your promise of protection. In this fallen world, there are so many trials and snares. We are never away from Your sight. You watch our every step.

So I shepherded the flock marked for slaughter, particularly the oppressed of the flock.
Zechariah 11:7

Father, only Your Son Jesus could have saved my sinful soul from the slaughter and hell to come. I thank you for Your grace and mercy that I could live an eternal existence with You as my shepherd.

The people of Jerusalem are strong, because the Lord Almighty is their God.
Zechariah 12:5

Father, we are only as strong as our relationship to You. Strength comes from knowing You and Your Word from the Holy Bible. I pray I will rely not on my feeble self but in the One True God Almighty today and each day I am on this earth.

They will call on my name and I will answer them; I will say,
'They are my people,' and they will say, 'The Lord is our God.'
Zechariah 13:9

Father, I called on Your name and You answered. You always
answer.

On that day there will be neither sunlight nor cold, frosty
darkness. It will be a unique day-a day known only to the
Lord-with no distinction between day and night. When evening
comes, there will be light.
Zechariah 14:6-7

One day Jesus will be the light of this earth for 1,000 years.
Thank You Father today for showing us Your light.

"For I am a great king, says the Lord Almighty, "and my name is to be feared among the nations.
Malachi 1:14

Father, You are great and wonderful. May You be recognized and acknowledged in each step Your children take today. We love You and live to worship Your Holy name.

Has not the one God made you? You belong to him in body and spirit. And what does the one God seek? Godly offspring. So be on your guard, and do not be unfaithful to the wife of your youth.
Malachi 2:15

Father, may we be the marriage partner You intended and love and honor our marriage vowels. May we raise and train our children to love only You as our God through a life free of hypocrisy. May we consistently walk with You.

On the day when I act," says the Lord Almighty, "they will be my treasured possession. I will spare them, just as a father has compassion and spares his son who serves him.
Malachi 3:17

Father, thank You for Your mercy and forgiveness. I am so unworthy of Your love. I will serve You today and acknowledge that You are my God. Help me Father.

But for you who revere my name, the sun of righteousness will rise with healing in its rays.
Malachi 4:2

Father, Jesus will come again in the future to take Your Children to heaven to be with others that have already left this earth to be with You. Thank You Father for allowing me and so many to live with You forever and ever through eternity. You are my God.

But after he had considered this, an angel of the Lord appeared to him in a dream and said, "Joseph son of David, do not be afraid to take Mary home as your wife, because what is conceived in her is from the Holy Spirit. She will give birth to a son, and you are to give him the name Jesus, because he will save his people from their sins."
Matthew 1:20-21

What wonderful parents Jesus had to love Him. Father, I pray that we will look to Mary and Joseph to pattern how to love our children. Thank You Father for being the perfect Father.

When they saw the star, they were overjoyed. On coming to the house, they saw the child with his mother Mary, and they bowed down and worshiped him. Then they opened their treasures and presented him with gifts of gold, frankincense and myrrh.
Matthew 2:10-11

Father, over 2000 years have passed since Your beloved Son Jesus was born on this earth. I thank You for Your perfect plan of salvation and I praise Jesus for leaving heaven to be the perfect sacrifice that only He could fulfill. I, like the Magi, offer the best today that I have. I worship only You.

As soon as Jesus was baptized, he went up out of the water. At that moment heaven was opened, and he saw the Spirit of God descending like a dove and alighting on him. And a voice from heaven said, "This is my Son, whom I love; with him I am well pleased."
Matthew 3:16-17

What a wonderful event when the trinity of God the Father, Jesus His beloved Son, and the Holy Spirit were all celebrating Jesus' baptism. Thank You Father, for allowing us to enter the waters of baptism as Your Son did over 2000 years ago.

At once they left their nets and followed Him.
Matthew 4:20

When Jesus called Peter and his brother Andrew to follow, they left their nets of fishing and followed.
Father, I pray we will follow the disciples' example and follow Your plan for our lives today.

"You are the light of the world. A town built on a hill cannot be hidden.
Matthew 5:14

Father, we were born in darkness but the light that comes from us is the Holy Spirit that You sent when we accepted Your salvation from our trespasses against Your holiness. May we shine for You today that others may see Your gift of salvation that was paid with the ultimate love of Your Son Jesus on the cross.

This, then, is how you should pray: Our Father in heaven, hallowed be your name, your kingdom come, your will be done, on earth as it is in heaven. Give us today our daily bread. And forgive us our debts, as we also have forgiven our debtors. And lead us not into temptation, but deliver us from the evil one.
Matthew 6:9-13

Father, thank You for allowing Jesus to demonstrate a prayer that reflects a pure heart. Thank You for hearing our prayers at any time.

Therefore everyone who hears these words of mine and puts them into practice is like a wise man who built his house on the rock.
Matthew 7:24

Thank You Jesus for being our rock that is never shaken or moved. Your teachings that came from our Father stand for eternity. I pray we will learn, obey and practice them today and use discernment that comes only from You.

Jesus reached out his hand and touched the man. "I am willing," he said. "Be clean!"
Matthew 8:3

Jesus, You alone are worthy to wash away the sins of the world. Thank You for cleansing me and so many in my family's sins. I pray for the ones that have not bowed down and believed by faith for the forgiveness of their sins against God. May today be the day they choose to follow You.

As Jesus went on from there, he saw a man named Matthew sitting at the tax collector's booth. "Follow me," he told him, and Matthew got up and followed him.
Matthew 9:9

What a day in Matthews life when he turned from the world of power and money to a life of following Jesus by faith. He walked instead of being carried. Went from luxury and feasts to sleeping on the ground. His life changed in that moment of accepting the Savior of the world. Now he lives with Jesus in paradise just as we will do one day. Let us walk as Matthew for Jesus today and proclaim Jesus as the King of kings and the Lord of Lords.

I am sending you out like sheep among wolves. Therefore be as shrewd as snakes and as innocent as doves.
Matthew 10:16

Father, protect and deliver us from evil today. We live in a world that is roamed by Satan and his demons. Your light in us can be seen by the ones that have not accepted You. May we shine bright today and bring honor and glory to Your Holy name.

Come to me, all you who are weary and ·burdened, and I will give you rest. Take my yoke upon you and learn from me, for I am gentle and humble in heart, and you will find rest for your souls. For my yoke is easy and my burden is light.
Matthew 11:28-30

How You love us Jesus. May we find rest in our souls today. Peace in spirit and mind.

Here is my servant whom I have chosen, the one I love, in whom I delight.
Matthew 12:18

Father, how Your Son Jesus fulfilled Your will. Help me Father to live life and make the right choices that pleases You. Thank you for my family and the many blessings You have bestowed on me. Thank You most for forgiveness of my sins and reconciliation to You. I have peace and joy in knowing I am your child and so many in my family will be with You for eternity.

No, he answered, because while you are pulling the weeds, you may uproot the wheat with them. Let both grow together until the harvest.
Matthew 13:29-30

Father, evil will be with us while on earth. It is so assuring that the Holy Spirit dwells within me and battles for me each day. May Your angels protect us today in spiritual warfare that we are unaware takes place. Thank You for the victory that comes only through Your Son Jesus Christ.

When Jesus landed and saw a large crowd, he had compassion on them and healed their sickness.
Matthew 14:14

Thank You Jesus for being compassionate. John the Baptist had just been beheaded and You seeked a solitary place but the people followed. You loved the people so much You went to them and healed their sickness. You are so so good. You are ever present and always available when we seek You.

How many loaves do you have?" Jesus asked. "Seven," they replied, "and a few small fish." He told the crowd to sit down on the ground. Then he took the seven loaves and the fish, and when he had given thanks, he broke them and gave them to the disciples, and they in turn to the people. They all ate and were satisfied. Afterward the disciples picked up seven basketfuls of broken pieces that were left over.
Matthew 15:34-37

God, You took 7 loaves of bread and a few small fish and fed 4,000 men that day as well as the women and children. You can do what is impossible for man. You are a God who satisfies.

"But what about you?" he asked. "Who do you say I am?"
Matthew 16:15

I believe as Peter answered Jesus, "You are the Messiah, the Son of the living God." Let today be a day we show our love and devotion to the Son of God. Let the s love as He loved. Let us see creation as He saw. Let us look to the Father as He did.

He replied, "Because you have so little faith. Truly I tell you, if you have faith as small as a mustard seed, you can say to this mountain, 'Move from here to there,' and it will move. Nothing will be impossible· for you."
Matthew 17:20

Jesus, I believe that You are the Son of God and I confess You as my Lord. I believe that God raised You from the dead. I have faith that You will always have me in the palm of Your loving and caring hands. Nothing is impossible for You.

See that you do not despise one of these little ones. For I tell you that their angels in heaven always see the face of my Father in heaven.
Matthew 18:10

Father, thank You for the angels that You have watching over Your children. I know we are safe and secure in Your care.

Jesus looked at them and said, "With man this is impossible, but with God all things are possible."
Matthew 19:26

Father, You made it possible to establish a relationship with You. Through the resurrection of Jesus, separation from You was ended and we were offered a place by Your side for eternity. Thank You Father for allowing the Holy Spirit to reside in Your children and help us to please You. You are a God of holiness and greatness beyond human understanding.

Whoever wants to become great among you must be your servant, and whoever wants to be first must be your slave- just as the Son of Man did not come to be served, but to serve, and to give his life as a ransom for many.
Matthew 20:26-28

How opposite Jesus teachings were to the ways that the world has developed since the Garden of Eden.
Jesus demonstrated and lived a life of helping and serving others. He put others before self. By His life we may live.

But when the chief priests and the teachers of the law saw the wonderful things he did and the children shouting in the temple courts, "Hosanna to the Son of David," they were indignant.
Matthew 21:15

Father, the children recognized Your Son Jesus while the priests rejected. This world blinds through its offerings of satan. I pray we'll see through the eyes of children your love today.

Jesus replied: "'Love the Lord your God with all your heart and with all your soul and with all your mind.' This is the first and greatest commandment. And the second is like it: 'Love your neighbor as yourself.' All the Law and the Prophets hang on these two commandments."
Matthew 22:37-40

Father, love is in both of the commandments Jesus gave us to follow. I thank You for Your love for us and the ability to love that You let us experience. Thank You so much for our families and the love that we have for each other. May we love today as You loved us.

Blessed is He who comes in the name of the Lord.
Matthew 23:39

Jesus thank You for coming to earth and redeeming mankind. Without Your sacrifice we would not have hope of escaping eternal death and hell. Heaven and being with You is our destination. How glorious it will be.

Heaven and earth will pass away, but My words will never pass away.
Matthew 24:35

Thank You Jesus for giving us Your words to live by and knowing that You never change. We have peace knowing we are Yours for eternity.

Truly I tell you, whatever you did for one of the least of these brothers and sisters of mine, you did for me.
Matthew 25:40

Father, may we look beyond the outside to see the need on the inside.

Then one of the Twelve-the one called Judas Iscariot-went to the chief priests and asked, "What are you willing to give me if I deliver Him over to you?
Matthew 26:14-15

May we ever learn from the betrayal of Judas. A man that had walked with Jesus for three years ultimately let his foolish selfish ideology come between him and his salvation that would climax tomorrow night with a kiss. Let us never let anything come between our relationship to Jesus.

At that moment the curtain of the temple was torn in two from top to bottom. The earth shook, the rocks split and the tombs broke open. The bodies of many holy people who had died were raised to life.
Matthew 27:51-52

What a moment on this earth, the Son of God's Spirit left His body and entered paradise. God would no longer reside in a tabernacle or temple but through the Holy Spirit reside in man. Not long after a thief would also die next to Jesus and meet Him as promised in paradise. Even to the point of death Jesus asked that mankind believe and accept God. Let us show that kind of love and compassion today until one day we also meet Jesus in heaven.

The angel said to the women, "Do not be afraid, for I know that you are looking for Jesus, who was crucified. He is not here; He has risen, just as He said.
Matthew 28:5-6

Jesus defeated death that day once and for all. Our hope is through the resurrection. We are free of the chains of death and can be certain that we will- spend eternity with our Father. Praise the name of Jesus, our deliverer.

He reached out his hand and touched the man. "I am willing," he said. "Be clean!" Immediately the leprosy left him and he was cleansed.
Mark 1:41-42

What compassion Jesus has for mankind. Jesus not only healed the leper outside but more important He healed the leper on the inside. I pray Father that we will look and help those today know You.

Why does he eat with tax collectors and sinners?
Mark 2:16

Thank You Jesus for loving us when we were living lives separated from the Father. You loved us while we were still sinners. Now by the covering of Your blood, even though we still live imperfect lives, we are clean through You. May today be our best day as we magnify and worship Your Holy name.

When his family heard about this, they went to take charge of him, for they said, "He is out of his mind."
Mark 3:21

The family of Jesus did not realize that they had been living with the Son of God for over 30 years. His brother James would not believe until after the resurrection. We must accept Jesus as little children and believe. Confess and believe. A lifetime of peace and joy awaits. Jesus never leaves once asked to be the Lord of your life. Just open the door and let Jesus enter.

He got up, rebuked the wind and said to the waves, "Quiet! Be still!" Then the wind died down and it was completely calm.
Mark 4:39

Jesus, even the wind and the waves and all of nature obey You. God the creator can alter nature at His choosing. You can part seas, create clouds of fire, and provide shelter in the belly of a fish at Your command. What a great God we serve. May we look to You in our storms for the calmness that only You can provide.

He took her by the hand and said to her, "Talitha koum!" (which means "Little girl, I say to you, get up!"
Mark 5:41

Jesus took synagogue leader Jarius's 12 year old daughter who had died by the hand and restored her life. A household that was full of grief and sorrow was filled with joy and laughter. Thank You Jesus for bringing our dead souls to life and many take Your hand and start living for You today.

Later that night, the boat was in the middle of the lake, and Jesus was alone on land. He saw the disciples straining at the oars, because the wind was. against them.
Mark 6:47-48

That night, after Jesus had been alone praying on a mountainside to His Father. He looked out through the darkness of night and saw His disciples in distress. Just like the disciples, thank you Jesus when we are in distress and the waves and winds of this life are tossing, we know You intercede from heaven, the Holy Spirit is our rudder and God controls all.

You have let go of the commands of God and are holding on to human traditions.
Mark 7:8

Father, may we read Your word and not get turned from how You wish Your children to live. Let us not add or take away. You know what is best.

"But what about you?" he asked. "Who do you say I am?
Mark 8:29

The one question mankind individually must decide. The most important question. The question that has eternal implications. Thank You Father for presenting the question and allowing us to answer. May many like Peter reply, "You are the Messiah."

Then a cloud appeared and covered them, and a voice came from the cloud: "This is my Son, whom I love. Listen to him!" Suddenly, when they looked around, they no longer saw anyone with them except Jesus.
Mark 9:7-8

Father, may we listen and obey to what pleases You this day. Never a moment goes by that You do not watch and care for us. Thank You for Your ever presence as we journey through this life.

What do you want me to do for you?" Jesus asked him. The blind man said, "Rabbi, I want to see." "Go," said Jesus, "your faith has healed you." Immediately he received his sight and followed Jesus along the road
Mark 10:51-52

Bartimaeus of Jericho received his sight that day but more importantly he followed Jesus. Thank You Father for allowing so many in our family to also follow You. I pray that many who are blinded by sin today receive Your gift of salvation. You are such a wonderful Father.

Blessed is He who comes in the name of the Lord!
Mark 11:9

Father, how the people celebrated as Your Son Jesus entered Jerusalem. May we spread our cloaks and branches today for all that Jesus has done for our lives. Let us shout thanksgivings for only what He could do on the cross: Defeat death, allow us the choice to accept You as our God and be forgiven for eternity of our sins.

David himself, speaking by the Holy Spirit.
Mark 12:36

Thank You Holy Spirit for living inside mankind who have received forgiveness of sins from God through Jesus dying and defeating death through the resurrection. We are a temple of God. May our lives bring honor and glory to our God today.

What I say to you, I say to everyone: 'Watch!
Mark 13:37

Jesus has told us that He will one day come back to this earth. Father, I pray that many will come to know You today. May we live lives today that are peculiar to the world and one that unbelievers will want what we possess through the acceptance of Jesus as Lord; a relationship with You.

"Abba, Father," He said, "everything is possible for You. Take this cup from Me. Yet not what I will, but what You will."
Mark 14:36

Jesus and the cross were the only way that mankind could be reconciled to a Holy God. There was no other way. God gave His perfect, sinless Son as an atonement for man's sins. There was nothing man could do but praise the Lamb: Jesus paid it all.

With a loud cry, Jesus breathed His last.
Mark 15:37

At that moment of time, the Son of God died for our sins. He took on Himself every sin that each person would ever commit on this earth. He took the punishment so we might have eternal life with God. Praise Jesus for doing what we could not.

Don't be alarmed," he said. "You are looking for Jesus the Nazarene, who was crucified. He has risen!
Mark 16:6

Thank You Father for the resurrection of Jesus. Death was defeated once and for all that early morning right after sunrise. Let each sunrise remind us of that day when the tomb no longer held death; Jesus arose.

Everyone who heard this wondered about it, asking.
"What then is this child going to be?"
For the Lord's hand was with Him.
Luke 1:66

Father, the Holy Spirit was with John the Baptist even before his birth. Thank You for allowing the same Holy Spirit to always live inside Your children watching and directing our daily lives.

May we , like John, live today the path You wish us to walk.
Today in the town of David a Savior has been born to you; he is the Messiah, the Lord.
Luke 2:11

Father, Your begotten Son was born and the angel came to proclaim the good news. Another group of the heavenly host appeared praising God. Baby Jesus was born. What a day on this earth. Our Savior had come.

When all the people were being baptized, Jesus was baptized too. And as He was praying, heaven was opened and the Holy Spirit descended on Him in bodily form like a dove. And a voice came from heaven: "You are My Son, whom I love; with You I am well pleased.
Luke 3:21-22

What a beautiful picture, the Trinity. God the Father, The Holy Spirit, and Jesus. Thank Father for loving mankind so much. A love that is timeless.

Jesus answered, "It is said: 'Do not put the Lord your God to the test.'" When the devil had finished all this temptation, he left him until an opportune time.
Luke 4:12-13

Father, the same devil that tempted Jesus is still on this earth with deception and cunning. Please help us as we live for You to resist temptations and keep our eyes focused on the will You have for our lives. Lives to worship and live only for You!

Jesus reached out his hand and touched the man. "I am willing," he said. "Be clean!" And immediately the leprosy left him.
Luke 5:13

Jesus, You touched the leper. No one would get close because of the man's disease but You touched him. You healed his physical leprosy but most important washed him spiritually clean of sins.

For the mouth speaks what the heart is full of.
Luke 6:45

Father, may the Holy Spirit help us to speak as You would have us to today. Words of love and kindness to help encourage.

I tell you, among those born of women there is no one greater than John; yet the one who is least in the kingdom of God is greater than he."
Luke 7:28

Father, what a man of God John the Baptist was for Your son Jesus to say that no one born of women was greater than he. John came to prepare the way for Jesus. He did his duty and baptized many. The greatest of which was Your son Jesus. What a sight it must have been when You, Jesus, and the Holy Spirit were there at the baptism. May many rise today and accept Jesus and be baptized. May they like John the Baptist proclaim the name of Jesus.

But the seed on good soil stands for those with a noble and good heart, who hear the word, retain it, and by persevering produce a crop.
Luke 8:15

Father, thank You for providing good soil. May the Holy Spirit help tend to us as we journey and persevere today to live for our Lord.

Whoever is ashamed of me and my words, the Son of Man will be ashamed of them when he comes in his glory and in the glory of the Father and of the holy angels.
Luke 9:26

Father, I pray that our words and deeds honor You today. May we worship and look only to You as we take each step today.

Rejoice that your names are written in heaven.
Luke 10:20

Father, thank You for allowing us the peace and security of eternal fellowship with You. May many turn from eternal separation to eternal life through Your Son Jesus Christ this day.

He replied, "Blessed rather are those who hear the word of
God
and obey it."
Luke 11:28

Father, thank You for the Bible that lets us learn about what
pleases You and how You wish us to live our lives. Lives
devoted to You and bringing our children up to honor and
praise only You. May today be a day that brings honor not to
ourselves but to You our Lord.

I tell you, whoever publicly acknowledges me before others,
the Son of Man will also acknowledge before the angels of
God.
Luke 12:8

Thank You Jesus for being our counselor and mediator. You
are
forever our Lord and we never leave Your sight. What a
peace
we have as we are brought before God by his beloved Son as
one of His.

Jerusalem, Jerusalem, you who kill the prophets and stone those sent to you, how often I have longed to gather your children together, as a hen gathers her chicks under her wings.
Luke 13:34

How wonderful to know we are under Your protective hands Jesus. The Father is in control at all times and the Holy Spirit resides in us. What assurance as we walk through this fallen world.

Then the master told his servant, 'Go out to the roads and country lanes and compel them to come in, so that my house will be full.
Luke 14:23

Father, You have sent prophets, angels, and Your Son Jesus to show Your love and desire for humanity to come and worship You. May today many come to know You and we do our part to show our love for You.

In the same way, I tell you, there is rejoicing in the presence of the angels of God over one sinner who repents.
Luke 15:10

How wonderful to know that we were once lost but now found. We are united with our creator through the blood of Jesus. All of heaven rejoices. That is how special each one of us is to God.

He said to them, "You are the ones who justify yourselves in the eyes of others, but God knows your hearts. What people value highly is detestable in God's sight.
Luke 16:15

Father, may we live in a pleasing way to You today.

When he saw them, he said, "Go, show yourselves to the priests." And as they went, they were cleansed.
Luke 17:14

Father, 10 lepers left that day cleansed by Jesus. Only one, a Samaritan, returned praising God in a loud voice, and threw himself at the feet of Jesus. May we today remember our cleansing of sins and praise our God.

Then Jesus told his disciples a parable to show them that they should always pray and not give up.
Luke 18:1

Father, thank You for always being in control at all times. Nothing goes on in our lives or on this earth without Your knowing. May the Holy Spirit help us to live out the plan for our lives. Whatever we do may it be unto the Lord.

So he ran ahead and climbed a sycamore-fig tree to see him,
since Jesus was coming that way.
Luke 19:4

Zacchaeus and his house found forgiveness through Jesus that
day. Jesus on His way to the Cross had compassion on a
despised man tax collector who climbed a tree to see this one
called The Son of Man. May we all climb a little higher in our
relationship to Jesus today, Amen

The stone the builders rejected has become the cornerstone.
Luke 20:17

Jesus, You are our cornerstone. All we are is built upon You
being the center and holding us up. Let us use Your strength to
overcome the desires and snares set in our path today. Thank
You for the security and hope we have with You holding us up.
Heaven and earth will pass away, but my words will never pass

Heaven and earth will pass away, but my words will never pass
away.
Luke 21:33

Father, You have given us Your words in the Holy Bible. How
we love to read about Your love for us and know that nothing
ever happens in our walk today that You're not aware. You
overshadow us in each step. When this earth is no longer, we
will be for eternity with You. What hope and assurance from
Your word.

But from now on, the Son of Man will be seated at the right
hand of the mighty God.
Luke 22:69

Jesus sits next to You Father as an intercessor for us each
moment. We asked through Your Son to help us through the
Holy Spirit to bring honor and glory to Your name this day.
May we do nothing that dishonors You. We love You and praise
You. In Jesus' name we pray.

Truly I tell you, today you will be with me in paradise.
Luke 23:43

As we remember Good Friday, let us not forget one of Jesus' final acts on earth. He allowed a sinner that hung on a cross next to Him to be forgiven of his sins. Up to His last breath Jesus did His fathers will. Let us do the same.

And they stayed continually at the temple, praising God.
Luke 24:53

Father, may today our children and the world see our love for You by our continuous praise and worship. Let each step and every word that leaves our mouth be pleasing to You. Nothing comes before our devotion to You.

Yet to all who did receive Him, to those who believed in His name, He gave the right to become children of God.
John 1:12

Thank You Jesus for coming to earth to dwell among Your creation. John says You were the Word that became flesh and
made Your dwelling among mankind. You came from the Father full of grace and truth. May we share that truth today.

His mother said to the servants, "Do whatever He tells you."
John 2:5

Mary had watched and cared for her son Jesus for 30 years. What joy she must have had to see Him perform His first sign to reveal His glory. She would watch for 3 more years as Jesus came to fulfill the will of His Father

For God so loved the world that He gave His one and only Son, that whoever believes in Him shall not perish but have eternal life.
John 3:16

Thank You Father for loving us so much that You gave us Your Son and now we have chosen Him for eternal life. Thank You for the Holy Spirit that resides in Your children. You provide what we need.

Jesus answered, "Everyone who drinks this water will be thirsty again, but whoever drinks the water I give them will never thirst.
John 4:13-14

Thank You Jesus for providing the Way to the Father. We have drunk from Your well the water of life through believing in You. We will never thirst again. Your well satisfies and will never run dry for eternity.

When Jesus saw him lying there and learned that he had been in this condition for a long time, he asked him, "Do you want to get well?
John 5:6

The man had been an invalid for 38 years. Lying beside the Pool of Bethesda when Jesus came into his presence. He chose to pick up his mat and walk as Jesus instructed. Let us also do today as Jesus instructed. Live today to please the Father.

For my Father's will is that everyone who looks to the Son and believes in Him shall have eternal life, and I will raise them up at the last day.
John 6:40

We have hope in Jesus.

Whoever speaks on their own does so to gain personal glory, but he who seeks the glory of the one who sent him is a man of truth; there is nothing false about him.
John 7:18

Jesus, You are the truth. There is nothing found false in You. Let us today live by Truth and follow Your teachings. Let today bring honor and glory to Your name that is above all names: Jesus.

When Jesus spoke again to the people, He said, "I am the light of the world. Whoever follows Me will never walk in darkness, but will have the light of life."
John 8:12

Jesus You are the light that leads to our Father. Let us carry that light to others today. May many choose to leave the darkness of sin and come to You this day.

He replied, "Whether He is a sinner or not, I don't know. One thing I do know. I was blind but now I see!"
John 9:25

A blind man from birth was not afraid or ashamed to tell others what Jesus had done for him. Even though his parents did not take a stand, for fear of being put out of synagogue. Later Jesus would find him and offer him the choice to believe in The Son of Man: the man believed and truly received sight that day that would last for eternity.

My sheep listen to My voice; I know them, and they follow Me. I give them eternal life, and they shall never perish; no one will snatch them out of My hand.
John 10:27-28

Thank you Jesus for knowing me by name and my inmost heart. Thank you for Your promises that are always kept. May we have hope and assurance today that Jesus is our shepherd. We are to listen and follow only Him. He will lead us to green pastures and protect us with His staff.

When He had said this, Jesus called in a loud voice, "Lazarus, come out!" The dead man came out, his hands and feet wrapped with strips of linen ,and a cloth around his face. Jesus said to them, "Take off the grave clothes and let him go."
John 11:43-44

Just days before our Lord was to give His life for mankind's sins He thought not of Himself but on the ones He loves. May we show such acts today and each day to come to our fellow man. We no longer wear grave clothes but by Jesus blood we wear garments of righteousness.

I have come into the world as a light, so that no one who believes in Me should stay in darkness.
John 12:46

Thank you Jesus for coming to earth to save us from the darkness of sin and death. We are to live in Your light each day that gives us hope and joy. Your light shines for eternity.
Jesus

Jesus answered, "Unless I wash you, you have no part with Me."
John 13:8

Jesus took on the part of a servant to wash the feet of His disciples. The One who was by the Father as creation was formed and will soon defeat death through His resurrection showed us how we should live. Let us humble ourselves today and serve others.

Jesus answered, "I am the way and the truth and the life. No one comes to the Father except through me.
John 14:6

Thank You Jesus for preparing the way to our Father. Truth is found in Your word and we can have abundant life through acceptance of You in our lives. May many come to the Father through the name of Jesus today.

This is My command: Love each other.
John 15:17

Father, may today I love others as Your Son Jesus loved. You gave your Son for a sinful humanity and He chose to obey Your will and die a crucifixion death. This shows Your desire that we made in Your image leave the bondage on sun and death and be reconciled to Your love. Thank You for giving so much that we will never again be separated from You.

But very truly I tell you, it is for your good that I am going away. Unless I go away, the Advocate will not come to you.
John 16:7

The Spirit glorifies Jesus and now resides in us who believe. Jesus called us by the Spirit and now we are His. Let's let the Spirit guide us in truth today.

Now this is eternal life: that they know You, the only true God, and Jesus Christ, whom You have sent.
John 17:3

Father, thank You for allowing us to know You through Your Son Jesus and the Holy Spirit. We are safe for eternity in Your arms. We are no longer of this world but have an eternal home and fellowship with You. You always listen and always want what is best for Your children. How wonderful and what peace to have such a Father.

"You are a king, then!" said Pilate. Jesus answered, "You say that I am a king. In fact, the reason I was born and came into the world is to testify to the truth. Everyone on the side of truth listens to Me." "What is truth?" retorted Pilate.
John 18:37-38

Jesus is truth. Nothing is false in Him. We can always find comfort and peace when we put our trust in Jesus.

Jesus answered, "You would have no power over Me if it were not given to you from above."
John 19:11

Jesus knew that Pilate or anyone else was in control as He stood before them. Jesus knew His Sovereign Father was always in control. What a peace we have as His children to know He is always watching over us.

Then he said to Thomas, "Put your finger here; see my hands. Reach out your hand and put it into my side. Stop doubting and believe." Thomas said to him, "My Lord and my God!"
John 20:27-28

Father, may we never doubt. May we believe and never be confused or uncertain. John wrote this book so that we may believe. Thank You for the peace we receive once we believe.

Then the disciple whom Jesus loved said to Peter, "It is the Lord!" As soon as Simon Peter heard him say, "It is the Lord," he wrapped his outer garment around him (for he had taken it off) and jumped into the water.
John 21:7

Father, may today we have the same love and passion for Jesus as Peter did that day as he leaped from the boat into the water that was 100 yards from shore. May our lives be pleasing and devoted to You this day and not drift from Your perfect will.

Then they prayed, "Lord, you know everyone's heart.
Acts 1:·24

Father, the apostles looked to You to replace Judas. Let us always be sensitive to the Holy Spirit's guidance as we take each step today. Let all our decisions be pleasing to You.

But God raised Him from the dead, freeing Him from the agony of death, because it was impossible for death to keep its hold on Him.
Acts 2:24

Father, agony is being separated from You. Nothing will ever come between You and Your children all because of Jesus nailing our sins to the cross. What a glorious third day when You raised Him from the dead.
Praise Jesus for sacrificing Himself that we might have abundant life today and forevermore.

By faith in the name of Jesus, this man whom you see and know was made strong. It is Jesus' name and the faith that comes through him that has completely healed him, as you can all see.
Acts 3:16

Father, may we have faith through Jesus that today our lives are watched and Your will be done. Let each step and every word spoken be pleasing to You. Let others see the healing in our lives from sin as they saw in the lame man from birth that through the name of Jesus began to walk and jump. What a powerful name, the name of Jesu

Jesus is "the stone you builders rejected, which has become the cornerstone.' Salvation is found in no one else, for there is no other name under heaven given to mankind by which we must be saved."
Acts 4:11-12

Jesus, the name above all names. The name that leads to salvation and release from the filth of sins. Let us fall to our knees and submit this day to the one that is worthy of all honor and glory and praise.

Day after day, in the temple courts and from house to house, they never stopped teaching and proclaiming the good news that Jesus is the Messiah.
Acts 5:42

The apostles had just been flogged for proclaiming Jesus but left rejoicing that they had been found worthy of the Name. Father, thank You for America where we can go today and proclaim Jesus and rejoice as the apostles.

But they could not stand up against the wisdom the Spirit gave him as he spoke.
Acts 6:10

The Jews brought false charges against Stephen and had men lie about him. Stephen however, stood before the false accusers with his face as an angel. Let us also let the Holy Spirit show through our lives this day.

But Stephen, full of the Holy Spirit, looked up to heaven and saw the glory of God, and Jesus standing at the right hand of God. "Look," he said, "I see heaven open and the Son of Man standing at the right hand of God."
Acts 7:55-56

Father, what a witness Stephen was for Your name. He allowed You to use him to address corruption and sin of Your chosen people. We will one day also stand before You and Jesus. May we be found faithful as Stephen.

Then Philip began with that very passage of Scripture and told him the good news about Jesus.
Acts 8:35

Philip listened to the angel of the Lord and shared the Good News with the Ethiopian eunuch. Let us share with others our love for Jesus today.

As he neared Damascus on his journey, suddenly a light from heaven flashed around him.
He fell to the ground. and heard a voice say to him, "Saul, Saul, why do you persecute me?" "Who are you, Lord?" Saul asked.
Acts 9:3-5

Saul thought he was doing right but after the Lord revealed Himself on the road to Damascus soon Saul would receive a new name Paul. His life was forever changed. He would no longer be the one persecuting but would be persecuted in the name of Jesus Let us take up our cross and live today with the same fervor as Paul.

Then Peter began to speak: "I now realize how true it is that God does not show favoritism but accepts from every nation the one who fears him and does what is right.
Acts 10:34-35

Thank You Father for accepting Cornelius, his family, and close friends. You showed Peter that salvation is for all mankind that accepts and believes in God through His Son Jesus Christ. I pray that many come to know this forgiveness today.

The disciples were called Christians first at Antioch.
Acts 11:26

After Stephen's death, many disciples dispersed telling the Good News. Barnabus and Saul spent a year in Antioch teaching and telling Jews and Greeks. Let us continue telling the Good News to others today. The work of being a Christian.

Suddenly an angel of the Lord appeared and a light shone in the cell. He struck Peter on the side and woke him up. "Quick, get up!" he said, and the chains fell off Peter's wrists.
Acts 12:7

Father, You can do what You want, when You want, and how You want. You have caused the sun to delay setting and gates to open by themselves. Events that cannot be explained by man are possible with You. What a peace to know that You are in total control of the seemingly impossible.

God testified concerning him: 'I have found David son of Jesse, a man after my own heart; He will do everything I want him to do'
Acts 13:22

Father,. David was a man that made mistakes but how he loved You. David faced hills and valleys just as all mankind since the fall of mankind at the Garden of Eden. I pray that You will look on each of us today and we will be men and women after Your own heart.

The people of the city were divided; some sided with the Jews, others with the apostles.
Acts 14:4

In the past as in today, God is patient with mankind. Salvation is for all who believe. Some choose to believe in Jesus and others do not. Jesus is the one and only way to the Father.

They had such a sharp disagreement that they parted company. Barnabas took Mark and sailed for Cyprus, but Paul chose Silas and left, commended by the believers to the grace of the Lord. He went through Syria strengthening the churches.
Acts 15:39-41

Father, man may be Your children but they are still man and fight the sinful nature. Two great Godly men even had sharp disagreements between each other. It is hard for me to understand how much they had done for You and not been on the same page in thought. I am glad to know in further reading they reconcile and Mark turns out to be back in good standing with Paul. Let us be considerate and kind today as we do Your work and may we do our best to keep the sinful nature doors closed.

Paul came to Derbe and then to Lystra, where a disciple named Timothy lived, whose mother was Jewish and a believer but whose father was Greek.
Acts 16:1

Father, how important are momma and daddy's that live You. Children look to their parents each day to learn what it means to love You. May we be the parents You want us to be today. Thank You for being our good good Father.

For in Him we live and move and have our being.
Acts 17:28

What joy and peace to know that not a moment will go by today that You are not watching over us Father. Thank You for valuing us so much as Your children.

For he vigorously refuted his Jewish opponents in public debate, proving from the Scriptures that Jesus was the Messiah.
Acts 18:28

Father, a Jewish believer Apollos used scripture to help prove to others who come to know you. Please help me today through the Holy Spirit understand what Your Living Word wants me to know. Through faith I believe, through Your word I come to know Your nature and love for mankind.

He told the people to believe in the one coming after him, that is, in Jesus.
Acts 19:4

Father, let the wonderful name of Jesus be proclaimed through Your children today. Let the world know what we believe and many confess their displeasing to You and commit their lives today. May Your beloved Son be honored today as 2000 years ago as Paul proclaimed to the Ephesians.

However, I consider my life worth nothing to me;my only aim
is to finish the race and complete the task the Lord Jesus has
given me-the task of testifying to the good news of God's grace.
Acts 20:24

Father, I pray that today we will run the race strong for You. Let
each step we take be run with the mindset that You are at the
finish line cheering us to the victory that comes through Your
Son Jesus Christ.

When he would not be dissuaded, we gave up and said, "The
Lord's will be done."
Acts 21:14

Father, may our actions today be pleasing to You. Let us follow
Your will. Paul had been told he would be bound in Jerusalem.
Paul was not deterred even to the point of giving his life for the
name Lord Jesus. Thank You Father for our country where we
can speak freely of the name Lord Jesus.

And now what are you waiting for? Get up, be baptized and wash your sins away, calling on his name!
Acts 22:16

Father, Paul thought he was doing right by going to synagogues and beating and putting in prison those who followed Jesus. Thank you for allowing Paul and all who have accepted Jesus to be washed of their sins and be with You forever.

The following night the Lord stood near Paul and said, "Take courage! As you have testified about me in Jerusalem, so you must also testify in Rome."
Acts 23:11

A group of 40 men were about to ambush Paul and kill him. They had taken an oath not to eat until they carried out their plan. Little did they know that God was not finished using Paul. Let us as Paul knew that day: God is in total control when things of life look out of control.

So I strive always to keep my conscience clear before God and man.
Acts 24:16

Father, let today be one that when finished we will be able to have a clear conscience before You. Holy Spirit help make each choice and step pleasing to our Father. May Your Holy scriptures flow through our minds when temptations come.

Instead, they had some points of dispute with him about their own religion and about a dead man named Jesus who Paul claimed was alive.
Acts 25:19

Father, Your Son was sent by You to this earth around 2,020 years ago. He came willingly to do Your will and give mankind a choice to turn to You, away from sin and death. How heaven rejoiced when Your Son was born not in a palace but a manger. You have revealed to us that Jesus will come again. Spiritual warfare will cease and all Your advisories will be locked in hell for eternity. May we rejoice and find peace that Jesus is alive and seated at Your right hand watching over us day and night.

That the Messiah would suffer and, as the first to rise from the dead, would bring the message of light to His own people and to the Gentiles.
Acts 26:23

The Messiah has come to this earth as a little baby born in a manger. The little baby grew into a man and lived a sinless life. The Son of God would die on a cross carrying the sins of the world. The third day he defeated death and arose from the grave. He now sits at the right hand of His Father as our intercessor awaiting His return to earth. Let us continue telling of our Savior until His return. Thank you Jesus.

So keep up your courage, men, for I have faith in God that it will happen just as He told me.
Acts 27:25

Father, You are a holy righteous God that if You speak then it is truth. My hope is found in Your truth that never changes. In You we have security and unconditional love.

"Therefore I want you to know that God's salvation has been sent to the Gentiles, and they will listen!"
Acts 28:28

Father, how You love Jews and Gentiles. We are all made in Your image. You have made the way to You through Your Son Jesus Christ. The messiah for mankind. May we listen today and take Your words to our hearts and please You.

For since the creation of the world God's invisible qualities-His eternal power and divine nature-have been clearly seen, being understood from what has been made, so that people are without excuse.
Romans 1:20

Father, You have let us have a glimpse of how great You are by creation. We marvel at how You spoke and the universe was. The impossible by man is possible through You.

God "will repay each person according to what they have done."
Romans 2:6

Father, You look upon us not because of what we have done but because of what Jesus has done for us. We did not deserve to be in Your presence due to sin but because of acceptance and belief in Jesus You will forever watch over us for ages to come. Praise the name of Jesus.

This righteousness is given through faith in Jesus Christ to all who believe. There is no difference between Jew and Gentile, for all have sinned and fall short of the glory of God, and all are justified freely by His grace through the redemption that came by Christ Jesus.
Romans 3:22-24

There was no way Father that we could cross the bridge over to You. You extended the bridge of salvation through Your Son Jesus. It is a one way bridge that once crossed, we are assured that we are safe in Your arms.

The words "it was credited to Him" were written not for Him alone, but also for us to whom God will credit righteousness-for us who believe in Him who raised Jesus our Lord from the dead. He was delivered over to death for our sins and was raised to life for our justification.
Romans 4:23-25

Father, may we bring worship and praise to You today. All our hope rests in You alone our God.

But God demonstrates His own love for us in this: While we were still sinners, Christ died for us.
Romans 5:8

Praise the name of Jesus. The law brought forth to man eternal punishment for disobedience to God. Through acceptance of Jesus, we are justified to stand before our Father. Again, praise the name of Jesus.

For the wages of sin is death, but the gift of God is eternal life in Christ Jesus our Lord.
Romans 6:23

Father, we are no longer separated from You. We know from Your word that we have been assured of the gift of eternal life with You through Your Son Jesus Christ. Thank You Father for loving us so much.

Thanks be to God, who delivers me through Jesus Christ our Lord!
Romans 7:25

Nothing we could have done could have forgiven us of our sins were it not for what Jesus did for us. We come to the Father through his Son. Praise the name of Jesus for who He is, what He has done, and what He will do.

Who then is the one who condemns? No one. Christ Jesus who died-more than that, who was raised to life-is at the right hand of God and is also interceding for us.
Romans 8:34

Father, we have access to You through Jesus who is at Your right hand interceding on our behalf. May we never let a day pass that our prayers are not raised to You. Thank You Father for never letting us be alone while on this earth.

It does not, therefore, depend on human desire or effort, but on God's mercy.
Romans 9:16

Father, we could not have come to you except by Your offer of mercy. Mercy that was extended to all mankind. May many ask in the name of Jesus to receive that mercy today and submit to a life devoted to serving You.

If you declare with your mouth, "Jesus is Lord," and believe in your heart that God raised Him from the dead, you will be saved.
Romans 10:9

Father, thank You for Your promise that salvation comes through Your Son Jesus Christ. You are a faithful Father that forever keeps His promises. Thank You for the peace in knowing truth that comes from Your word.

Oh, the depth of the riches of the wisdom and knowledge of God!
Romans 11:33

Father, may Your Spirit help us understand Your living words. Let them remove anxiety and fear. May knowing that You are in control bring hope and peace.

Love must be sincere. Hate what is evil; cling to what is good.
Romans 12:9

Father, may we run from evil this day and anything that is
displeasing to You. May the Holy Spirit guide us in each
decision we make that it lead to Your good and perfect will.

Let everyone be subject to the governing authorities, for there is
no authority except that which God has established.
Romans 13:1

Father, when things look out of control, You are in total control.
Thank You for the peace in knowing that nothing happens that
You do not know.

If we live, we live for the Lord; and if we die, we die for the Lord. So, whether we live or die, we belong to the Lord.
Romans 14:8

Father, through belief and acceptance of Your Son Jesus we are Your children that will live with You for eternity. What peace to know we are Yours forever.

May the God of hope fill you with all joy and peace as you trust in Him, so that you may overflow with hope by the power of the Holy Spirit.
Romans 15:13

All our hope is in You Father. Having been set apart from sin and death through the Holy Spirit, we uplift honor and praise to You.

So that all the Gentiles might come to the obedience that comes from faith - to the only wise God be glory forever through Jesus Christ! Amen.
Romans 16:26-27

Father, You made mankind a way to have a relationship with You. From the first walks with Adam in the garden, You have wanted mankind to worship and know You. May many come to you through faith in Your Son Jesus today.

It is because of Him that you are in Christ Jesus, who has become for us wisdom from God-that is, our righteousness, holiness and redemption.
1 Corinthians 1:30

Father, all goodness comes from You. May we work and let our choices be acceptable to You today. Let us have peace deep in our souls that only comes when we are in fellowship with You.

What we have received is not the spirit of the world, but the Spirit who is from God, so that we may understand what God has freely given us.
1 Corinthians 2:12

Father, thank You for sending the Holy Spirit to help us discern while on earth. Before salvation, mankind is foolish and can't understand things that come from You. Holy Spirit may we accept and understand the deep things of God today.

Don't you know that you yourselves are God's temple and that God's Spirit dwells in your midst?
1 Corinthians 3:16

Father, may Your temple be found in order today. Let us remove all that is not pleasing to You.

Now it is required that those who have been given a trust must
prove faithful.
1 Corinthians 4:2

Father, may we prove faithful to You this day. Thank You for
your great love and care.

What business is it of mine to judge those outside the church?
1 Corinthians 5:12

Father, You are the great judge that knows each heart. May we
let the judgment of the world be kept to Your perfect justice.

Do you not know that your bodies are temples of the Holy Spirit, who is in you, whom you have received from God? You are not your own; you were bought at a price. Therefore honor God with your bodies.
1 Corinthians 6:19-20

Father, may we treat our bodies in a way that will honor You today. From what we choose to read to what we eat and drink, let it be wholesome and pleasing to You.

Were you a slave when you were called? Don't let it trouble you-although if you can gain your freedom, do so.
1 Corinthians 7:21

Father, thank You for freedom from sin and its death. Thank You for the United States that allows us to worship You in freedom. Thank You that slavery was abolished in our country through Men of God such as Martin Luther King that used Your living words to change hardened hearts and minds.

Yet for us there is but one God, the Father, from whom all things came and for whom we live; and there is but one Lord, Jesus Christ, through whom all things came and through whom we live.
1 Corinthians 8:6

Father, You are the one true God. All that is and ever will be was created by You. How magnificent is Your works. May we live for You today and live through Jesus Christ to please You.

But we did not use this right. On the contrary, we put up with anything rather than hinder the gospel of Christ.
1 Corinthians 9:12

Father, we strive to get our reward, the true reward, one day You will tell us well done my good and faithful servant. Let us not look to any other gratification but strive to please you today.

No one should seek their own good, but the good of others.
1 Corinthians 10:24

Father, may we look and see others today. Let us see mankind as Jesus. Mankind with physical, material and spiritual needs.

Everyone ought to examine themselves before they eat of the bread and drink from the cup.
1 Corinthians 11:28

Father, may we examine our lives today and act and think to please You.

Now you are the body of Christ, and each one of you is a part of it.
1 Corinthians 12:27

Father, we as believers in Your Son Jesus Christ were all baptized by one Spirit to form one body. May we function in our gifts today to bring honor and glory to Your name.

And now these three remain: faith, hope and love. But the greatest of these is love.
1 Corinthians 13:13

Father, You demonstrated love when You sent Your Son to die for our sins. Jesus loved us so much He died not for His sins but in the place of ours. The Holy Spirit shows His love for us daily by residing with us. Thank You Father for Perfect love.

For God is not a God of disorder but of peace-as in all the congregations of the Lord's people.
1 Corinthians 14:33

Father, thank You for the peace that comes from knowing that You are a God of order. In You, we align our lives this day. Lives of order and not chaos. Lives that look to You and not the world. We will have trials and live in a fallen world, but with our focus on You Father, we have peace knowing You are always in control.

Therefore, my dear brothers and sisters, stand firm. Let nothing move you. Always give yourselves fully to the work of the Lord, because you know that your labor in the Lord is not in vain.
1 Corinthians 15:58

Father, from sunrise till sunset let us stand firm. Let us lay down our head tonight knowing we gave ourselves fully to You.

Be on your guard; stand firm in the faith; be courageous; be strong. Do everything in love.
1 Corinthians 16:13-14

Father, today let us use Your word and the guidance of the Holy Spirit to represent You in a way that You are pleased. Thank You Jesus for the perfect example.

Now it is God who makes both us and you stand firm in Christ. He anointed us, set His seal of ownership on us, and put His Spirit in our hearts as a deposit, guaranteeing what is to come.
2 Corinthians 1:21-22

Father, what is to come is our hope. As we wade through this world and its ups and downs, let us always remember to stand firm in only You. We are Your children and You are our God.

Now when I went to Traos to preach the gospel of Christ and found that the Lord had opened a door for me, I still had no peace of mind, because I did not find my brother Titus there.
So
I said goodbye to them and went on to Macedonia.
2 Corinthians 2:12

Father, thank You for Your guidance as we walk for You today.
May Your doors be opened and our minds be at peace.

Now the Lord is the Spirit, and where the Spirit of the Lord is, there is freedom.
2 Corinthians 3:17

Thank You for freedom of sin Father. Freedom of mind knowing we are not squeezed by the pressures and bondage of
the consequences of sin. By the precious blood of Jesus, we are
free indeed.

So we fix our eyes not on what is seen, but on what is unseen, since what is seen is temporary, but what is unseen is eternal.
2 Corinthians 4:18

Father, may we not look to the world but to You this day. Let us focus on eternal rewards.

God made Him who had no sin to be sin for us, so that in Him we might become the righteousness of God.
2 Corinthians 5:21

Praise to God for allowing mankind the choice to be reconciled to Him through Jesus. Jesus, the name above all names.

I tell you, now is the time of God's favor, now is the day of salvation.
2 Corinthians 6:2

Father, thank You for the age of grace we live in. May many accept Your gift of salvation today. Let our lives reflect Your love this day.

Therefore, since we have these promises, dear friends, let us purify ourselves from everything that contaminates body and spirit, perfecting holiness out of reverence for God.
2 Corinthians 7:1

Father, thank You for accepting us as sinners. We are now Your children who" are loved unconditionally. We strive to honor and please You as our Father. We will never reach perfection as Jesus but let us try to make pleasing choices today with guidance from Your Holy Spirit. May Your name be glorified and no other.

For you know the grace of our Lord Jesus Christ, that though He was rich, yet for your sake He became poor, so that you through His poverty might become rich.
2 Corinthians 8:9

Thank You Jesus for Your willingness to do Your Fathers will. You left heaven to a sinful earth to defeat death and give us a choice to accept the Fathers gift of salvation and freedom from the bondage of sin. Praise the name of Jesus.

Thanks be to God for His indescribable gift!
2 Corinthians 9:15

Father, thank You for using Your children to help so many on this earth. Through obedience to You, may Your children show a dying world love and compassion today. May our actions point the lost to the greatest gift You gave: Your Son Jesus.

But, " Let the one who boasts boast in the Lord." For it is not the one who commends himself who is approved, but the one whom the Lord commends.
2 Corinthians 10: 17-18

Father, only You are worthy of praise. We strive to please You and bring honor and glory to Your name. Let our work and actions point only to You.

In fact, you even put up with anyone who enslaves you or exploits you or takes advantage of you or puts on airs or slaps you in the face.
2 Corinthians 11:20

Father, let us have discernment on this day and not be deceived by satan and his servants. Let us be coherent of Your Spirit and direction. We are Your children who wish to follow only You.

But he said to me, "My grace is sufficient for you, for my power is made perfect in weakness.
2 Corinthians 12:9

Father, thank You for Your grace that is always sufficient in all we will go through this day. You are with us and all is in Your control. May Your power be manifested through our weaknesses and we grow stronger for you today.

May the grace of the Lord Jesus Christ, and the love of God, and the fellowship of the Holy Spirit be with you all.
2 Corinthians 13:14

Father, we can step into this day with the assurance that You have provided all we need to make it through this day.

Am I now trying to win the approval of human beings, or of God? Or am I trying to please people? If I were still trying to please people, I would not be a servant of Christ.
Galatians 1:10

Father, may we look to please only You this day. Let us make choices that bring honor only to You.

I have been crucified with Christ and I no longer live, but Christ lives in me. The life I now live in the body, I live by faith in the Son of God, who loved me and gave Himself for me.
Galatians 2:20

We have life through Jesus. A life as God intended. One that allows us to be separated from sin and allows our Holy Father to look upon us. Our Father knows us by name and desires our fellowship. What a wonderful day to live for Him.

There is neither Jew nor Gentile, neither slave nor free, nor is there male and female, for you are all one in Christ Jesus.
Galatians 3:28

Father, thank You for seeing us as your children. We are all one in Jesus. Nothing will ever separate us from You. Thank You for another day of life on this earth to worship and honor Your name.

So you are no longer a slave, but God's child; and since you are His child, God has made you also an heir.
Galatians 4:7

Father, no one on earth loves a child like their father and mother. To know You love with a greater love is beyond understanding. What a blessing to be Your Child.

So I say, walk by the Spirit, and you will not gratify the desires of the flesh.
Galatians 5:16

Father, each day there is conflict with the flesh and the Spirit. May we make choices today that please You. We will only be able to make those choices if our relationship is strong with You.

Whoever sows to please their flesh, from the flesh will reap destruction; whoever sows to please the Spirit, from the Spirit will reap eternal life.
Galatians 6:8

Father, may we do good to all today. Goodness that comes from the Spirit and not our flesh. You're a good good Father.

And God placed all things under His feet and appointed Him to be head over everything for the church, which is His body, the fullness of Him who fills everything in every way.
Ephesians 1:22-23

Father, how wonderful to know through Your word that Jesus has done all needed to bring us into fellowship with You. Jesus has authority and is the head of us as Your children. We could never have been in Your presence if not for Jesus. Eternal praise to the name of Jesus.

And in Him you too are being built together to become a dwelling in which God lives by his Spirit.
Ephesians 2:22

Father, I pray that we allow things that are pleasing to You in our thoughts and hearts today. May today we build rather than tear down.

In Him and through faith in Him we may approach God with freedom and confidence.
Ephesians 3:12

Father, through Jesus Your Son we are able to come before Your throne with our thoughts and prayers. Knowing You hear our every word and know our every thought is beyond wonderful. Let us go and lift Your name to others for what You have done for us.

Do not let any unwholesome talk come out of your mouths, but only what is helpful for building others up according to their needs, that it may benefit those who listen.
Ephesians 4:29

Father, may we only speak words today that would honor You.

Be very careful, then, how you live -not as unwise but as wise, making the most of every opportunity, because the days are evil.
Ephesians 5:15-16

Father, You have shown us through Your Son Jesus how we should live on this earth. Let us follow His teachings this day and bring honor to Your name.

Finally, be strong in the Lord and in His mighty power. Put on the full armor of God, so that you can take your stand against the devil's schemes.
Ephesians 6:10-11

Father, let us put on the full armor that You provide. Our struggles against the powers of this dark world can only be won with Your perfect equipment.

For to me, to live is Christ and to die is gain.
Philippians 1:21

Father, thank You for the assurance that You are with us each moment of every day. True life began by acceptance of Your Son Jesus. We will worship You through eternity.

Therefore God exalted Him to the highest place and gave Him the name that is above every name, that at the name of Jesus every knee should bow, in heaven and on earth and under the earth, and every tongue acknowledge that Jesus Christ is Lord, to the glory of God the Father.
Philippians 2:9-11

May the name of Jesus be on our minds and hearts as we go through this day. May we honor and praise the name above all names. Jesus Christ is Lord.

But our citizenship is in heaven. And we eagerly await a Savior from there, the Lord Jesus Christ, who, by the power that enables Him to bring everything under His control, will transform our lowly bodies so that they will be like His glorious body.
Philippians 3:20-21

Father, thank You for the assurance we will be with You for eternity. We will no longer experience evil and pain. We will be in glorified bodies. What a day that will be.

Whose names are in the book of life.
Philippians 4:3

Father, praise Your Holy name that we have life through Your Son Jesus Christ.

For He has rescued us from the dominion of darkness and brought us into the kingdom of the Son He loves, in whom we have redemption, the forgiveness of sins.
Colossians 1:13-14

Thank You Father for your perfect plan that was a mystery for so many until Jesus came and fulfilled prophecy. Through Jesus, we have become without blemish and free from accusation.

My goal is that they may be encouraged in heart and united in love, so that they may have the full riches of complete understanding, in order that they may know the mystery of God, namely, Christ, in whom are hidden all the treasures of wisdom and knowledge.
Colossians 2:2-3

Father, may we grow in wisdom and knowledge by following Jesus today. Let us hold to Jesus each step and breathe we take.

Whatever you do, work at it with all your heart, as working for the Lord, not for human masters.
Colossians 3:23

Father, whatever and whoever You put before us today let us see as You see and do as You do. May we be sensitive to the pull of the Holy Spirit and be drawn to Your perfect will.

Devote yourselves to prayer, being watchful and thankful.
Colossians 4:2

Father, what a blessing to know that we can talk to the creator of all the universe through Jesus. You care and know each of Your children by name. Each word we utter in prayer is sweet incense. Thank You for answering our prayers according to Your perfect will.

They tell how you turned to God from idols to serve the living and true God, and to wait for his Son from heaven, whom He raised from the dead-Jesus, who rescues us from the coming wrath.
1 Thessalonians 1: 9-10

Father, we as the Thessalonians live in the age expecting the return of Jesus. Each day we live our lives with the hope that today is the day Your church will be raptured. Thank You Father for Your great love and plan for Your children.

We are not trying to please people but God, who tests our hearts.
1 Thessalonians 2:4

Father, may all we do today be for Your glory and not the world, power, or riches. Let our work honor You.

May He strengthen your hearts so that you will be blameless and holy in the presence of our God and Father when our Lord Jesus comes with all His holy ones.
1 Thessalonians 3:13

May our heart be strengthened knowing that Jesus is our rock that never moves or is shaken.

Make it your ambition to lead a quiet life: You should mind your own business and work with your hands, just as we told you, so that your daily life may win the respect of outsiders and so that you will not be dependent on anybody.
1 Thessalonians 4:11-12

Father, today is a day like all others to show our love to You by our actions and deeds. May Your name be honored today.

Rejoice always, pray continually, give thanks in all circumstances; for this is God's will for you in Christ Jesus.
1 Thessalonians 5:16-18

Father. may we live and practice today the will that You have shown us in Your word. Let us stay focused and let not our will but Yours be done.

We pray this so that the name of our Lord Jesus may be glorified in you, and you in Him, according to the grace of our God and the Lord Jesus Christ.
2 Thessalonians 1:12

Father, may the choices we make this day honor You and not men. May we stand firm in Your teachings and bring glory to Your name. Let us shine for You.

So then, brothers and sisters, stand firm and hold fast to the teachings we passed on to you, whether by word of mouth or by letter.
2 Thessalonians 2:15

Father, help us to stand firm today. May we tell and show others today about You and how our lives are devoted to serving You.

But the Lord is faithful, and He will strengthen you and protect you from the evil one.
2 Thessalonians 3:3

Father, just as Paul asked prayer that they be delivered from wicked and evil people as the evil one, knowing You are with us today gives peace and strength to try our best to live the life you expect from Your children.

The grace of our Lord was poured out on me abundantly, along with the faith and love that are in Christ Jesus.
1 Timothy 1:14

Father, thank You for bathing us in Your grace and mercy. We have our names in The Book of Life and have eternity to spend with You.

This is good, and pleases God our Savior, who wants all people to be saved and to come to a knowledge of the truth.
1 Timothy 2:3-4

Father, thank You for wanting all of mankind to accept salvation through Your Son Jesus Christ. May many come to You this day.

Here is a trustworthy saying: Whoever aspires to be an overseer desires a noble task.
1 Timothy 3:1

Father, we pray for the overseer's of Your church. Let us be encouragers to them and lift them up as they minister and preach.

Don't let anyone look down on you because you are young, but set an example for the believers in speech, in conduct, in love, in faith and in purity.
1 Timothy 4:12

Father, You can do great things through the young and the old. May we, regardless of age grow each day in our knowledge of Your word to refrain from the snares of satan and live a life fully devoted to Your perfect will.

Do not rebuke an older man harshly, but exhort him as if he were your Father. Treat younger men as brothers, older women as mothers, and younger women as sisters, with absolute purity.
1 Timothy 5:1-2

Father, may we treat others in a way that is pleasing to You.

God, the blessed and only Ruler, the King of kings and Lord of lords, who alone is immortal and who lives in unapproachable light, whom no one has seen or can see. To Him be honor and might forever. Amen.
1 Timothy 6:15-16

Father, You are beyond my understanding. You love with perfect love, protect with a mighty hand, and dwell within our very soul.

I know whom I have believed, and am convinced that He is able
to guard what I have entrusted to Him until that day.
2 Timothy 1:12

Praise the name of Jesus, the destroyer of death and bondage to
sin. May we live today with gladness and security in knowing
Jesus can be trusted to never leave or forsake us.

Nevertheless, God's solid foundation stands firm, sealed with
this inscription: "The Lord knows those who are His."
2 Timothy 2:19

Father, thank You for delivering us from the penalty of
wickedness and sin. Let our actions be pleasing to You today.
Actions that are from love that You have shown us.

All Scripture is God-breathed and is useful for teaching, rebuking, correcting and training in righteousness, so that the servant of God may be thoroughly equipped for every good work.
2 Timothy 3:16-17

Father, may we read Your Word and be equipped to do good this day.

Now there is in store for me the crown of righteousness, which the Lord, the righteous Judge, will award to me on that day -and not only to me, but also to all who have longed for His appearing.
2 Timothy 4:8

Father, how we long for the appearing of Jesus Your Son and being in Your presence for eternity. The day is coming and let us live today in anticipation and hope.

In the hope of eternal life, which God, who does not lie, promised before the beginning of time.
Titus 1:2

Father, it is beyond our understanding of eternity and before the beginning of time. We put our trust in You and know You are our creator and there is nothing that is that You have not created.

I————————————I

For the grace of God has appeared that offers salvation to all people. It teaches us to say "No" to ungodliness and worldly passions, and to live self-controlled, upright and godly lives in this present age, while we wait for the blessed hope-the appearing of the glory of our great God and Savior, Jesus Christ, who gave Himself for us to redeem us from all wickedness and to purify for Himself a people that are His very own, eager to do what is good.
Titus 2:11-14

Father, may we say no today when ungodliness enters our minds and comes before us. Let us be eager to do what is good.

But when the kindness and love of God our Savior appeared, He saved us, not because of righteous things we had done, but because of His mercy.
Titus 3:4

Father, we thank You for kindness and love. You showed us mercy we did not deserve but out of love for us You sent Your Son. Salvation made possible through Your love.

Your love has given me great joy and encouragement, because you, brother, have refreshed the hearts of the Lord's people.
Philemon 1:7

Father, thank You for Your children that are in our lives that refresh our hearts with love and encouragement. May we go today and give joy and hope to the world through the message of Jesus.

The Son is the radiance of God's glory and the exact
representation of His being, sustaining all things by His
powerful
word.
Hebrews 1:3

Jesus now sits by the Majesty in heaven. Jesus came to
provide
a way to You Father. We no longer have to be told by
prophets
but You have spoken through Your Son. Praise the name of
Jesus.

How shall we escape if we ignore so great a salvation?
Hebrews 2:3

Jesus, You have shown Your great love and mercy for
mankind
by coming to earth and giving Your life so mankind could
choose to have forgiveness for their sins. Praise Your name
for
demonstrating the ultimate sacrifice and true love.

Therefore, holy brothers and sisters, who share in the heavenly calling, fix your thoughts on Jesus, whom we acknowledge as our apostle and high priest.
Hebrews 3:1

Father, may we look to Jesus today and stay clear of things that displease You. Thank You Holy Spirit for helping us fight spiritual battles. Let our thoughts stay fixed on Jesus.

For the word of God is alive and active. Sharper than any double-edged sword, it penetrates even to dividing soul and spirit, joints and marrow; it judges the thoughts and attitudes of the heart.
Hebrews 4:12

Father, Your word is our bread and water to survive. It gives us strength to fight battles, to feel love, to experience joy, and to live in peace. May we eat and drink of it each day we live.

During the days of Jesus' life on earth, He offered up prayers and petitions with fervent cries and tears to the one who could save Him from death, and He was heard because of his reverent submission.
Hebrews 5:7

Thank You Jesus for submission to the Father. May we choose today to submit to our Fathers will.

We have this hope as an anchor for the soul, firm and secure. It enters the inner sanctuary behind the curtain, where our forerunner, Jesus, has entered on our behalf. He has become a high priest forever, in the order of Melchizedek.
Hebrews 6:19-20

Thank You Jesus for being our high priest who cares and carries our petitions before our Father. You are for us and not against us.

Unlike the other high priests, He does not need to offer sacrifices day after day, first for his own sins, and then for the sins of the people. He sacrificed for their sins once for all when He offered himself.
Hebrews 7:27

Thank You Father for Your promise that Jesus will be our high priest forever. Jesus is made perfect forever. Once we were washed of our sins they were removed forever. We became a child of God.

For if there had been nothing wrong with that first covenant, no place would have been sought for another. But God found fault with the people.
Hebrews 8:7-8

Father, Your creation of man did not keep the first covenant with You. You always keep Your promises. Thank You for allowing mankind a second chance and establishing the second covenant that we celebrate this week with Easter. Praise the name of Jesus.

How much more, then, will the blood of Christ, who through the eternal Spirit offered Himself unblemished to God, cleanse our consciences from acts that lead to death, so that we may serve the living God!
Hebrews 9:14

Father, the High Priest would go once a year into the Most Holy Place of the tabernacle and offer blood for the sins of himself and people. Today we praise the name of Jesus who entered heaven itself with his own shed blood. The perfect sacrifice. Praise the name of Jesus.

Their sins and lawless acts
I will remember no more." And where these have been forgiven, sacrifice for sin is no longer necessary.
Hebrews 10:17-18

Father, we are told by the Holy Spirit that we are no longer slaves to sin and fear. Jesus died for our sins and transgressions in the cross of Calvary. Our sins are at the foot of the cross and never is another sacrifice needed. Praise the name of Jesus.

And without faith it is impossible to please God, because anyone who comes to Him must believe that He exists and that He rewards those who earnestly seek Him.
Hebrews 11:6

Father, we come to You this day to worship and uplift Your Holy name. Praise the name of Jesus whom You raised from the grave and defeated sin and death forever.

And let us run with perseverance the race marked out for us, fixing our eyes on Jesus, the pioneer and perfecter of faith.
Hebrews 12:1-2

Father, may we go about this day looking to Jesus and be mindful of pleasing You. May the Holy Spirit's guidance be accepted and done. Let us run to You and Your will be done.

Jesus Christ is the same yesterday and today and forever.
Hebrews 13:8

Thank You Jesus for being perfect and for never changing. You have and always will be the perfect Son of God. You bore our sins that we may be saved by mercy and grace. Praise Your name that is worthy of all honor and praise: Jesus.

If any of you lacks wisdom, you should ask God, who gives generously to all without finding fault, and it will be given to you.
James 1:5

Father, true wisdom comes from following Your words and will. May we seek You today with all our being and be pleasing with our thoughts and actions.

For whoever keeps the whole law and yet stumbles at just one point is guilty of breaking all of it.
James 2:10

Father, how we want to please You. We try so hard and still can not meet Your holiness. We have peace in knowing You love us as we are and know our hearts. You are so proud of Your children even though we are imperfect.

But the wisdom that comes from heaven is first of all pure; then peace-loving, considerate, submissive, full of mercy and good fruit, impartial and sincere.
Peacemakers who sow in peace reap a harvest of righteousness.
James 3:17-18

Father, may we seek the wisdom You offer.

Come near to God and He will come near to you.
James 4:8

Father, how wonderful to know that You like us for who we are.
Even in our shortcomings, you wish to fellowship with us.
Thank You for being patient in our faults and showing grace
and mercy. You are the perfect Father.

You too, be patient and stand firm, because the Lord's coming is
near.
James 5:8

Father, only You know the day, hour, and second that You will
rapture Your church. Let us live today in anticipation of that
wonderful day. May many come to know You today and be
among Your children that will be taken up to You in a twinkling
of an eye.

Though you have not seen Him, you love Him; and even though you do not see Him now, you believe in Him and are filled with an inexpressible and glorious joy.
1 Peter 1:8

Father, there is joy knowing we are Your children and You know each step we will take today. Thank You for protection and guidance as we live to honor You today.

He himself bore our sins" in His body on the cross, so that we might die to sins and live for righteousness; "by His wounds you have been healed."
1 Peter 2:24

We are no longer held in the bondage of sin. We have been set free by the Cross. Praise the name of Jesus.

But in your hearts revere Christ as Lord. Always be prepared to give an answer to everyone who asks you to give the reason for the hope that you have. But do this with gentleness and respect.
1 Peter 3:15

Father, let us live today prepared to give witness to the love You have shown us. A love that is beyond understanding but is felt in our inner souls.

So then, those who suffer according to God's will should commit themselves to their faithful Creator and continue to do good.
1 Peter 4:19

Father, thank you for the blessing of living in our country where we have the freedom to worship You without fear of suffering torture or death. Freedom is always paid with a high price.

Cast all your anxiety on Him because He cares for you.
1 Peter 5:7

Father, thank You for loving us and caring about every aspect of our lives. It is comforting to know that the things that we struggle with are all possible to overcome with You.

He received honor and glory from God the Father when the voice came to Him from the Majestic Glory, saying, "This is My Son, whom I love; with Him I am well pleased." We ourselves heard this voice that came from heaven when we were with Him on the sacred mountain.
2 Peter 1:17-18

Father, Jesus always was in perfect fellowship with You and did Your perfect will. Let us look to Jesus example and strive today to follow only You.

But there were also false prophets among the people, just as there will be false teachers among you.
2 Peter 2:1

Father, help us to use discernment in this world we live in of false teachers and ones that do deeds falsely in Your name. We wish to only follow You and Your will.

The Lord is not slow in keeping His promise, as some understand slowness. Instead He is patient with you, not wanting anyone to perish, but everyone to come to repentance.
2 Peter 3:9

Father, thank You for your patience that will allow many to come and know You today. Let all we do today not hinder but help in telling others about You. Thank You for Your indescribable love for mankind.

If we confess our sins, He is faithful and just and will forgive us our sins and purify us from all unrighteousness.
1 John 1:9

Father, thank You for the assurance of Your forgiveness. You say it and it is so.

My dear children, I write this to you so that you will not sin. But if anybody does sin, we have an advocate with the Father-Jesus Christ, the Righteous One.
1 John 2:1

Father, we have Jesus our advocate that sits at Your right hand. How we want to please only You Father. May we show our love for You today by our actions and choices. Let today be a day of worship and praise to the name above all names.

See what great love the Father has lavished on us, that we
should be called children of God!
1 John 3:1

Father, we are Your children. What a wonderful feeling to know
our names are in the Book of Life. May we go this day into the
world and proclaim Your great love.

If anyone acknowledges that Jesus is the Son of God, God lives
in them and they in God. And so we know and rely on the love
God has for us.
1 John 4:15-16

Father, our hope relies on our relationship with You made
possible through acceptance of Your son Jesus Christ. May the
Holy Spirit help lead us today in Your perfect will.

We know also that the Son of God has come and has given us understanding, so that we may know Him who is true. And we are in Him who is true by being in His Son Jesus Christ. He is the true God and eternal life.
1 John 5:20

Father, thank You for sending understanding and insight into Your plan for mankind, may we search Your Word and hear Your great love for us.

Anyone who runs ahead and does not continue in the teaching of Christ does not have God; whoever continues in the teaching has both the Father and the Son.
2 John 1:9

Father, may we follow Your Word and the teachings of Jesus. Let us not be deceived by false teachings of the world. We can only do this by the Holy Spirit. Thank You for providing all we need to follow You.

Dear friend, do not imitate what is evil but what is good.
3 John 1:11

Father, may we do what is good today. We know good because
we know You.

But you, dear friends, by building yourselves up in your most
holy faith and praying in the Holy Spirit, keep yourselves in
God's love as you wait for the mercy of our Lord Jesus Christ to
bring you to eternal life.
Jude 1:20-21

Father, may we stay strong in Your word and through praying in
the Holy Spirit. Thank You for providing Your word to help us
make choices for You this day.

"I am the Alpha and the Omega," says the Lord God, "who is, and who was, and who is to come, the Almighty."
Revelation 1:8

Father, we honor You and praise You for Your great love for us that is indescribable. Knowing that You love us and watch over us brings peace and joy.

Whoever has ears, let them hear what the Spirit says to the churches. To the one who is victorious, I will give the right to eat from the tree of life, which is in the paradise of God.
Revelation 2:7

Father, victory comes through the acceptance of Your Son Jesus Christ. The victory has been won and the future is certain. Your church is Yours and paradise in heaven awaits. May many become a part of Your church today.

To the one who is victorious, I will give the right to sit with Me on my throne, just as I was victorious and sat down with My Father on his throne.
Revelation 3:21

Father, how we want to be victorious today and each day to one day sit with Jesus in His throne. Thank You Holy Spirit in your guidance to victory as we grow stronger in our relationship to Jesus. Let us finish the race strong.

Day and night they never stop saying: "'Holy, holy, holy is the Lord God Almighty,' who was, and is, and is to come."
Revelation 4:8

Father, we bow at Your holiness. We look to Your creation and see a glimpse of Your greatness. You are holy.

Then I heard every creature in heaven and on earth and under the earth and on the sea, and all that is in them, saying: "To Him who sits on the throne and to the Lamb be praise and honor and glory and power, for ever and ever!"
Revelation 5:13

Father, Your creation worships You. May mankind cry out in worship today as You intended before we let sin destroy our relationship with You. By the blood of Jesus we have been restored, our praise and worship once again is lifted to You.

I watched as the Lamb opened the first of the seven seals.
Revelation 6:1

Worthy is the Lamb.

For the Lamb at the center of the throne will be their shepherd;
'He will lead them to springs of living water.' And God will
wipe away every tear from their eyes.'
Revelation 7:17

Thank You Jesus for living water that allows eternal fellowship
with You. The Lamb of God is worthy of all honor and praise.
We shall worship our compassionate Father through eternity
with happiness and thanksgiving.

The smoke of the incense, together with the prayers of God's
people, went up before God from the angel's hand.
Revelation 8:4

Father, You hear the prayers of Your children. All the billions of
prayers lifted today are important to You. We are never alone.

The rest of mankind who were not killed by these plagues still did not repent of the work of their hands; they did not stop worshiping demons, and idols of gold, silver, bronze, stone and wood-idols that cannot see or hear or walk. Nor did they repent of their murders, their magic arts, their sexual immorality or their thefts.
Revelation 9:20-21

Father, I pray that our hearts will be sensitive to the pull and movement of the Holy Spirit. You give us free will to live our lives for You and make choices that show our love for You. May our actions today reflect our devotion for what Jesus has done to make it possible to be in fellowship with You.

And when the seven thunders spoke, I was about to write; but I heard a voice from heaven say, "Seal up what the seven thunders have said and do not write it down."
Revelation 10:4

Father, may we have obedience as John this day. Let us do as Your word directs. Let us live today in a way pleasing to You.

But after the three and a half days the breath of life from God entered them, and they stood on their feet, and terror struck those who saw them.
Revelation 11:11

Father, You are the breath of life. With Your breath You gave life to Adam and tell us of a time when You will breathe life into Your two witnesses who have been dead for 3 and a half days during the first 3 and a half years of the tribulation period. You have given us insight into the things to come. We will be in heaven during the tribulation period and we pray many will come to know You today and never take the chance of experiencing such a terrible time.

Then the dragon was enraged at the woman and went off to wage war against the rest of her offspring–those who keep God's commands and hold fast their testimony about Jesus.
Revelation 12:17

Father, what a wonderful mother Mary was to Jesus. We thank You for mother's today that protect and love. May many women come to know You that they may prepare their children for the snares of this life and show them the love of Jesus each day in the way they live for You.

This calls for patient endurance and faithfulness on the part of God's people.
Revelation 13:10

Father, may we be found faithful to You today. Let us make choices that are pleasing to You.

And I heard a sound from heaven like the roar of rushing waters and like a loud peal of thunder. The sound I heard was like that of harpists playing their harps.
Revelation 14:2

Father, how wonderful the sound John heard coming from heaven. You are the creator of sound and music. Our ears have heard the sound of Your creation and imagine how much more beautiful the sounds will be in Your perfect heaven. May we take time to listen today and sing songs of praise to You.

Great and marvelous are Your deeds, Lord God Almighty. Just and true are Your ways, King of the nations.
Revelation 15:3

Father, we want to follow Your ways and not our own. Following Your ways provides peace even when in the storms. Holy Spirit, our hearts are filled with joy knowing You are guiding us this day.

And I heard the altar respond: "Yes, Lord God Almighty, true and just are your judgments."
Revelation 16:7

Father, how assuring to know Your judgements are true and just. We fall before You today in the name of Jesus our Lord and Savior and ask forgiveness for our transgressions. Thank You for the mercy and grace You extended to us through Your beloved Jesus. May many come to You today and not face the judgment of unbelievers in Your Word.

They will wage war against the Lamb, but the Lamb will triumph over them because He is Lord of lords and King of kings -and with Him will be His called, chosen and faithful followers."
Revelation 17:14

Father, there has never been nor ever be any war that You have not won. You are our Almighty God who we put our trust and hope. Thank You for allowing us to be born again as Your followers through the blood of Jesus. We are victorious over death by the acceptance of Your son Jesus Christ through the cross and resurrection.

She will be consumed by fire, for mighty is the Lord God who judges her.
Revelation 18:8

Father, a time will come that the sins of man will be judged. We are to worship You and live lives joyfully as servants of Your Holy name. May we have the passion to grow closer to You today and submit to Your perfect will for our lives. Lives to please you and live as You intended as laid out in Your Word through the Bible.

Then the angel said to me;'Write this:Blessed are those who are invited to the wedding supper of the Lamb!" And he added, "These are the true words of God."
Revelation 19:9

Father, how wonderful it will be when we sit down with You one day and eat the wedding supper of the Lamb. We will be reunited with loved ones and worship' You our God for eternity. May many come to know You this day and reserve their seat at the table.

And I saw the dead, great and small, standing before the throne, and books were opened. Another book was opened, which is the Book of Life.
Revelation 20:12

Father, all of mankind that have turned from sin to You through acceptance of Your Son Jesus Christ have their name written in the Book of Life. May many have their names added today to the most important book to be a part of, a book that will determine a soul's eternal destiny.

And I heard a loud voice from the throne saying, "Look! God's dwelling place is now among the people, and He will dwell with them. They will be His people, and God Himself will be with them and be their God.
Revelation 21:3

Father, You have made known to us that we will spend eternity with You in heaven that John described. It is beyond our understanding what a place it will be. Streets of gold and Your glory gives it light and the Lamb is its lamp. What a day that will be and may many have their names written in the Lambs Book of Life today.

The Spirit and the bride say, "Come!" And let the one who hears say, "Come!" Let the one who is thirsty come; and let the one who wishes take the free gift of the water of life.
Revelation 22:17

Father, may many come to You today and taste the water of life. Water that allows eternal worship of You. How beautiful heaven must be.

About the Author

Dr. Lance Boyd accepted Jesus as his personal Savior in April, 1986 while in high school. Since that day, he has devoted his life to being a servant for his Lord and Savior. Dr. Boyd has taught Sunday School and Wednesday night Bible studies for over 33 years. After graduating from Hanceville High School in Cullman, Alabama, he attended Wallace State Community College on a baseball scholarship and was recently inducted into the Cullman County Sports Hall of Fame. After receiving an Associates in Science Degree from Wallace State Community College, he attended Athens State University receiving a Bachelor of Science Degree in Mathematics and Biology. Dr. Boyd taught 9 years at Fairview School and also coached football, basketball, and math teams. He earned his Masters in Administration from The University of Alabama and was assistant principal of Fairview Elementary and Middle Schools. He earned a Masters Degree in Mathematics from Alabama A&M and taught 17 years and advised Education Majors at Wallace State Community College. It was there he earned his Educational Leadership and Doctorate Degree from The University of Alabama in Higher Education Administration. He spent three years at Cullman Christian School as a Mathematics and Physics teacher and Headmaster. He most recently spent time at West Point Middle School helping with Math Intervention and also Cullman Christian School teaching History. Dr. Boyd has had the opportunity to speak at numerous churches, schools, and conferences during his years of service. He is most proud of his wife Kristi, son Truman(wife Alivia), daughter Sadie(husband Trett), grandson Walt, and granddaughter Palmer.

Made in the USA
Columbia, SC
21 November 2024

47248933R00328